Pleasure

OXFORD **PHILOSOPHICAL** CONCEPTS

OXFORD PHILOSOPHICAL CONCEPTS

Christia Mercer, Columbia University

Series Editor

PUBLISHED IN THE OXFORD PHILOSOPHICAL CONCEPTS SERIES

Efficient Causation
Edited by Tad Schmaltz

Eternity
Edited by Yitzhak Y. Melamed

Sympathy
Edited by Eric Schliesser

Self-Knowledge
Edited by Ursula Renz

The Faculties
Edited by Dominik Perler

Embodiment
Edited by Justin E. H. Smith

Memory
Edited by Dmitri Nikulin

Dignity
Edited by Remy Debes

Moral Motivation
Edited by Iakovos Vasiliou

Pleasure
Edited by Lisa Shapiro

FORTHCOMING IN THE OXFORD PHILOSOPHICAL CONCEPTS SERIES

Persons
Edited by Antonia LoLordo

Love
Edited by Ryan Hanley

Evil
Edited by Andrew Chignell

Human
Edited by Karolina Hübner

Health
Edited by Peter Adamson

Animals
Edited by G. Fay Edwards
and Peter Adamson

Space
Edited by Andrew Janiak

The World-Soul
Edited by James Wilberding

Teleology
Edited by Jeffrey K. McDonough

Pleasure

A HISTORY

Edited by Lisa Shapiro

OXFORD
UNIVERSITY PRESS

OXFORD
UNIVERSITY PRESS

Oxford University Press is a department of the University of Oxford. It furthers
the University's objective of excellence in research, scholarship, and education
by publishing worldwide. Oxford is a registered trade mark of Oxford University
Press in the UK and certain other countries.

Published in the United States of America by Oxford University Press
198 Madison Avenue, New York, NY 10016, United States of America.

Library of Congress Cataloging-in-Publication Data
Names: Shapiro, Lisa, editor.
Title: Pleasure : a history / edited by Lisa Shapiro.
Description: New York : Oxford University Press, 2018. |
Series: Oxford handbooks | Includes bibliographical references and index.
Identifiers: LCCN 2017047686 (print) | LCCN 2018008898 (ebook) |
ISBN 9780190225131 (online course) | ISBN 9780190225124 (updf) |
ISBN 9780190882495 (epub) | ISBN 9780190225117 (pbk. : alk. paper) |
ISBN 9780190225100 (cloth : alk. paper)
Subjects: LCSH: Pleasure.
Classification: LCC B105.H36 (ebook) | LCC B105.H36 P54 2018 (print) |
DDC 128/.4—dc23
LC record available at https://lccn.loc.gov/2017047686

1 3 5 7 9 8 6 4 2

Paperback printed by Webcom Inc., Canada
Hardback printed by Bridgeport National Bindery, Inc., United States of America

Contents

Illustrations

Figures

Series Editor's Foreword

Oxford Philosophical Concepts (OPC) offers an innovative approach to philosophy's past and its relation to other disciplines. As a series, it is unique in exploring the transformations of central philosophical concepts from their ancient sources to their modern use.

OPC has several goals: to make it easier for historians to contextualize key concepts in the history of philosophy, to render that history accessible to a wide audience, and to enliven contemporary discussions by displaying the rich and varied sources of philosophical concepts still in use today. The means to these goals are simple enough: eminent scholars come together to rethink a central concept in philosophy's past. The point of this rethinking is not to offer a broad overview, but to identify problems the concept was originally supposed to solve and investigate how approaches to them shifted over time, sometimes radically. Recent scholarship has made evident the benefits of reexamining the standard narratives about western philosophy. OPC's editors look beyond the canon and explore their concepts over a wide philosophical landscape. Each volume traces a notion from its inception as a solution to specific problems through its historical transformations to its modern use, all the while acknowledging its historical context. Each OPC volume is a history of its concept in that it tells a story about changing solutions to its well-defined problem. Many editors have found it appropriate to include long-ignored writings drawn from the

Islamic and Jewish traditions and the philosophical contributions of women. Volumes also explore ideas drawn from Buddhist, Chinese, Indian, and other philosophical cultures when doing so adds an especially helpful new perspective. By combining scholarly innovation with focused and astute analysis, OPC encourages a deeper understanding of our philosophical past and present.

One of the most innovative features of OPC is its recognition that philosophy bears a rich relation to art, music, literature, religion, science, and other cultural practices. The series speaks to the need for informed interdisciplinary exchanges. Its editors assume that the most difficult and profound philosophical ideas can be made comprehensible to a large audience and that materials not strictly philosophical often bear a significant relevance to philosophy. To this end, each OPC volume includes Reflections. These are short stand-alone essays written by specialists in art, music, literature, theology, science, or cultural studies that reflect on the concept from their own disciplinary perspectives. The goal of these essays is to enliven, enrich, and exemplify the volume's concept and reconsider the boundary between philosophical and extraphilosophical materials. OPC's Reflections display the benefits of using philosophical concepts and distinctions in areas that are not strictly philosophical, and encourage philosophers to move beyond the borders of their discipline as presently conceived.

The volumes of OPC arrive at an auspicious moment. Many philosophers are keen to invigorate the discipline. OPC aims to provoke philosophical imaginations by uncovering the brilliant twists and unforeseen turns of philosophy's past.

Christia Mercer
Gustave M. Berne Professor of Philosophy
Columbia University in the City of New York

Abbreviations

Aristotle

NE   *Nicomachean Ethics.* Translations are based on *Aristotle: Nicomachean Ethics*, translated with commentary by T. H. Irwin (Indianapolis: Hackett, 1999), and have sometimes been modified.

Avicenna

DA   *Avicenna's De Anima, Being the Psychological Part of Kitāb al-Shifā'.* Edited by F. Rahman. London: Oxford University Press, 1959.

Thomas Aquinas

ST   *Summa Theologiae.* In *Opera omnia.* Editio Leonina. Rome: Commissio Leonina, 1888–1906.

George Berkeley

All works can be found in George Berkeley, *The Works of George Berkeley, Bishop of Cloyne,* 9 vols., edited by A. A. Luce and T. E. Jessop (London: Thomas Nelson, 1948–57).

ALC   *Alciphron.* Passages are referred to by dialogue and section number.

DHP   *Three Dialogues between Hylas and Philonous.* Passages are referred to by page number in *Works*, vol. 2.

NB   *Notebooks.* Passages are referred to by section number.

PHK   *Principles of Human Knowledge.* Passages are referred to by part and section number.

RENÉ DESCARTES

Citations are by volume and page in AT, followed by volume and page in CSM(K).

AT   *Oeuvres Complètes.* 11 vols. Edited by Charles Adam and Paul Tannery. Paris: Vrin, 1996.

CSM   *The Philosophical Writings of Descartes.* 2 vols. Edited and translated by John Cottingham, Robert Stoothof, and Dugald Murdoch. Cambridge: Cambridge University Press, 1985.

CSMK   *The Philosophical Writings of Descartes.* Vol. 3. Edited and translated by John Cottingham, Robert Stoothof, Dugald Murdoch, and Anthony Kenny. Cambridge: Cambridge University Press, 1991.

IMMANUEL KANT

Citations are to the title or abbreviated title of the work, followed by the volume and page number of the *Ak.* Unless otherwise noted, citations from Kant's texts are quoted from the following translations, with modifications noted in the text.

Ak   *Akademie Ausgabe: Kants gesammelte Schriften.* Hrsg. von der Königlich Preußischen Akademie der Wissenschaften. Berlin: de Gruyter, 1902–.

CPJ   *Critique of the Power of Judgment.* Edited and translated by Paul Guyer and translated by Eric Matthews. Cambridge: Cambridge University Press, [1790] 2000.

CPrR   *Critique of Practical Reason.* Edited and translated by Mary Gregor. In *Practical Philosophy.* Cambridge: Cambridge University Press, [1788] 1996.

FI   Kant's first draft of the introduction to *Critique of the Power of Judgment,* found in CPJ.

LM   *Kant's Lectures on Metaphysics.* Edited as *Metaphysik Dohna, Metaphysik Vigilantius (K₃),* and *Metaphysik L₂,* in *Lectures on Metaphysics.* Edited and translated by Karl Ameriks and Steve Naragon. Cambridge: Cambridge University Press, [1792–93 and 1794–95] 1997.

MM   *The Metaphysics of Morals.* Edited and translated by Mary Gregor. In *Practical Philosophy.* Cambridge: Cambridge University Press, [1797] 1996.

NICOLAS MALEBRANCHE

Citations are to the volume and page number in OC, followed by the location in the work and the page number in the translation of that text.

DMR   *Dialogues on Metaphysics and Religion.* Cited by dialogue and section numbers.

JS   *Dialogues on Metaphysics and Religion.* Edited and translated by Nicholas Jolley and David Scott. Cambridge: Cambridge University Press, 1997.

LO   *The Search after Truth.* Edited and translated by Thomas Lennon and Paul Olscamp. With *Elucidations of the Search after Truth.* Edited and translated by Thomas M. Lennon. Cambridge: Cambridge University Press, 1997.

OC   *Oeuvres Complètes de Malebranche.* Edited by André Robinet. Paris: Vrin, 1958–84.

ST   *The Search after Truth.* Cited by book and chapter or Elucidation.

John Stuart Mill

The standard edition is the thirty-three-volume *Collected Works of John Stuart Mill*, ed. J. M. Robson (Toronto: University of Toronto Press, 1963–1991). Specific works are cited as follows.

APHM 1/2   Mill, James. *Analysis of the Phenomena of the Human Mind.* Edited with notes by John Stuart Mill and Alexander Bain. 2 vols., 2nd ed. London: Longman, Green, Reader and Dyer, 1869. 1 or 2 indicates the volume number.[1]

SL   Mill, John Stuart. *System of Logic, Ratiocinative and Inductive.* In *Collected Works,* vols. 7–8, 1843.

U   Mill, John Stuart. *Utilitarianism.* In *Collected Works,* vol. 10, 203–259, 1861.

---

1. The first edition was published by James Mill in 1822 (Vol.1) and 1829 (Vol.2). The second edition, cited in this volume as APHM, includes extensive notes by John Stuart Mill and Alexander Bain.

Contributors

MURAT AYDEDE is Professor of Philosophy at the University of British Columbia. He works primarily in philosophy of psychology/cognitive science and, more generally, philosophy of mind, and he has increasingly focused on perceptual and affective consciousness. His current research involves developing a theory of sensory affect that would also illuminate perceptual consciousness.

SUSANNA BERGER is Assistant Professor of Art History at the University of Southern California. Her book, *The Art of Philosophy: Visual Thinking in Europe from the Late Renaissance to the Early Enlightenment*, was published by Princeton University Press in 2017. She was previously a member of the Society of Fellows at Princeton University and has held a Robert Lehman Fellowship at Villa I Tatti, the Harvard University Center for Italian Renaissance Studies, a Panofsky Fellowship at the Zentralinstitut für Kunstgeschichte in Munich, a Frances A. Yates fellowship at the Warburg Institute, and an Andrew W. Mellon fellowship at the Huntington Library.

EMILY FLETCHER is Assistant Professor of Philosophy at the University of Wisconsin-Madison. She works on Plato, focusing on the psychology and ethics of the late dialogues. She has published several articles about the *Philebus*, which contains Plato's most comprehensive account of pleasure and its role in the good life.

MELISSA FRANKEL is Associate Professor of Philosophy at Carleton University. She specializes in early modern philosophy and philosophy of perception.

KEREN GORODEISKY is Associate Professor at Auburn University. She has published work on Kant, aesthetic pleasure, aesthetic value, aesthetic rationality, and Romanticism. She is currently completing a book on the significance of Kant's notion of aesthetic judgment, focusing on this judgment's logical form and *sui generis* type of rationality. For this book project, Gorodeisky received the Philip Quinn Fellowship at the National Humanities Center.

ROGER MATHEW GRANT is Assistant Professor of Music at Wesleyan University. His articles have appeared in *Critical Inquiry, Music Theory Spectrum, Eighteenth-Century Music,* and the *Journal of Music Theory.* His first book, *Beating Time and Measuring Music in the Early Modern Era* (Oxford University Press, 2014), won the Emerging Scholar Award of the Society for Music Theory.

ANN M. KRING is Professor and Chair in the Department of Psychology at the University of California, Berkeley. She studies social-emotion-cognitive processes and how they do (and do not) go awry in psychological disorders, with a particular focus on schizophrenia.

DOMINIQUE KUENZLE is Adjunct Professor at the Institute of Philosophy, University of Zürich. His publications include a monograph on metaepistemology (*Refurbishing Epistemology*, 2017), an edited volume on the role of emotions in epistemology (*Epistemology and Emotions*, 2008), and a book-length introduction to the philosophy of John Stuart Mill (in German, 2009).

MARTIN PICKAVÉ is Professor of Philosophy and Medieval Studies at the University of Toronto and Tier 2 Canada Research Chair in Medieval Philosophy. Most of his published work deals with issues in metaphysics and philosophy of mind in later medieval philosophy, but he also has research interests in ancient and early modern philosophy. He is currently writing a book on medieval theories of the emotions.

SAJJAD RIZVI is Associate Professor of Islamic Intellectual History and Islamic Studies at the University of Exeter. His work focuses on Islamic intellectual history in the wider Persianate world. He is currently completing three projects: an intellectual history of philosophy in Iran and North India on the cusp of colonialism, an analysis of the noetics of Mullā Ṣadrā, and a short monograph on Mīr

Dāmād. His next major projects are mapping Islamic philosophical traditions in India, 1450–1850, and writing an intellectual history of apophasis in Islamic thought.

AMY H. SANCHEZ is a doctoral student in psychology at University of California, Berkeley.

LISA SHAPIRO is Professor of Philosophy at Simon Fraser University. Her research has two foci: early modern accounts of the passions as illuminating of the metaphysics of the human being and accounts of mind in the period, and integrating early modern women philosophers into the narratives of philosophy.

MATTHEW STROHL is Associate Professor of Philosophy at the University of Montana. He specializes in ancient Greek philosophy and aesthetics.

CHAPTER ONE

Introduction

Lisa Shapiro

What is pleasure? In what way is pleasure philosophically interesting? Some familiar contemporary answers to these questions characterize pleasure as a paradigm example of a mere feeling that is, as such, unanalyzable. Utilitarian and emotivist ethical theories, which each take pleasure to be motivating of action, provide illustrative cases of this sort of answer. Though utilitarians admit that pleasures come in degrees, they do not consider what might distinguish different kinds of pleasures, beyond a simple distinction of higher and lower pleasures. Emotivists acknowledge that there are different kinds of pleasures, but insofar as they conceive of pleasures as feelings without content they are hard pressed to explain what distinguishes one pleasure from another. On both theories, any differences in pleasures are simply primitive, raising the question of how to understand what they share to make them all pleasures. Other familiar answers take pleasure as antithetical to reason. A dominant stream in aesthetics takes pleasures to be unanalyzable responses to objects presented to us, mere matters of taste. The task of aesthetics, on this view, is to determine the causes of pleasurable (and unpleasant) responses to objects, as well as to articulate the standards of taste, or norms governing these experiences of pleasures. Equally, in contemporary epistemology, it has been assumed that affective states, which presumably include pleasure, are opposed to rationality insofar as they interfere with our ability to understand how things are independently of us, and so are opposed to our ability to arrive at knowledge. Thus, on received views, pleasures are taken to be principally motivating of action, themselves unanalyzable, caused, rather than responsive to reasons, and, perhaps because of that, antithetical to rationality.

This book challenges these received views. It provides a fresh perspective on our current way of thinking about pleasure by better contextualizing our contemporary views within the extended conversation that is the history of philosophy, and thereby helps us to understand the tacit assumptions that figure in these contemporary views. If the history of philosophy demonstrates anything about the concept of pleasure, it is the complexity of understanding just what pleasure is. Reminders of how preceding philosophers thought about the concept of pleasure can also bring back into view positions that have fallen out of fashion, stimulating new lines of inquiry as well as new ways of approaching standing issues.

The essays that make up this book tell a story in four acts. The first three acts mark moments in central philosophical concerns about pleasure that lead to pleasure being folded into scientific psychology. In the fourth act, we see in both contemporary psychology and philosophy recognition of the shortcomings of the current scientific accounts and a return to questions that start the story in an effort to enrich those accounts.

The first act, the chapters of the first third of the volume, demonstrates how philosophers became centrally concerned with unifying the variety of pleasures. Plato's dialogues contain an array of concerns about pleasure: the relation of pleasure and pain, and so to the condition of the body, the relation of pleasure to false beliefs, and so to knowledge and truth, the proper objects of pleasure, and so how pleasure ought to be experienced, and the unity of the varieties of pleasure. Of all these issues, the one that proves most compelling, to Aristotle but also to philosophers within Islamic traditions and the medieval Latin tradition, is that of how to unify the variety of experiences that are all called "pleasure." While the other issues also figure in the discussions, and in particular the relation of pleasure to knowledge, the key concern to ensure the unity of pleasurable phenomena constrains the answers to those issues.

The second act, the chapters of the second third of the volume, focuses on the early modern period and shows how pleasure begins to be treated psychologically rather than logically. The discussions of the philosophers considered here—Malebranche, Berkeley, and Kant—shift the focus to the relation of pleasure to knowledge and truth. While these philosophers clearly acknowledge the particular feeling of pleasure, none of them reduce pleasure to mere feeling. The challenge for them is to understand the relation between pleasures and other sensory experiences and thereby to explain just how pleasure figures in our cognition of the world. Human cognition is acknowledged to be imperfect, and understanding just how our cognition works is key to recognizing our epistemic limits and achieving knowledge as best we can. Understanding the role of pleasure in human cognition is part of that project.

The third act takes us into the eighteenth and nineteenth centuries and the development of scientific psychology. It is during this period that the conception of pleasure as an unanalyzable feeling begins to flourish, perhaps as a way of distinguishing pleasures and pains from sensations, or perhaps as a way of modeling the motivational role of pleasure as a force. The development of scientific psychology in the nineteenth century brings with it the need to ensure that the objects of the new science are well defined, and thinking of pleasure as a mere feeling gets a grip. With this, the dominant philosophical concept of pleasure narrows to occlude the many varieties of pleasure that so concerned the ancient and medieval discussions.

However, it is not as if the varieties of pleasure disappear, and as the Reflections demonstrate, artists, whether etchers of frontispieces of textbooks or musicians, recognize just how experiences of pleasure can engage the mind, and through these experiences the idea that pleasures involve if not reason then aspects of cognition remains in the background. And equally the range of occasions for us to experience pleasure makes clear that pleasure as an unanalyzable feeling does little justice to the phenomena.

It is thus perhaps not surprising, in the fourth act, that in both contemporary scientific psychology and contemporary philosophy there is a renewed concern with recognizing the heterogeneity of pleasure, the intertwining of pleasure in both our understanding of the world around us and our actions in the world, and with revising the concept of pleasure in a way that does justice to this multidimensional role in human life.

I will now summarize the chapters themselves, before concluding with some brief thoughts about the historiography of philosophy exemplified in this book, as well as a recognition of central figures, and so storylines, that are omitted.

Emily Fletcher provides in chapter 2 the historical starting point of the book with her consideration of Plato's account of pleasure. Rather than assigning Plato a settled view, she shows how, through the development of Plato's thinking, an array of philosophical problems associated with the concept of pleasure emerge over the full range of the Platonic dialogues. In *Phaedo* and *Gorgias* we are presented with a notion of pleasure as essentially linked with pain, the satisfaction of a painful desire restoring the body to its equilibrium state. In virtue of this link, pleasure is also linked to false beliefs. While this aspect of Plato's view might appear to anchor the contemporary view of pleasure as compromising the objectivity required for knowledge, Fletcher shows that these earlier dialogues are not Plato's last word on pleasure. The earlier dialogues hint at the possibility of beneficial pleasures, and first in *Republic* then later in *Philebus* Plato develops this suggestion, broadening his conception of the nature and types of pleasure. In *Republic*, he opens a space of beneficial pleasures, including philosophical pleasures, which are both pure, in being independent of pain, and aligned with truth, in connecting pleasures with their objects, allowing for the distinction of real and illusory pleasures. Plato thus confronts the heterogeneity of pleasure. In *Philebus* the point that the word "pleasure" does not single out a unified concept is made more strongly. The dialogue distinguishes those pleasures akin to the restoration model presented in *Phaedo* from the anticipatory pleasures we feel at the prospect of a future satisfaction of a desire; it also distinguishes pleasures whose value is aligned with their objects from those whose value is tied to the character of the individual experiencing the pleasure. Plato's dialogues thus set up the following set of questions: What are the varieties of pleasure? How ought pleasure to be experienced? What are the proper or real objects of pleasure? How can pleasure contribute to our grasp of the truth?

Aristotle, as Matthew Strohl shows in chapter 3, begins his account of pleasure where Plato left off, recognizing that there are many varieties of pleasure. However, whereas Plato's discussion of pleasure seems reconciled to a variety that cannot be unified under one concept, Aristotle aims to articulate a principle that effectively explains the variety. Aristotle holds what Strohl calls the covariance thesis: that pleasures differ with kinds of activities. So there are as many kinds of pleasures as there are kinds of activities. Strohl argues that pleasure is best understood as an aspect of an activity, rather than a feeling that attaches to it. In particular, it is the aspect that reflects the fit between a capacity for activity and the object of that activity. The more an activity realizes its nature as an activity, that is, the more an object activates a capacity to realize its nature, the more perfect the activity is. This fit between activity and object is identified with pleasure. So pleasure is not a consequence of the perfection of an activity, as it might be tempting to think; it *is* the perfection. Insofar as pleasure is identified with the fit between a subject's capacity and the object activating the capacity, it makes sense that pleasures will covary with the activities of our capacities. The covariance thesis precludes the view that identifies pleasure as a phenomenological feeling, since it is implausible that feelings differ that much. However, understanding pleasure as perfection does not preclude pleasures having a phenomenal character; pleasure on this view still can involve a feeling. Moreover, because pleasure is perfection in the fit between activity and object, all pleasures, though they may feel different, increase the pleasure simply in virtue of being pleasant: the pleasure of perfection furthers the pleasure.

In chapter 4, Sajjad Rizvi considers the concept of pleasure in the Islamic tradition, and in particular the way in which that concept is tied to the conception of embodiment, contrasting the Islamic Aristotelian tradition with the scriptural Sufi and Shiʿi traditions. On the former, Islamic thinkers followed Aristotle and Plato, as their works were conveyed in Arabic, and privileged pleasures aligned with the good of a philosophical way of life and the understanding of higher causes of existence, so eschewing bodily pleasures in favor of intellectual pleasures. Al-Rāzī and later al-Ṭūsī marshal the idea of pleasure as a restoration of a natural human state, put forward in the Platonic account and discussed by Fletcher, to advocate for those intellectual pleasures that realize the nature of the soul, the essence of a human being. Miskawayh takes the privileging of a disembodied intellectual life further, making virtue and happiness proprietary to the intellect. All things bodily are identified with ignorance and pain, whereas knowledge and pleasure go together, and are in fact perfections of human activity. We thus see how in this Islamic tradition, a reading of Aristotle aligned with that offered by Strohl is appropriated to further a rejection of embodiment and a promotion of intellectual pursuits. However, the suggestion that any sensory pleasures are illusory or perverse is problematized by considerations of the nature of human subjectivity, and in particular that of Avicenna in his "floating man" thought experiment. Although

Avicenna recognizes that a disembodied soul constitutes the nature of the human subject, he also recognizes that each soul has a proper body that is central to its development and ultimately its path to the afterlife. For him, the soul's self-awareness is essential to the soul. While Avicenna's account is initially aligned with the assertion of the primacy of disembodied pleasures, Mullā Ṣadrā in the seventeenth century also insists that the soul does not exist without the body. In the second part of his chapter, Rizvi highlights scriptural Islamic traditions that privilege the self as essentially embodied. Sufi and Shi'i writings focus on bodily pleasure as a means to encountering the divine. Some accounts translate Avicenna's model into a system through which to control bodily pleasures, in some cases setting out a system of etiquette and rules to ensure that humans pursue pleasure while remaining within the constraints of the moral law articulated in the Qur'an, in other cases acknowledging human carnal desires and advocating the self-discipline required to master them. The Sufi tradition of Ibn 'Arabī on the other hand celebrated love, and in particular carnal love, holding that human sexual love reflected divine love and so was a means to seek the One. This wholesale endorsement of bodily pleasure was appropriated by Indo-Persian authors, and in particular Nakhshābī, and in sex manuals that follow that tradition, with an aim of leveraging this understanding of one's embodied self into a recognition of the divine.

Susanna Berger's "Engraving Pleasure in Philosophy Teaching Aids" highlights the role of sensual pleasure in facilitating knowledge in her Reflection on the art of seventeenth-century broadsides that were designed to serve the pedagogical function of making the study of philosophy pleasurable. These are intricate images; some of them guide the reader into an intellectually pleasant activity (of wending one's way through a landscape), and others more overtly evoke sexual pleasure even while representing a warning of its dangers. They resonate with the accounts of pleasure in the Islamic tradition in chapter 4, as well as with the Aristotelian accounts of pleasure that Martin Pickavé discusses in chapter 5.

Pickavé considers how the problem of unifying the diversity of pleasant phenomena that concerned Aristotle gets picked up by later medieval philosophers in the Latin tradition, and in particular Thomas Aquinas. Pickavé's chapter, in the light of Strohl's, demonstrates just how interpreting Aristotle informs the Thomist account. For the two philosophers are presented as wrestling with similar questions: How can we understand pleasure as both passive and as aligned with our nature? In what sense is pleasure to be understood as a perfection of an activity, raising both the question of the sense in which it is a perfection and of the way as a passion it is aligned with an activity? Pickave's chapter also begins to look forward, both to the contemporary context and to the focus of early modern accounts of pleasure. On Pickavé's reading, Aquinas's view is neither a motivational theory of pleasure nor a desire satisfaction account of pleasure, for even though the satisfaction of desire is necessary for pleasure, pleasure, for him, does not reduce to perception and desire. Equally, that Aquinas's account is silent about the phenomenology, or feeling, of pleasure follows from his taxonomy of the human mind. For pleasure to be a feeling it would need to be a perception, and so part of the sensitive part of the soul, rather than the appetitive part. Pickavé argues that though, for Aquinas, pleasure is proper to the appetitive part of the soul, it can interact with our perceptions and beliefs, either focusing attention or reinforcing beliefs or, equally, interfering with reasoning. The chapter concludes by highlighting two thinkers—Adam Wodeham and Peter Auriol—whose taxonomies of mind allow them to align pleasure with cognition and with freedom, respectively.

While echoes of the Thomist tradition are found in the early modern period, and in particular in the writings of Locke and Hume, the essays in this book that are focused on that period resonate more with views like that of Wodeham and Auriol that align pleasure and cognition. In chapter 6, I consider Malebranche's version of the Fall of Man as presented the *Search after Truth* as a locus of problematizing the relation between pleasure and other sense modalities. On Malebranche's account, Adam's fall is not a matter of his experience of pleasure—for Malebranche, Adam does experience bodily pleasures in his Edenic state—but rather a matter of some change in his experience of the world. I suggest that, for Malebranche, the pleasure that leads to the Fall is intimately connected to our awareness of objects. The Fall of Man involves lending primacy of perception to something other than God, and thereby coming to perceive the world as constituted by the particular things perceived and losing sight of God. In our fallen state, we perceive things through natural judgments, rather than perceiving intelligible extension, or things in the mind of God. That Malebranche offers an interpretation of the role of pleasure in the Genesis story to make a philosophical point about human cognition also resonates with the appeals to pleasure in the Qur'an by thinkers in the Islamic traditions as discussed by Sajjad Rizvi in chapter 4.

Malebranche's suggestion that pleasure is in some way integral to sensory perception of objects resonates with Berkeley's account of our perception of sensible qualities. Melissa Frankel in chapter 7 situates pleasures (and pains) within Berkeley's account of sensible qualities and perception of those sensible qualities. It seems clear that Berkeley wants to deny that our sensory perceptions have an act-object structure and to maintain that they are sensations, that is, feelings. This position has epistemological implications, for it is not clear how ideas that do not represent can afford knowledge of anything outside the mind. On Frankel's account, understanding Berkeley's view involves drawing an important distinction between what is external to the mind, (i.e., the nonmental), and that which is external to a self that perceives. While Berkeley rejects the former, he does not reject the latter. Frankel uses this distinction to show how, for Berkeley, sensations, including pleasures, do afford knowledge of things outside us, selves that perceive. While knowledge of things is grounded in self-knowledge, it is properly about the existence and nature of objects, and sensory pleasures afford this knowledge just as much as other sensible qualities; pleasures and pains can be constituents of objects. This commitment implies further that pleasures and pains exhibit the sort of regularity proper to laws of nature.

Keren Gorodeisky, in chapter 8, reconsiders Kant's views on pleasure, showing that in his account of the power of judgment Kant moves away from thinking of pleasure and pain as mere sensations and develops an account that takes pleasure as rational. On this account, sensory pleasures depend on practical reason, and the way in which aesthetic pleasures are conscious, Gorodeisky argues, entail that they are responsive to reasons. In particular, she argues that Kant is properly understood to claim that aesthetic pleasures, while being both receptive and affective, are both grounded in judgments and grounding of judgments, and she understands this reciprocal relationship as contained in the awareness proper to these pleasures. So, for Kant, aesthetic pleasures are not to be understood as states of awareness causally related to a theoretical commitment. Equally, on Gorodeisky's interpretation, aesthetic pleasure exhibits an internal causality, wherein as a self-conscious state it depends on reflective endorsement for being felt and sustained, and so aesthetic pleasures are rational active states. While there is an affinity between this Kantian account of aesthetic pleasure and what my chapter highlights in Malebranche, for Malebranche it is not clear that the natural judgments in which our fallen pleasure figures are fully rational.

Roger Mathew Grant's Reflection, "Musical Pleasure, Difficult Music," provides a context through which we not only can understand Kant's aesthetics but also can situate the early modern shift in accounts of sensory representation and the rationality of pleasure. Grant considers how a complex melody in J. S. Bach's *Well-Tempered Clavier* represents a shift in musical aesthetics in the eighteenth century. In a context in which melodies are paired with text, the musical tones can be taken to imitate features of the natural world, including emotions, in a way complementary to what is depicted in the text. Without a text to guide the listener, however, what the music is meant to represent can be difficult to determine, even when the music itself is painstakingly constructed, as with a Bach fugue. Music whose meaning is indeterminate in this way was understood as designed to evoke pleasure just by opening up a space of possibilities in which listeners choose how they experience the music. John Stuart Mill's account of pleasure as an integral part of his utilitarian moral theory has been well worked over. Dominique Kuenzle, in chapter 9 approaches Mill's account of pleasure from another angle, Mill's philosophy of science and language. The utilitarian calculus demands a science of pleasure, whereby pleasure as a concept is defined and appropriate measures determined. Kuenzle's aim is to explicate the semantic and epistemic theoretical frameworks through which the content of "pleasure" is determined within an associationist psychology. In particular, he shows that, for Mill, "pleasure" is a scientific term with a denotation and connotation, which, though drawn from ordinary use, are not left imprecise but rather are fixed to be appropriate to scientific contexts. What counts as appropriate to scientific contexts, in turn, depends on the scientific method adopted, and for Mill that method is an associationist psychology through which human behavior can be explained, predicted, and ultimately, governed. The associationist psychology Mill adopts, that of his father, James Mill, requires that pleasures be inductively linked with other mental states, be reducible to their physiological causes, and explain actions. These demands pressure Mill to hold that pleasures are but a quality of sensations. Reading Mill through his philosophies of language and of science can help in understanding the tensions surrounding "pleasure" in Mill's moral philosophy. Mill's account effectively narrows down to one sense the many related but different kinds of pleasure that philosophers from Plato and Aristotle forward have tried to unify into a single account. Nonetheless, because Mill singles out the scientific sense of "pleasure" as the central one, he also admits that sense can evolve with the empirical findings and development of scientific psychology.

The last two chapters demonstrate just how the development of scientific psychology is leading both psychologists and philosophers to move away from the view that pleasure is a mere qualitative feeling.

Ann M. Kring and Amy H. Sanchez, in their Reflection "Pleasure Experience in Schizophrenia," detail both how anhedonia, or the lack of pleasure, is identified and measured in a clinical setting and just how this symptom manifests in schizophrenia. Rather than failing to experience pleasure, schizophrenics fail to anticipate future pleasures, and so may be less likely to seek out pleasurable experiences. Anticipating pleasure is connected with a range of cognitive skills—imagination, reflection, memory, drawing on past experience, maintaining an image—that connect to motivational processes. While the motivational implications are important, understanding the cognitive processes that figure in anhedonia sheds light not only on schizophrenia but also on how pleasure, and in particular anticipatory pleasure, figures in cognitive functioning, and moves us away from models of pleasure as a mere feeling. It would also be interesting to consider how this contemporary notion of anticipatory pleasure interfaces with the anticipatory pleasure marked by Plato and Malebranche.

In chapter 10 Murat Aydede presents an account of pleasure that draws on both felt-quality views, which take sensory pleasure to be a feeling, and attitudinal views, which identify pleasures with inclinations toward a sensation, while avoiding their pitfalls. Aydede's account has three dimensions: an adverbial dimension that conceptualizes the phenomenology of pleasure; a functionalist dimension that addresses how this phenomenology is realized in our physiology; and a descriptive experiential-desire dimension that takes a pleasant sensation to be an experienced desire paired with belief that both are directed to the same stimulus in the world. While synthesizing contemporary philosophical discussion, Aydede's account also is attuned to the problems we have seen vexing historical philosophical discussion: including the heterogeneity of pleasurable feelings that so puzzled Aristotle, as well as the objects of pleasure and the relation of pleasure and sensation, introduced by Plato and taken up by Malebranche, Berkeley, and Kant.

Christia Mercer, in her series foreword, notes that each book offers *a* history of a concept. This is most certainly the case in this book. In an effort to show what has gone missing in contemporary discussions of pleasure, the story presented here has intentionally discounted the questions about the motivational role and about the feeling of pleasure that have so dominated discussion. Another history focused on those questions might well have taken a different shape.

The series as a whole, along with this book, is committed to contextualizing philosophical positions. However, while the series remains neutral with regard to other historiographical commitments, this book is not, again, making it one history among many possible ones. The story told here is not a progressive one: it does not presuppose that there is a correct conception of pleasure toward which the arc of philosophical thought tends. Nor is it focused on articulating the causal connections between the different philosophers and their views. Clearly, there are causal connections between Plato and Aristotle, and between those two and thinkers in the Islamic and Latin traditions, just as there are between Malebranche and Berkeley, but such lines of influence are not threads binding this book together. Rather, the book aims to highlight different moments in the philosophical consideration of pleasure, to present some associations between these moments. In this way, it can be helpful to think of each chapter as a snapshot of a conception of pleasure and all of them together as forming a kind of album that is representative enough to capture a slice of a life of the concept of pleasure. And just as a photo album invites us to find out more about the events captured on film, so too can the snapshots presented here prompt readers to consider other philosophical discussions of the same moment and so to consider just how views about pleasure tie into other philosophical concepts and questions.

Further, just as there are inevitably omissions in a photo album, this book neither is comprehensive nor aims to be so. I want to conclude this introduction by mentioning some of the more obvious missing figures. There is no chapter on Epicurus, whose identification of happiness with pleasure and focus on the way in which pleasure comes in degrees, has been tremendously influential. To contemporary philosophers, Epicurus is perhaps most associated with the development of utilitarianism, but he was also taken up, through his atomism, by Pierre Gassendi in the late seventeenth century and Karl Marx in the early nineteenth century. There is certainly another history of pleasure to be told there. Equally, there is no chapter on Augustine, who defines pleasure as an assent to what one wills, and as such integral to happiness. A story could well have been told that brought out more clearly the relations between Augustine, Malebranche, and Kant on pleasure. In this book, the two essays on Malebranche and Kant suggest a role for pleasure, or perhaps simply aesthetic pleasure in our consciousness of objects, and a story could have unfolded that brought them into conversation with the phenomenological tradition of the early twentieth century, which has much more to say about how pleasure helps to constitute our subjective experience. Such a story could have included figures such as Edmund Husserl, Max Scheler, Edith Stein, and Maurice Merleau Ponty, as well as Simone de Beauvoir and Luce Irigaray. Also omitted from this book are chapters on Spinoza and Hume, though both take pleasure as fundamental. Each of these figures has relatively little to say about pleasure in isolation, but they situate pleasure within the network of associations of our complex affective responses, and so within the complex social relationships through which those affective responses arise. It would be interesting to situate those thinkers in relation to the work of Marx and Nietzsche, as well as that of Michel Foucault, whose works *The History of Sexuality, The Use of Pleasure,* and *The Care of the Self* situate the experience of pleasure within sets of social structures and forces that, through the culture we inhabit, shape our experiences.

Perhaps this all too brief recognition of what this book leaves out nonetheless offers preliminary gestures at the other histories that might have been written and, indeed, that others might go on to write. This book aims simply to remind us of the many varieties of thinking about pleasure there are.

CHAPTER TWO

Two Platonic Criticisms of Pleasure

Emily Fletcher

Pleasure plays a prominent role in many of Plato's dialogues, yet it is an open question whether we can identify a single, distinctively Platonic account of pleasure. Pleasure comes up in many different contexts, and in some cases remarks about pleasure play a subordinate role to the main topic of discussion. The resulting treatments of pleasure are inconsistent in both scope and substance. For example, far from presenting a consistent view about the value of pleasure, Plato depicts Socrates elaborating a sophisticated form of hedonism in one dialogue, while arguing against hedonism in others.[1] However, one can still detect some broad similarities among the treatments of pleasure

---

1 See *Protagoras* 351b–d for Socrates's introduction of a hedonistic value theory and *Gorgias* 492e–499b and *Philebus* 20e–22c for arguments against various forms of hedonism. Translations of all Plato's dialogues are found collected in *Plato: Complete Works*, ed. John Cooper and D. S. Hutchinson (Indianapolis: Hackett, 1997). Throughout this chapter, I quote these translations, with occasional modifications.

in Plato's corpus. Plato consistently emphasizes that one cannot evaluate pleasure without first giving an account of what pleasure is.[2] In
addition, the nature of pleasure is usually examined in order to determine what role, if any, pleasure plays in the good human life. Beyond
observations such as these about Plato's general approach to pleasure,
scholars have doubted whether it is possible to make any substantive
claims about pleasure that hold true throughout the corpus.

In this chapter, I argue that there is an important continuity in Plato's
thought about pleasure that has gone unnoticed. He consistently raises
two compelling criticisms of pleasure: (1) pleasure is essentially linked
with pain or painful desire, and (2) pleasure produces false beliefs.[3]
A common objection to hedonism is that some pleasures are worthless
or bad, but Plato is distinctive in arguing that many pleasures are bad
for the person who experiences them. While a sadist's pleasures seem
bad because of the harm they cause to others, and the pleasures of a
pig seem insignificant and worthless, we do not necessarily think these
pleasures are bad for the subject in question. By contrast, Plato argues
that certain pleasures inflict direct physical and cognitive harms, such
as disease or madness, on their subject.[4] On Plato's view, pleasure is not
a possession that we can keep at arm's length and evaluate objectively;
instead, it has the power to distort our perceptions, beliefs, and values.

---

2 See, for example, *Gorgias* 500e–501a. Many philosophers interested in the value of pleasure fail to
provide a satisfactory account of what pleasure is. One could accuse Plato of this very mistake in the
Protagoras. I do not discuss the *Protagoras* in this chapter, since it does not contain an account of the
nature of pleasure, and it is beyond the scope of this essay to determine the precise role that hedonism
plays in Socrates's argument. That said, Socrates's defense of the art of measurement in the *Protagoras*
is an important precursor to the hedonistic calculus developed by Bentham and Mill.

3 These observations only count as criticisms of pleasure if one evaluates pain and false belief as bad.
They are criticisms from the point of view of hedonism in particular, for hedonists usually disvalue
pain and have instrumental reasons for excluding false belief from the best life, since it inhibits a
subject's ability to maximize pleasure. Even from a nonhedonistic perspective, pain and false belief are
very often evaluated as bad. Plato relies on this intuition in the choice of lives thought experiments
in the *Gorgias* (493e–494a), *Republic* II (360d–362c), *Philebus* (20b–22c) and *Laws* V (732d–734e),
which are only compelling to the extent that most people would choose to remove both pain and false
belief from their lives.

4 E.g., *Philebus* 44e–47b.

Recognizing Plato's two central criticisms of pleasure reveals many connections between his apparently dissimilar accounts of the nature and value of pleasure. On the whole, Plato's attitude toward pleasure improves over the course of his career; in contrast with the refutations of hedonism in the *Gorgias* and the asceticism of the *Phaedo*, we find arguments that the best life is the most pleasant in the *Republic*, and certain pleasures join limit and knowledge in the ranking of goods at the end of the *Philebus*.[5] Despite Plato's increasing recognition of pleasure's positive value, the same criticisms of pleasure put forward in the *Gorgias* and *Phaedo* reappear in the *Philebus*, a late dialogue containing Plato's most sophisticated account of pleasure. I argue that the changes in Plato's attitude toward pleasure do not result from a new appreciation of pleasures that he once rejected as harmful, but rather from a broadening conception of the nature and types of pleasure. Plato distinguishes new types of pleasure that are immune to one or both of his central criticisms and even characterizes some of these pleasures as beneficial. Ultimately, he explains the fact that some pleasures are good and others are bad by positing fundamental differences between the natures of these pleasures. For example, in the *Republic* we find a distinction between real and illusory pleasures, and the *Philebus* directly challenges the assumption that pleasure has a single nature at all.

I. THE TWO CRITICISMS OF PLEASURE

Pleasure, pain, and desire all come under attack in the *Phaedo*, and yet the first discussion of pleasure in the dialogue focuses on its nature,

---

5 The precise chronology of Plato's dialogues is controversial, but we can confidently identify a group of late dialogues, which includes the *Timaeus, Critias, Sophist, Statesman, Philebus,* and *Laws*, by tracking subtle changes in Plato's writing style. See L. Brandwood, "Stylometry and Chronology," in *The Cambridge Companion to Plato*, ed. R. Kraut (Cambridge: Cambridge University Press, 1992), 90–120, for a helpful introduction to the use of stylometry for dating Plato's works. The *Gorgias* and *Hippias Major* are generally thought to be written before the *Phaedo* and *Republic*, on the basis of developments in Plato's philosophical views rather than stylistic variation; as a result, the relative dating of these dialogues is less certain.

not its value. At the beginning of Phaedo's account of Socrates' last day in prison, we find Socrates reflecting on the relationship between pleasure and pain.

> What a strange thing that which men call pleasure seems to be, and how astonishing the relation it has with what is thought to be its opposite, namely pain! They do not tend to come to a man at the same time.[6] Yet if he pursues and catches the one, he is almost always bound to catch the other also, like two creatures with one head. I think that if Aesop had noted this he would have composed a fable that a god wished to reconcile their opposition but could not do so, so he joined their two heads together, and therefore when one arrives, the other follows later. This seems to be happening to me. My bonds caused pain in my leg, and now pleasure seems to be following. (*Phaedo* 60b3–c7)

Socrates makes two observations about the relationship between pleasure and pain in this passage, which together lead him to a novel view of their nature: (1) pleasure and pain do not usually come to a person at the same time, and (2) they almost always follow one another. When Socrates refers to "that which men call pleasure" and "what is thought to be its opposite, namely pain," he is not expressing doubt about the existence of pleasure or pain, nor is he referring to pleasures and pains that are in some way unreal or illusory. On the contrary, Socrates is talking about a concrete, real experience that he undergoes as his bonds are removed; the mistake is to assume there are two things there instead of one. The fable reveals the truth about pleasure, that it is half of a whole creature; what we call "pleasure" is really pleasure-pain. Most people are not only oblivious to this fact, but they even treat pain as the

---

6 In this line I depart from Grube's translation "A man cannot have both at the same time." The Greek is τὸ ἅμα μὲν αὐτὼ μὴ 'θέλειν παραγίγνεσθαι τῷ ἀνθρώπῳ (60b5–6).

opposite of pleasure, rather than viewing it as essentially attached to pleasure.[7]

Socrates's revisionary image of pleasure and pain as two halves of a single creature does not in itself constitute a criticism of pleasure. However, Socrates's insight into the nature of pleasure, and in particular his claim that it is inseparable from pain, has important consequences for any inquiry into pleasure's value. If pleasure is not an independent thing, then we should not evaluate it as such, and the question of whether pleasure is good or bad is misguided, or at least misleadingly incomplete. Socrates does not restrict the scope of his remarks in this passage to particular types of pleasure and pain. However, the one example he provides is the pleasure-pain caused by the bonds on his ankles, and so this account may apply primarily, or even exclusively, to pleasures and pains connected to the body.[8]

In the *Gorgias* we find a similar observation that pleasure and pain are essentially linked with one another. Socrates provides a more specific model for the relationship between the two, associating pleasure with the filling of a painful lack or desire in the soul. Socrates again uses a myth to illustrate the relationship between pleasure and pain. He compares the lives of two men, each of whom possesses many jars. One of these men successfully fills his jars, and gives them no further thought, whereas the other man has leaky jars and so must constantly fill them. Socrates's preference for the first life is evident, for he says

---

7 Socrates does not deny that pleasure and pain appear to be opposed to one another, and the fable he tells even provides an explanation for their apparent opposition. According to the story he tells, "a god wished to reconcile their opposition *but could not do so*, so he joined their two heads together" (60c2–4, my emphasis). Socrates not only says that pleasure and pain used to be separate, warring parties but also indicates that a certain tension or opposition remains between them, even now that they form a single creature. See G. Betegh, "Tale, Theology and Teleology in the *Phaedo*," in *Plato's Myths*, ed. C. Partenie (Cambridge: Cambridge University Press, 2009), 77–100, for further discussion of this passage.

8 Many of Socrates's critical remarks about pleasure in the *Phaedo* seem to be directed at bodily pleasures in particular, which goes along with his generally negative attitude toward the body and its care (e.g., 64d–e, 65e, 67a, 82c, 83b–d). Furthermore, Socrates praises the pleasures of learning as beneficial to philosophers (114d8–15a2), and he never claims that they are either preceded or followed by pain. See section 2 for further discussion of the pleasures of learning in the *Phaedo*.

the first man "can relax over [his jars]" (493e5–6), whereas the second is "forced to keep filling them, day and night, or else he suffers extreme pain" (493e8–494a1). However, Socrates fails to convince his recalcitrant interlocutor, Callicles. When asked whether Socrates has persuaded him that "the orderly life is better than the undisciplined one," Callicles replies: "you do not, Socrates. The man who has filled himself up has no pleasure any more, and when he's been filled up and experiences neither joy nor pain, that's living like a stone, as I was saying just now. Rather, living pleasantly consists in this: having as much as possible flow in" (*Gorgias* 494a6–b2). In Socrates's illustration of Callicles's ideal, the leaky jars represent insatiable desires, and Socrates uses the myth to make three observations about these desires: (1) unsatisfied desires are painful, (2) the process of satisfying these desires requires a lot of effort, and (3) if one constantly increases one's desires, there will be no rest from this trouble. Callicles accepts the filling model of the relationship between pleasure and painful desire, and he chooses the pleasant life with all of its inevitable pain. Callicles does not make the mistake of evaluating pleasure independently of pain, but he nevertheless chooses "living pleasantly." He justifies this choice by emphasizing another consequence of this necessary link: if one does not accept the pain that comes with pleasure, then one must give up both. Callicles does not choose a life in which pleasure outweighs pain, nor does he choose a life that contains an equal but moderate amount of each in preference to one that contains neither. Instead, he chooses a life that contains the extremes of both pleasure and pain. Since the size of a particular pleasure correlates directly with the size of the preceding desire, Callicles's pursuit of larger pleasures necessarily involves the pursuit of larger and more painful desires.[9]

---

9 B. Sommerville helpfully sets the leaky-jar image in its dialectical context and provides an insightful account of the central disagreement between Callicles and Socrates: "Callicles' happy man is not the sort who pursues pleasure and avoids pain. Rather, he pursues both pleasure and pain in equal measure" Sommerville, "The Image of the Jars in Plato's *Gorgias*," *Ancient Philosophy* 34.2 (2014): 245–246.

The filling model of pleasure accommodates Socrates's observation about the necessary link between pleasure and pain in the *Phaedo*, and it also provides an explanation for their interdependence. If we connect pleasure with the process of filling desires, and desires are painful, then pain necessarily precedes pleasure. There are also some differences between the two accounts. In the *Phaedo* Socrates claims not only that pleasure and pain almost always follow one another but also that "they do not tend to come to a man at the same time" (60b5–6). Socrates does not say that pleasure and pain never occur at the same time, and yet he emphasizes that they usually occur sequentially, rather than simultaneously. In the *Gorgias*, by contrast, one of Socrates's arguments against Callicles's brand of hedonism relies on the premise that "we stop feeling pains and pleasures at the same time" (497c). Socrates treats this premise as a direct consequence of the filling model of pleasure, according to which lacks are always painful, even when they are in the process of being filled. In other words, the filling model suggests that we always experience pleasure against a backdrop of pain.[10] According to this model, even while I enjoy eating a meal, I continue to experience the pain of hunger until my desire for food is fully satisfied. Despite the apparent disagreement between the *Phaedo* and the *Gorgias* about whether the relationship between pleasure and pain is primarily sequential or simultaneous, the two dialogues share an important insight: if pleasure and pain are essentially linked with one another, then we cannot evaluate them independently.

The *Phaedo* contains a second criticism of pleasure, which Socrates calls "the greatest and most extreme evil." When asked what this great evil is, Socrates explains:

That the soul of every man, when it feels violent pleasure or pain in connection with some object, inevitably believes at the same

---

10 Notice that this account of the relationship between pleasure and pain is not symmetrical. One can experience pain in the absence of pleasure, when one is in the process of being emptied.

time that what causes such feelings must be very clear and very true, which it is not . . . every pleasure and pain provides, as it were, another nail to rivet the soul to the body and to weld them together. It makes the soul corporeal, so that it necessarily believes the truth is what the body says it is. As it shares the beliefs and delights of the body, I think it comes to share its ways and manner of life and is unable ever to reach Hades in a pure state. (*Phaedo* 83c5–8 and d4–9)

The criticism of both pleasure and pain in this passage is that they produce false beliefs in the soul. Socrates claims that this cognitive harm has the further consequence of changing the very nature of the soul, binding it to the body and "making it corporeal." Socrates is not clear about the precise relationship between pleasure and false belief; however, he claims that the link is inevitable, the pleasure and belief are directed at the same object, and they occur "at the same time." Although Socrates initially makes these claims about "violent" pleasure and pain, he goes on to say that "every pleasure and pain" rivets the soul to the body. This comment suggests that all pleasures and pains have these negative effects, although perhaps to greater or lesser degrees.

The image of pleasures and pains riveting the soul to the body provides a vivid reason for viewing pleasure and pain as harmful and bad. Perhaps it is unsurprising to learn that pleasures and pains have some sort of impact on our beliefs. However, the *Phaedo* presents an alarming picture, according to which even mild pleasures and pains influence our beliefs in subtle ways that we often fail to detect. Over time, these pleasures and pains can change one's basic values and pursuits, thus impacting one's entire way of life.[11]

---

11 See D. Ebrey, "The Asceticism of the *Phaedo*: Pleasure, Purification and the Soul's Proper Activity," *Archiv für Geschichte der Philosophie* 99.1 (2017): 1–30, for an illuminating account of the way in which intense bodily pleasures and pains affect the soul in the *Phaedo*.

2. BENEFICIAL PLEASURES

Alongside Plato's persistent concern about pleasure's harmful nature, he consistently recognizes that some pleasures are exceptions to one or both of his two central criticisms. In fact, he sometimes characterizes a narrow class of pleasures not as merely harmless, but as positively beneficial elements in the best human life. These beneficial pleasures, which gain increasing prominence throughout the corpus, raise a puzzle about Plato's earlier accounts of the nature and value of pleasure: what differentiates the beneficial pleasures from the pleasures that are essentially linked with pain or produce false beliefs? In the *Phaedo*, the *Gorgias*, and the *Hippias Major*, Plato proposes a number of candidates for the feature that distinguishes beneficial pleasures from harmful ones, and yet he does not provide a full explanation of how they are immune to his two criticisms. In sections 3 and 4, I argue that answering this question shapes Plato's views about the nature and value of pleasure in the *Republic* and the *Philebus*, the two most comprehensive discussions of pleasure in the corpus.

As I have shown, in the *Phaedo* Socrates launches a vehement attack on pleasure; however, even in one of the most critical treatments of pleasure in the corpus, there is one exception. The dialogue contains a single reference to the pleasures of learning, which Socrates endorses as beneficial to the soul and associates with virtue and happiness. "That is the reason why a man should be of good cheer about his own soul, if during life he has ignored the pleasures of the body and its ornamentation as of no concern to him and doing him more harm than good, but has seriously concerned himself with the pleasures of learning, and adorned his soul not with alien but with its own ornaments, namely, moderation, righteousness, courage, freedom and truth, and in that state awaits his journey to the underworld" (*Phaedo* 114d8–115a2). Socrates does not provide a detailed account of the pleasures of learning, nor does he explain why they are exempt from the criticisms that apply to bodily pleasures. According to this brief remark, the important feature that differentiates the pleasures of learning from the pleasures of the body is that they belong to the soul. Socrates groups the pleasures of learning with the soul's own ornaments, as opposed to the pleasures that are "alien" (*allotrios*) to the soul. Presumably, belonging to the soul guarantees that these pleasures do not bind the soul to the body, forcing it to adopt the body's beliefs, values, and manner of life. In addition, the characterization of these pleasures of the soul as pleasures of learning suggests that they do not give rise to false beliefs. On the other hand it is unclear whether or not the pleasures of learning are, like bodily pleasures, essentially linked with pain. It certainly seems plausible that the pleasures of learning are preceded or followed by some corresponding pain, such as the pain of recognized ignorance or forgetting.[12] It is possible that Socrates does not view the pleasures of learning as exceptions to the account of pleasure and pain as two halves of a single entity in this passage, but instead evaluates the pleasures of learning together with their corresponding pains as good.

In the *Gorgias*, Socrates criticizes the unrestrained pursuit of pleasure, and he argues against Callicles's identification of pleasure with the good; however, he does not conclude that pleasure is always bad. Rather, he argues that there is a distinction between good and bad pleasures.[13] Socrates nowhere challenges the filling model of pleasure, according to which pleasure is always accompanied by painful desire.

---

12 See J. Warren, *The Pleasures of Reason* (Cambridge: Cambridge University Press, 2014): 29–32, who points to the allegory of the cave in the *Republic* as a place where Plato clearly recognizes that learning can be difficult and painful.

13 See K. Vogt, "What Is Hedonism?," in *Pain and Pleasure in Classical Antiquity*, ed. William Harris (Leiden: Brill, forthcoming), for a helpful distinction between antihedonism and nonhedonism. Both positions reject hedonism, or the view that pleasure is the only good that does not derive its value from another good. However, while antihedonism holds that pleasure is bad, nonhedonism holds merely that pleasure is not the good, either because there are some bad pleasures, or because there are other nonderivatively good things besides pleasure. Vogt identifies Plato as a nonhedonist, correcting a tendency in the literature to characterize him as an antihedonist. Plato's dialogues consistently present as an alternative to hedonism the view that there are both good and bad pleasures, not that all pleasures are bad. In the *Philebus* Socrates explicitly rejects an antihedonist position (44c–d).

Like Callicles, he seems to accept pain as a necessary side effect of pleasure, and he even evaluates some pains as good (499e1–3). The primary difference between Socrates and Callicles is that Socrates evaluates as good only those pleasures and pains that lead to good conditions, such as health or strength, and he calls these pleasures and pains "beneficial" (499d). The description of the "disciplined" man in the earlier comparison of lives provides a further explanation of the difference between good and bad pleasures. Like the undisciplined man, the disciplined man possesses a series of jars (i.e., desires) that he must fill, but his jars are sound and whole, rather than leaky and rotten (493e–494a). The important differentiating feature of beneficial pleasures is that they are inherently limited in size and duration. Unlike the insatiable appetites and unlimited pleasures pursued by Callicles, the pleasures of a disciplined man come to an end as soon as the corresponding desire has been satisfied and a good condition has been reached.[14]

In the *Hippias Major* Socrates attributes a new feature to beneficial pleasures, which is that they have beautiful objects.[15] Pleasure comes up in the *Hippias Major* in the context of a search for the definition of "the beautiful" (*to kalon*). After a series of failed attempts, Socrates himself proposes to define the beautiful as "what is pleasant through sight and hearing" (298a). The pleasures of sight and hearing Socrates has in mind have very particular objects, which are in all cases beautiful (*kala*) and include human beings, pictures, sculptures, music, and speeches (298a). The corresponding pleasures

---

14 Socrates and Callicles not only value different types of pleasure (limited and unlimited, respectively), but they also value these pleasures in different ways. According to Socrates, pleasure has at most derivative value; thus, the pleasure of eating is beneficial when it leads to a state of health, but it would be a mistake to value and aim at the pleasures of eating for their own sake. By contrast, Callicles treats pleasure as itself valuable and worthy of pursuit, without reference to health or anything else; as a result, he might recommend the pursuit of a morbid condition, such as excessive hunger, as a means of achieving more pleasure. In other words, Callicles thinks pleasure is the goal, whereas for Socrates the goal is a state that is neither pleasant nor painful, even if some pleasures are good to the extent that they lead to this state.

15 Socrates explicitly identifies these pleasures as beneficial at 303e.

are themselves also called beautiful (299a–b). Socrates does not explain the connection between the beauty of an object of pleasure and the beauty of the pleasure itself, and in fact he moves back and forth freely between claims about the beauty of what is "pleasant" (*hedu*) through sight and hearing and the beauty of "pleasures" (*hedonai*) through sight and hearing (303d–e). However, the idea that we can evaluate a pleasure on the basis of its objects, and indeed that pleasure and its object share the same nature, remains important for the evaluation of pleasure in both the *Republic* and the *Philebus*.

The group of pleasures identified as beneficial in the *Hippias Major* does not seem to coincide, or even overlap, with the pleasures identified as beneficial in either the *Gorgias* or the *Phaedo*. Examples of beneficial pleasures in the *Gorgias* include many ordinary appetitive pleasures, as long as they are limited in their nature and lead to good conditions. In the *Hippias Major*, Socrates introduces the new idea that pleasures take on the character of their objects, and beneficial pleasures are distinctive in that they involve the perception of beautiful objects. As a result, Socrates contrasts the pleasures of sight and hearing with appetitive pleasures in general, characterizing the former as beautiful and the latter as ugly (298d–299a). Socrates does not distinguish between good and bad appetitive pleasures in the *Hippias Major*, despite evaluating the inherently limited ones as beneficial in the *Gorgias*. There is also a striking contrast between the pleasures of perceiving beauty in the *Hippias Major* and the pleasures of learning in the *Phaedo*. As I showed, the most distinctive feature of the pleasures of learning is that they belong to the soul itself, as opposed to the body. Socrates does not explicitly assign the pleasures of sight and hearing to either the body or the soul in the *Hippias Major*. However, since they are "through sight and hearing," they at least require the use of sense perception and the body, in contrast with the pleasures of learning in the *Phaedo*.

3. The Nature and Value of Pleasure in the *Republic*

The *Republic* is the first dialogue that provides a comprehensive account of pleasure, rather than focusing on a narrow class of pleasures, such as appetitive pleasures or the pleasures of sight and hearing. At the end of book 9, Socrates gives two arguments that the philosopher's life is the most pleasant. I focus here on the second one, which contrasts philosophical pleasures with all others on the basis of two criteria, purity and truth. According to Socrates, the pleasures of a philosopher are pure in the sense that they arise independently of pain, whereas other pleasures are "reliefs from pain" (584b–c). Socrates goes on to argue that pleasures differ from one another in "truth" (*alētheia*), which he connects to a difference in "being" or "reality" (*ousia*, 585c12). In drawing this distinction, Socrates proposes a new account of what pleasure is, according to which pleasures do not all share the same ontological status; instead, some pleasures are mere "shadow-paintings" of others (583b, 586b). If Socrates's argument is successful, then pleasures vary not only along familiar dimensions such as intensity or duration; more radically, they differ in how much "being" they possess. Plato directly connects the two central criticisms of pleasure in the *Republic*, because the pleasures that are mixed with pain are for this very reason productive of false beliefs. He also provides an integrated account of those pleasures that are immune to these two criticisms, drawing on the idea from the *Hippias Major* that the nature of a pleasure depends crucially on the nature of its object.

The argument begins with a distinction between pleasure, pain, and an intermediate condition, which is neither a pleasure nor a pain (583c). Pain is described as "the opposite of pleasure" (583c), and Socrates does not suggest that there is any inevitable link between the two, as we find in the fable of the two-bodied creature in the *Phaedo* or the leaky-jar image in the *Gorgias*. On the contrary, Socrates claims that some pleasures are "pure" and thus arise independently of pain. Socrates does suggest that pleasure and pain are alike in that they are both a sort of motion (*kinēsis tis*, 583e10) in the soul, whereas the intermediate condition is "a sort of calm [*hēsuchia tis*] of the soul concerning these things" (583c7–8). The first stage of the argument turns on Socrates's observation that sick people say that nothing is more pleasant than health, just as people in extreme pain say nothing is more pleasant than the cessation of their suffering (583c10–d4). He likewise observes that the cessation of pleasure can appear painful, and so the intermediate condition can appear to be either pleasant or painful, depending on whether it is preceded by pain or pleasure (583e). He concludes that these appearances are misleading, both because it seems impossible "for that which is neither to become both" (583e7), and because pleasure and pain are motions, whereas the intermediate condition is a rest from all motion (583e9–584a6).

Socrates's conclusion is radical, for it suggests that many experiences commonly taken to be pleasures are something else: reliefs from pain. Regarding the apparent pleasures of the intermediate state, he says that "there is nothing sound[16] in these appearances as far as the truth about pleasure is concerned, only some sort of magic [goēteia tis]" (584a9–10). The only feature shared by the relief from pain and pure (i.e., actual) pleasure is their phenomenology: the intermediate condition "appears" (*phainetai*) pleasant when it is preceded by pain, and so it is often mistakenly judged to be a pleasure (584a). Notice that Socrates can only distinguish between pure pleasure and relief from pain, privileging one as real pleasure and criticizing the other as an illusion, because he gives an account of the underlying nature of pleasure that does not reduce it to an appearance or feeling. Many things might appear pleasant, but for something to count as a real pleasure it must have a particular nature, that is, it must be a certain sort of motion in the soul.[17]

---

16 *Hugies*; literally "healthy."

17 See J. Butler, "On Whether Pleasure's Esse Is Percipi: Rethinking Republic 583b–585a," *Ancient Philosophy* 19 (1999): 285–298, for a detailed argument that Socrates denies in this passage that pleasure just is a feeling or sensation.

The distinction between pure pleasures and the relief from pain does not coincide with any distinction among pleasures that we find prior to the *Republic*. In the argument, Socrates alludes to a distinction between bodily and psychic pleasure, such as we found in the *Phaedo*; however, the distinction in the *Phaedo* does not map onto the distinction between pure pleasures and reliefs from pain, because there are bodily and psychic examples of both. Socrates classifies a large group of bodily pleasures (i.e., the "greatest" ones, 584c6) as reliefs from pain,[18] as well as the pleasures of anticipation, which are psychic rather than bodily (584c9–11). Furthermore, Socrates claims that the pleasures of smell are "especially good examples" of pure pleasure, and his conclusion implies that pleasures of learning, which are psychic pleasures, also belong to the class of pure pleasures (585e–586b).

The pleasures of smell are Socrates's prime example of pure pleasures, and yet they do not receive universal praise throughout the corpus. For one thing, they are linked with the body and sense perception, both of which come under harsh criticism in the *Phaedo*. In the *Hippias Major*, the very idea of calling pleasant smells not only pleasant but also beautiful is described as laughable (299a1–3). The *Republic* seems to be a turning point in Plato's estimation of the pleasures of smell, and it is even possible that they were the example that initially alerted him to the possibility of pure pleasure, which arises independently of pain. The pleasures of smell are included among the class of pure and true pleasure in the *Philebus*, although Socrates calls them "less divine" than the pure pleasures of sight, hearing, and learning (51e1). This may be connected to the fact that, unlike the other pure and true pleasures, the pleasures of smell do not have beautiful objects.[19]

---

18 See *Philebus* 45a–e. In both passages, "the greatest" (*megistai*) pleasures are associated with disease, and in the *Philebus*, Socrates connects them with the greatest desires (45b4). These particularly intense bodily pleasures resemble the pleasures praised by Callicles in the *Gorgias*, which come from filling insatiable desires.

19 The pleasures of sight and hearing are explicitly linked with beautiful objects in the *Philebus*. While the pleasures of learning are not explicitly linked with beauty, learning is characterized

In the second stage of the argument, Socrates argues that the philosopher's pleasures are superior in both "truth" (*alētheia*) and "being" (*ousia*). The adjective usually translated "true" (*alēthēs*) seems to have the sense of "truthful," "trustworthy" or "nonmisleading" in this argument, the relevant contrast being with pleasures that are illusory and deceptive (see 585e). In other words, the philosopher's pleasures are not subject to the second criticism that pleasure produces false beliefs. Socrates's argument focuses on comparing bodily pleasures of eating and drinking with the psychic pleasures of learning. He introduces a filling model of pleasure that applies to both of these examples, and then argues that the pleasures of learning "partake more of pure being" than the pleasures of eating and drinking (585b12). Socrates explains that they are fillings of a more real vessel (the soul as opposed to the body), and they are fillings *with* what is more real (knowledge and understanding as opposed to food and drink).

The filling model of pleasure is reminiscent of the leaky-jar model in the *Gorgias*. However, in the *Republic* not all pleasures are accompanied by pain, and so the pursuit of pleasure does not necessarily go along with pain. Socrates states that "being filled with what is appropriate to our nature is pleasure" (585d11), but he does not say that empty states of the body or soul are necessarily painful. In fact, the possibility of pure pleasures, which are not merely reliefs from pain, requires that at least some empty states are not painful. Thus, the *Republic* provides an alternative to the choice presented in the *Gorgias* between a tortured life of constantly filling insatiable appetites and what Callicles contemptuously calls the life of a stone, in which one experiences neither pleasure nor pain.

While the distinction between pure pleasures and reliefs from pain does not correspond to that between pleasures of the body and those of the soul, Socrates does ultimately argue that fillings of the soul are

---

as "beautiful" in the *Symposium* (211c6) and *Gorgias* (475a1), and in the *Hippias Major* wisdom is described as "the most beautiful thing of all" (ἡ σοφία πάντων κάλλιστον, 296a5).

more valuable than fillings of the body. In the *Phaedo*, pleasures of learning are valued over appetitive pleasures, because they belong to the soul rather than the body. The *Republic* introduces the closely related criteria of being and truth to distinguish between the pleasures of the body and those of the soul, rather than relying solely on the claim that certain pleasures are more natural or appropriate to the soul. In the *Republic*, Socrates connects the being and truth of a pleasure to the permanence and stability of its objects. The objects of learning are always the same and immortal, and so the pleasures connected with these objects likewise share these characteristics. By contrast, food and drink are changing, mortal things, and appetitive pleasures are as impermanent and lacking in "being" as their objects (585c1–5).

According to both parts of the argument in *Republic* 9, there are examples of experiences that resemble pleasures, and yet are only pleasures in some deficient sense. Socrates concludes the argument by identifying the pleasures that are "mixed with pain" as "mere images and shadow-paintings of true pleasures" (586b7–8). These pleasures are subject to both of the criticisms of pleasure described in section 1. Since they are mixed with pain, they are deceptive and "appear intense, so that they give rise to mad erotic passions in the foolish" (586c1–3). At the same time, a single group of pleasures—the pleasures of learning characteristic of a philosopher—are immune to both of Plato's central criticisms of pleasure. The philosopher's pleasures do not appear to be the most intense; however, because they arise independently of pain, they do not deceptively appear to be something they are not. They are also the most real and unchanging pleasures, as a result of having the most real and unchanging objects.

According to the account of pleasure in the *Republic*, pleasures that are mixed with pain are not entirely different things from the pure and true pleasures of the philosopher, but nor are they pleasures to the same degree. Interestingly, Socrates does not merely conclude that intense bodily pleasures are less good than philosophical pleasures, as a result of having less truth and being. Instead, he criticizes them as emphatically bad. The deceptive character of mixed pleasures helps to explain why they are bad, and not merely less good than pure and true pleasures. After all, part of the danger of mixed pleasures is that they deceptively appear to be the greatest and most intense pleasures, and thus more worthy of pursuit than the pure and true pleasures of a philosopher.

4. THE NATURE AND VALUE OF PLEASURE IN THE *PHILEBUS*

As I have shown, Plato's two central criticisms of pleasure are firmly rooted in his conception of what pleasure is. If pleasure is by its very nature linked with pain and deceptive, then how can some pleasures be immune to these criticisms? In the *Republic* Plato provides an initial response to this question, offering a general account of pleasure that accommodates both good and bad pleasures. In the *Philebus* Plato develops a different solution to the puzzle of how there can be good and bad pleasures. I argue that the same considerations that lead Plato in the *Republic* to downgrade bodily pleasures to mere shadow-paintings of true pleasure lead him in the *Philebus* to challenge the basic assumption that the diverse experiences we call "pleasures" share a common nature at all.[20] As in the *Republic*, the distinction between good and bad pleasures in the *Philebus* does not correspond to the distinction between pleasures of the soul and those of the body; instead, it corresponds to the distinction between the pleasures characteristic of wise people and those pursued by fools. Socrates ultimately argues that good pleasures have a fundamentally different nature from bad pleasures, because they possess an inherent limit.

Socrates's first remark about pleasure in the dialogue is that it comes in many forms, and he cautions his interlocutor Protarchus not to

---

20 See E. Fletcher, "The Divine Method and the Disunity of Pleasure in the *Philebus*," *Journal of the History of Philosophy* 55.2 (2017): 179–208, for a more detailed defense of this thesis.

assume that all pleasures have the same nature, simply because they share a single name: "but as to pleasure, I know it is variegated and, just as I said, we must make it our starting point and consider carefully what sort of nature it has. If one goes by the name it is one single thing, but in fact it comes in many forms that are in some way even quite unlike each other" (*Philebus* 12c4–8). Socrates does not reject the possibility that pleasure might be a single thing—it is just this question, what sort of nature it has, that he wants to consider—but he makes it clear that we cannot draw any conclusions about the nature of pleasure from its name. Socrates goes on to contrast the pleasures of an intemperate person and those of a temperate one, as well as those of a fool and those of a wise person, claiming that they are "unlike" one another (12c8–d6). Protarchus replies: "Well, yes, Socrates—the pleasures come from opposite things. But *they* are not at all opposed to one another. For how could pleasure not be, of all things, most like pleasure? How could that thing not be most like itself?" (*Philebus* 12d7–e2). Protarchus resists the suggestion that pleasures are "unlike" one another in any respect, explaining Socrates's examples in terms of the different sources of these pleasures, rather than any inherent differences in the pleasures themselves. However, he does not heed Socrates's cautionary tale about names, for he immediately characterizes pleasure as a single thing, without providing an account of what pleasure is. Socrates asks Protarchus to identify the "common element" in good and bad pleasures that allows him to call them all good (13a). Socrates's request reveals his central concern about the unity of pleasure, that pleasures differ in value in a way that precludes them from sharing a single nature. This is because he thinks that pleasures are good or bad as a result of features that belong to the pleasures themselves, rather than their sources or effects.

In order to avoid Protarchus's mistake, Socrates undertakes a lengthy investigation into the nature of pleasure before drawing any conclusions about its value. After introducing a new methodology for conducting the inquiry (16a–19b), Socrates presents a novel division

of all being into four classes, (1) limit, (2) the unlimited, (3) mixtures
of limit and the unlimited, and (4) the cause of these mixtures (23c–
27c). A detailed discussion of this fourfold division of being is beyond
the scope of this chapter,[21] but it is significant that pleasure is initially
assigned to the class of the unlimited (27c–28a; 31a). While Socrates
does not frame this classification of pleasure explicitly as a criticism,
the imposition of limit on the unlimited produces good products, such
as health, beauty, and strength (26a–27b). Limit is also associated with
goodness and beauty later in the dialogue (65a). Socrates hints early on
that some pleasures could be saved by having limit imposed on them
(26b–c). The comparison between the disciplined and undisciplined
men in the *Gorgias* anticipates this identification of limit, as opposed
to unlimitedness, as a positive feature of pleasure. At this point in the
Philebus, Socrates has yet to actually provide an account of pleasure
that would confirm whether it is inherently unlimited, or whether at
least some pleasures can be "saved" by the imposition of limit.

Socrates examines pleasure in a piecemeal manner, gradually
introducing new types of pleasure and refining his account of pleasure's
nature as he goes. He first characterizes bodily pleasures as processes
of restoration and destruction of the harmony in a living organism
(32b–c).[22] This account has clear resonances with the "filling" account
in the *Republic* and the leaky-jar image in the *Gorgias*. In one respect,
the *Philebus*'s restoration account is more general than the *Republic*'s
account, for the relevant processes of restoration include warming
and cooling, drying and moistening, as well as "fillings" (31e–32a).
The restoration account also provides a unified explanation of bodily
pleasure and bodily pain. By contrast, in the *Republic* not all pleasures

---

21 See E. Fletcher, "Plato on Pure Pleasure and the Best Life," *Phronesis* 59 (2014): 113–142, for discussion of the significance of the fourfold division for the subsequent analysis and evaluation of pleasure in the *Philebus*.

22 Socrates does not explicitly restrict the restoration account to bodily pleasures; however, all of the examples he provides are physiological processes. He also distinguishes the psychic pleasures of anticipation as "another kind" of pleasure at 32b–d, and he never explains how the restoration account might apply to them.

are a return to the intermediate state of calm—some are movements into the "true above." Just before introducing the restoration account, Socrates claims that "we will not be able to provide a satisfactory examination of pleasure if we do not study it together with pain" (31b). This certainly seems to be the case for those pleasures that are restorations of a preceding destruction. On this account, every pleasure seems to presuppose pain, just as every process of restoration presupposes a process of destruction.[23]

Socrates next introduces a different kind of pleasure to which the restoration account does not seem to apply (32b–d). He clearly identifies the pleasures and pains connected with processes of restoration as "one kind" (*hen eidos*) of pleasure, and he distinguishes the pleasures of anticipating these processes as "another kind" (*heteron eidos*). Socrates does not say that the pleasures and pains of anticipation are themselves processes of restoration or destruction, and the distinctive features of these pleasures and pains tell against this interpretation. For one thing, these pleasures and pains belong entirely to the soul, rather than involving bodily processes, like warming or cooling. But most important, they arise "pure and unmixed with one another" (32c7–8).[24] If Socrates were thinking of the pleasures and pains of anticipation as restorations and destructions, only of a different type, then he would need to explain how these pleasures and pains could occur independently of one another.[25] After all, a

---

23 Later in the *Philebus*, Socrates refines the restoration account, identifying pleasures and pains only with those processes of restoration and destruction that are large enough to penetrate through the body and affect the soul (42e–43b). Movements of the body that are too small or gradual to move the soul are not perceived, making room for the possibility of pleasures of restoration that are preceded by unfelt (rather than painful) destructions.

24 Many scholars have argued that the restoration account is a general account that applies to all pleasures. See, for example, D. Frede, "Rumpelstiltskin's Pleasures: True and False Pleasures in Plato's *Philebus*," *Phronesis* 30 (1992): 151–180, T. Tuozzo, "The General Account of Pleasure in the *Philebus*," *Journal of the History of Philosophy* 34 (1994): 495–513, and M. Evans, "Plato's Anti-hedonism," *Proceedings of the Boston Area Colloquium of Ancient Philosophy* 22 (2007): 121–145. See Fletcher, "Plato on Pure Pleasure and the Best Life," for arguments against this view.

25 Note that at this point in the dialogue Socrates has not yet countenanced the possibility of unperceived restorations or destructions.

process of restoration just is the restoration of a previous process of destruction. It later becomes clear that the pleasures and pains that belong to the soul alone include those directed at the past and present, as well as the pleasures and pains involved in anticipating the future (39d–e). This indicates that Socrates is distinguishing between bodily and psychic pleasures in general in this passage, rather than giving an account that applies solely to the pleasures and pains of anticipation. Bodily and psychic pleasures do not differ from one another in a superficial way—it is not just that they have different sources, objects, or effects—but in what they are. Bodily pleasures are processes of restoration of the organism, and they are essentially linked with pain, whereas psychic pleasures are not essentially linked with pain and share the structure and many of the characteristics of beliefs. I will argue that bodily and psychic pleasures are also subject to different kinds of criticisms as a direct result of these differences in their natures.

The evaluation of pleasure in the *Philebus* is complex, for the dialogue puts forward both of the criticisms of pleasure that I outlined in section 1, while also isolating a narrow class of pleasures that are immune to these criticisms. As in the *Phaedo* and *Republic*, Socrates emphasizes the connection between certain pleasures and false beliefs, and yet he presents a new criticism of pleasure when he argues that pleasure itself can be false. The details of the argument in the *Philebus* that some pleasures can be evaluated as true or false are controversial, but the upshot is that at least some pleasures have the same structure as beliefs (*doxai*) and can be mistaken in a parallel way.[26] Protarchus resists Socrates's suggestion that pleasure can make a mistake, and he insists that falsity should always be attributed to a belief that accompanies

---

26 Most scholars argue that Socrates conceives of pleasure as a propositional attitude in this argument, e.g., T. Penner, "False Anticipatory Pleasures: *Philebus* 36a3–41a6," *Phronesis* 15 (2005): 166–178, D. Frede, "Rumpelstiltskin's Pleasures," and V. Harte, "The *Philebus* on Pleasure: The Good, the Bad and the False," *Proceedings of the Aristotelian Society*, 104 (2006): 111–128. F. Muniz, "Propositional Pleasures in Plato's *Philebus*," *Journal of Ancient Philosophy* 8 (2014): 49–75, is an exception and argues extensively against the propositional interpretation.

the pleasure (38a). In the elaborate comparison of the soul to an illustrated book, Socrates compares beliefs to statements written in the soul and pleasures to pictures that illustrate these statements. He argues that when the statements written in the soul are false, then the corresponding pictures are also false, even though they do not represent independent assessments of the world (39a–c).[27] The comparison between a pleasure and a picture allows Socrates to emphasize the integral relationship between a pleasure and its object. If pleasure is as inseparable from its object as a painting is from what it is a painting of, then one cannot evaluate a pleasure apart from its object any more than one could evaluate a belief apart from its object. Socrates evaluates both beliefs and pleasures as false when they are "about things that do not exist (40d). Although we find an anticipation of this criticism of pleasure in the *Phaedo*, where pleasures are said to arise simultaneously with false beliefs and to be directed at the same objects, in the *Philebus* Plato goes even further in attributing falsity directly to the pleasures themselves.

Unlike psychic pleasures, bodily pleasures cannot be false in the way that beliefs are false.[28] However, both bodily and psychic pleasures are subject to the now familiar criticisms that they are experienced together with pain and as a result produce false beliefs.[29] According to Socrates, when pleasure is experienced in proximity to pain, the juxtaposition of these two experiences distorts the pleasure and makes it appear larger than it is (42a–b). The problem is that

---

27 See E. Fletcher, "Pleasure, Judgment, and the Function of the Painter-Scribe Analogy" (unpublished), for a defense of this interpretation of the analogy.

28 The true-false distinction is not exhaustive of all pleasures, but applies only to psychic pleasures (39c, 40c4–6). Unlike bodily pleasures, psychic pleasures are directed at or "about" objects (37a–b). This feature of psychic pleasures makes them subject to a distinctive kind of defect: like beliefs, psychic pleasures can be mistaken about their objects.

29 Like false pleasures, mixed pleasures arise with false beliefs, and yet they produce false beliefs rather than being parasitic on them (42b). Socrates refers to pleasures with both types of defects as "false" (*pseudēs*), and yet he explicitly distinguishes between them (41a). See E. Fletcher, "Plato on False and Deceptive Pleasures," *Archiv der Geschichte der Philosophie* (forthcoming), for a more detailed defense of the claim that these are two distinct criticisms of pleasure.

mixed pleasures do not feel like mixtures, but rather like extremely
intense pleasures. It is unfortunate that the mixed pleasures do not
lead to a subjectively bad life, because the person who pursues these
pleasures does not recognize the cognitive and physical harms they
cause (47b). Socrates describes a person devoted to intense mixed
pleasures as foolish; like Callicles, such a person ends up irrationally
seeking painful, morbid conditions in order to experience ever more
intense pleasures.

At the end of the examination of pleasure, Socrates finally introduces
a narrow class of pleasures that are immune to all of the above criticisms.
These pleasures do not just happen to be true and unmixed with pain;
they are guaranteed to have these characteristics by their very nature.
The primary examples Socrates gives of this new class of pleasures are
certain pleasures of sight and hearing, specifically those connected
with pure and absolutely beautiful objects.

> SOCRATES: By the beauty of a shape, I do not mean what the many
> might presuppose, namely that of a living being or of a picture.
> What I mean, what the account says, is rather something
> straight or round and what is constructed out of these with a
> compass, rule and square, such as plane figures and solids. Those
> things I take it are not beautiful in a relative sense, as others
> are, but are by their very nature forever beautiful by themselves.
> They provide their own specific pleasures that are not at all
> comparable to those of rubbing! And colors are beautiful in an
> analogous way and import their own kinds of pleasures.
> PROTARCHUS: I am really trying to understand, Socrates, but will
> you also try to say this more clearly?
> SOCRATES: What I am saying is that those among the smooth and
> bright sounds that produce one pure note are not beautiful
> in relation to anything else but in and by themselves and that
> they are accompanied by their own pleasures, which belong to
> them by nature. (*Philebus* 51c–d)

The pleasures described in this passage are taken in objects of sense perception, but they are not processes of restoration. Instead, they are pure pleasures that belong to the soul alone.[30] Although psychic pleasures can arise together with pain, the purity of these pleasures is guaranteed by their objects, which are described as "by their very nature beautiful by themselves" and "not beautiful in relation to anything else." Since the objects of these pleasures are absolutely beautiful and not at all ugly, there is no danger they will give rise to a mixed rather than a pure pleasure. These pleasures are true, as well as pure, both in the sense that they do not appear larger or smaller than they really are, and in the sense that they are taken in absolutely beautiful objects about which a subject cannot be mistaken. This narrow class of pleasures does not include all pure pleasures, because many pure psychic pleasures are false, since they are taken in objects that do not exist. Likewise, it does not include all true pleasures, because there is nothing to stop a true pleasure of anticipation, for example, from arising in conjunction with pain.

Socrates ultimately draws a sharp distinction between the nature of pure and true pleasures and the nature of the pleasures that he criticized earlier in the dialogue. "But now that we have properly separated the pure pleasures and those that can rightly be called impure, let's add to our account the attribution of immoderation to the violent pleasures, but moderation, in contrast, to the others. That is to say, we will assign those pleasures which display high intensity and violence, no matter whether frequently or rarely to the class of the unlimited, the more or less, which affects both body and soul. The other kinds of pleasure we will assign to the class of things that possess measurement" (*Philebus* 52c). Although Philebus insisted earlier in the dialogue that pleasure belongs to the unlimited class, Socrates has shown that some pleasures have limit or measure inherent in their nature. As it turns out, pleasures do not all belong to the same class in the most

---

30 Socrates later describes them as "the soul's own pure pleasures" (66c).

fundamental division of being. Socrates does not fully explain what limits the pure and true pleasures, but their limited nature seems to come in part from their purity and in part from the nature of their objects. Since they are pure, they do not give rise to an irrational pursuit of ever more intense mixtures of pleasure and pain. They also have beautiful objects, and Socrates associates beauty very closely with limit and proportion (64e). As in the *Hippias Major*, here also the nature of a pleasure seems to be linked to the nature of its object. The distinction between limited and unlimited pleasures corresponds closely to the distinction Socrates made at the beginning of the dialogue between the pleasures characteristic of moderate, wise subjects and those of intemperate fools. However, through the lengthy investigation of pleasure Socrates has given an account of the difference in the underlying natures of these two groups of pleasure that explains and justifies his evaluation of them as good and bad, respectively.

5. CONCLUSION

There is substantial development in Plato's views about pleasure, but it comes as a result of his increasing recognition of the diversity of pleasures, rather than any substantive changes in his attitude toward specific types of pleasure. In the *Philebus*, Plato recognizes that pleasures do not all have the same nature, and as a result they are not subject to the same criticisms. Many of the details of the evaluation of pleasure in the *Philebus* are anticipated in earlier dialogues, including the two main criticisms of pleasure and some of the features that differentiate good pleasures. However, the evaluation of pleasure in the *Philebus* is still striking in a number of ways. For one thing, the ultimate distinction between good and bad pleasures does not coincide with any distinctions that sound familiar to contemporary ears, such as that between psychic and bodily pleasures or intellectual and sensory pleasures. On the contrary, Socrates evaluates only a narrow class of pure pleasures, which are taken in very specific objects, as good. The restriction of good pleasures to such a narrow class may seem unmotivated at first; after all, why not include the pleasure of seeing a beautiful painting, in addition to pure colors or perfect shapes? By carefully considering Plato's two central criticisms of pleasure throughout the corpus, we can begin to understand why in the end he evaluated these pleasures, and only these pleasures, as good. Plato insists that pleasures have the same nature as their objects. As a result, the best pleasures must not only arise independently of pain, but they must also have the most pure, real, and beautiful objects.

CHAPTER THREE

Aristotle on the Heterogeneity of Pleasure

Matthew Strohl

Aristotle famously claims that pleasures differ from one another in kind in accordance with differences in kind among the activities they arise in connection with—call this the covariance thesis. This aspect of Aristotle's theory of pleasure contrasts sharply with the prevalent conception of pleasure as a phenomenally characterized type of feeling. It seems quite clear that to maintain the covariance thesis, Aristotle must deny that pleasure is a phenomenally characterized type of feeling, as it is hard to imagine that the phenomenal character of the feelings associated with reading a nineteenth-century Russian novel on the one hand and eating a cupcake on the other could differ in a way that reflects the difference in kind between these two activities. The former activity is primarily cognitive while the latter is primarily sensory, and it does not seem plausible that this fundamental difference in kind could be reflected by phenomenal differences between two feelings.

Aristotle denies that pleasure is any type of feeling that arises in connection with our activities and instead takes pleasure to be an aspect of the activities themselves.[1] In particular, he takes pleasure to be the character that activities gain when there is a certain type of fit between the condition of the capacity being activated and the object that it is active in relation to. The paradigm case is one where the capacity is in the best possible condition and the object is the best or finest (most *kalon*) of the range of objects that the capacity engages with. In such cases, there is a fit between capacity and object in the sense that the capacity is in a condition to be activated in a manner that most fully realizes its nature as the capacity that it is and the object is such as to enable the full engagement of the capacity in such a condition. Such activities are considered "perfect" in virtue of this fit, and pleasure is identified with their very perfection.

I take it that Aristotle's understanding of pleasure as the perfection of perfect activity grounds his assertion of the covariance thesis. That is, he thinks that the relationship between pleasure and the activity it arises in connection with entails their covariance in kind. In this essay, I will defend this claim by developing an interpretation of the series of arguments that Aristotle gives for the covariance thesis in *Nicomachean Ethics* 10.5. In section 1, I explain Aristotle's account of pleasure as the perfection of perfect activity in greater detail. In section 2, I discuss Aristotle's first argument for the covariance thesis, according to which it follows from his account of pleasure as an aspect of perfect activity. When activities vary in kind, so too does this aspect. Because of pleasure's nature as an aspect of activity that varies in kind along with it, pleasure must be phenomenally heterogeneous in much the same manner as mental activity is. In section 3, I discuss his second argument, according to which the covariance thesis follows from the fact that the proper pleasure "increases" activity. Pleasure, in virtue of being the perfection of a perfect activity,

---

1 Matthew Strohl, "Pleasure as Perfection: *Nicomachean Ethics* X.4–5," *Oxford Studies in Ancient Philosophy* 41 (2011): 257–287.

bears a special relation to the activity it arises in connection with, such that it amplifies it in certain respects. This argument indicates that while Aristotle denies that pleasure is a phenomenally characterized type of feeling, he *does* think that pleasures have a phenomenal structure in common. In section 4, I discuss Aristotle's third argument, according to which the covariance thesis follows from the fact that an alien pleasure destroys activity. This argument sheds further light on the second argument and brings out additional details concerning the phenomenal structure of pleasure and the causal relationships between pleasures arising in connection with distinct activities. Finally, in section 5 I consider the difficult question of whether Aristotle's acceptance of the covariance thesis entails that pleasures differing in kind cannot be compared in pleasantness. I point to strong textual evidence that he thinks that pleasures differing in kind can indeed be compared in pleasantness, and suggest how his account might allow for this.

1. Pleasure and Perfect Activity

Aristotle's most famous remark on the nature of pleasure is the notorious simile of the bloom: "Pleasure perfects [τελεοῖ] the activity—not, however, as the state does, by being present in (the activity), but as a sort of added perfection [ἐπιγινόμενόν τι τέλος], like the bloom on those in the prime of youth" (NE 1174b31–33). Many commentators have found this passage to be unclear or confused.[2] It may seem as though Aristotle is struggling to express an important idea with a vague simile rather than spelling it out clearly because he does not in fact have a coherent view about what pleasure itself is. He is committed on the one hand to denying that pleasure is identical to pleasant activity and on the other hand to denying that pleasure is separate from pleasant activity (NE 1175b30–33). Elizabeth

---

2 W. F. R. Hardie, *Aristotle's Ethical Theory* (Oxford: Oxford University Press, 1980), 314; C. C. W. Taylor, "Pleasure: Aristotle's Response to Plato," in *Plato and Aristotle's Ethics*, ed. R. Heinaman (Aldershot, England: Ashgate, 2003): 19–20; David Bostock, "Pleasure and Activity in Aristotle's Ethics," *Phronesis* 32 (1988): 251.

Anscombe famously remarked that he was reduced to "sheer babble" by the lack of options he is left with due to these two commitments.[3]

I claim, on the contrary, that Aristotle is in fact stating an intelligible view reasonably clearly in this passage. To understand his meaning, it is necessary to interpret the simile in close connection with the preceding text. Aristotle has already established a connection between an activity's pleasantness and its *perfection*:

> Every perceptual capacity is active in relation to its perceptible object, and perfectly active when it is in good condition in relation to the finest of its perceptual objects. For this above all seems to be the character of perfect activity, and it doesn't matter if we ascribe it to the capacity or to the subject that has it. Hence for each capacity the best activity is the activity of the subject in the best condition in relation to the best object of the capacity. This activity will be the most perfect and the most pleasant (NE 1174b14–20).

He tells us clearly in this passage that an activity is perfect when the capacity being activated is in a good condition in relation to a fine object. The idea, I take it, is that when the capacity being activated is in a good condition it becomes possible to more fully utilize the capacity in question with respect to its natural end. The natural end of our capacity for sight is seeing, and when the capacity is in a good condition it is possible to more fully realize this end. It is not sufficient for a capacity to be in a good condition for it to fully realize its natural end, however, since it also needs an object that is apt fully to make use of this good condition. A capacity for seeing in the best possible condition would not be perfectly activated if its object were something ugly or mundane.[4] In order for the

---

3 G. E. M. Anscombe, "Modern Moral Philosophy," in *The Collected Philosophical Papers of G. E. M. Anscombe*, vol. 3, *Ethics, Religion, and Politics* (Minneapolis: University of Minnesota Press, 1981), 27.
4 To fully activate a capacity, it is not sufficient to merely utilize it completely. (A thoroughly ugly object could perhaps do this.) The full activation of a capacity entails fully realizing its nature as the capacity that it is and as a part of human nature more broadly. This generates normative constraints

resultant activity to be *perfect*, a capacity in a good condition must be active in relation to a fine object, one that is apt in virtue of its fineness to fully utilize the good condition that the capacity is in.[5] A capacity in a good condition is, as it were, more capacious, and thereby requires a more demanding object for full activation.

The point of the simile of the bloom is to express the idea that pleasure is the *very perfection* of a perfect activity. When the capacity being activated is in a good condition and is active in relation to a fine object, the resultant activity is thereby perfected. Aristotle states in the simile: "pleasure perfects [τελεοῖ] the activity—not, however, as the state [i.e., the condition of the capacity being activated] does, by being present in (the activity), but as a sort of added perfection [ἐπιγινόμενόν τι τέλος]" (NE 1174b15–17). Pleasure perfects activity not by being one of the conditions that bring about the activity's perfection, but rather by being the very perfection that the activity attains when these conditions are met. An activity of seeing is not necessarily pleasant, but rather is pleasant when the relevant perfecting conditions are in place. When the activity is perfected, pleasure is the perfect character that it has in virtue of the joint contribution of the good condition of the capacity being activated and the fineness of the object that it is active in relation to. It is the aspect of a perfect activity that distinguishes it from an activity of the same type that falls short of perfection. "The bloom on those in the prime of youth" is another example of an added perfection. A young person has the bloom when their sexual attractiveness is perfected in virtue of the set of features that come along with being at the prime of youth. These features bring about the perfection of their sexual attractiveness, whereas the bloom is identified with this perfection.

---

on the condition that the capacity must be in and the character of the object that it must be active in relation to. See section 1 of Strohl, "Pleasure as Perfection," for a fuller explanation.

5 I give an account of why fineness is required for the full activation of a capacity in a good condition in Strohl, "Pleasure as Perfection," 263–265.

One may worry that this account of pleasure is too narrow to accommodate a vast range of cases that we ordinarily consider to be pleasant. I can report with great confidence that I have taken pleasure in many objects that were not at all fine on occasions when my faculties were not in a good condition. Sometimes, for instance, I crave a cheap diner breakfast. When this craving strikes, I would not enjoy a nice breakfast at a fancy bistro as much as I would a plate of cheap diner food. Is Aristotle committed to denying that I experience pleasure on such occasions? The answer is surely that he is not.[6] At NE 1126a10–29, Aristotle clearly states that people who are in a deficient condition also take pleasure, but they take it in inferior objects that match their condition. I take it that the idea is that in these deficient cases, the relation between the condition of the subject's faculties and the object that they are active in relation to is *analogous* to the relation between faculties in a good condition and a fine object. Aristotle is happy to call such derivative cases instances of "perfection," just as we speak of someone being a "perfect thief" even though being a thief is not a good thing.[7] What unites all cases where an activity is pleasant is that there is a *fit* between the condition of the subject's faculties and the object they are active in relation to. When one's faculties are in a good condition, they fit with a fine object; when they are in a deficient condition, they fit with an inferior object.[8] He calls cases where the fit is between a good condition and a fine object *unqualified pleasures* and derivative cases *qualified pleasures* because in derivative cases the pleasantness of the activity depends on the subject being in a deficient condition and so we can only say that the activity is pleasant *for a subject in a given condition*, whereas in unqualified cases the activity is pleasant for human beings when they are in a condition that fulfills their essential

---

6 Here I disagree strongly with Gerd Van Riel, *Pleasure and the Good Life* (Leiden: Brill, 2000), 77.

7 See *Metaphysics*, Δ16, 1021b17–19.

8 This is not to say that an inexperienced listener could not take pleasure in Mahler's Ninth Symphony, but rather that in such a case the listener would not be engaging with the same object as the practiced music lover, because the piece would not be apprehended in its full fineness.

nature, and so no qualification is needed and the activity can simply be said to be pleasant.

2. THE SIGNIFICANCE OF ARISTOTLE'S CONCEPTION
OF PLEASURE AS AN *ASPECT OF* ACTIVITY

After presenting his theory of pleasure in NE 10.4, Aristotle turns in 10.5 to give a series of arguments for the covariance thesis. These arguments help to clarify what his theory of pleasure is and what he takes its significance to be. They are also our best evidence about Aristotle's understanding of the way pleasure is experienced. The overall picture of the phenomenology of pleasure that emerges from these arguments is that there is no phenomenal element that all pleasant experiences have in common, but that all pleasant experiences do share a certain phenomenal structure. In this section, I will be concerned with the first argument, according to which the covariance thesis follows from the nature of pleasure as the perfection of perfect activity. Aristotle's basic reasons for denying that all pleasures share a common phenomenal element emerge from this argument.

Aristotle writes:

> Hence pleasures also seem to differ in kind. For we suppose that things that differ in kind are perfected by different things. This is how it appears, both with natural things and artifacts, such as animals, trees, a painting, a statue, a house, or an implement. Similarly, activities that differ in kind are perfected by things that differ in kind. Activities of thought differ from activities of perception in kind, and these activities of perception differ from each other in kind; and so the pleasures that perfect these activities also differ in kind (NE 1175a21–28).

The word "hence" (ὅθεν) refers back to the claim made in the last sentence of the previous chapter, where Aristotle says that there is no pleasure without activity and that pleasure perfects every activity (which is not to say that every activity is perfect, but rather that every activity, when it is perfect, is perfected by pleasure). This indicates that his argument here hinges on his identification of pleasure with the perfection of perfect activity. In NE 10.4, at 1174b23–26, he clarified that the way in which pleasure perfects activity is not the same as the way in which the perceptual capacity and perceptual object perfect it, just as health and a doctor are not causes of being healthy in the same way. A doctor is the cause of being healthy in the sense that the doctor brings it about that a patient becomes healthy, but there are other ways of being a cause of being healthy. Health is also the cause of being healthy, not by bringing it about that a patient becomes healthy, but rather by being the condition that the patient acquires when she becomes healthy. The analogy should not be taken to imply that pleasure is in some sense a *cause* of perfect activity. The point is rather that just as there are several ways of causing something, there are several ways of perfecting something. Pleasure perfects activity, not by bringing it about that it becomes perfect, but rather by being the very perfection that it gains when there is the right kind of fit between object and capacity.

When Aristotle refers in the passage quoted above to the "different things" that perfect things that are different in kind, I take it he is referring *not* to the things that bring perfection about, but rather to the very perfection that things gain when they are perfected. He makes it very clear in the analogy with health discussed above that pleasure does not perfect activity by bringing it about that an activity becomes perfect, and so the first argument for the covariance thesis is invalid if he is using the verb "perfect" in the sense of "bringing it about that something becomes perfect." The correct interpretation of the argument, I take it, is that just as the perfection of one kind of *thing* is different in kind from the perfection of another kind of *thing*, so too this is true for *activities*. The perfection of an activity of thought differs in kind from that of an activity of perception, and the perfection of an activity of hearing differs in kind from the perfection of an activity of seeing. Since pleasure is the perfection of a perfect activity, it follows that pleasures differ from one another in kind.[9]

This argument sheds light on the basis of the covariance thesis and on its significance. Pleasure, for Aristotle, is not something that we experience *as a result* of performing an activity, as a sort of reward or incentive. Rather, pleasure is identified with an aspect of the activity itself, namely, the perfection that it gains in virtue of the fit between the condition of the subject's capacity and the object it is active in relation to. When activities vary in kind, this aspect varies along with them. The pleasure associated with an activity of seeing differs in kind from the pleasure associated with an activity of smelling in much the same way as the perfection of a well-designed bed differs in kind from the perfection of a particularly effective blender. Beds and blenders are different kinds of things, and the aspects of beds and blenders that contribute to their respective perfection are also different in kind. A bed is perfect (let us suppose) if it is supportive enough to promote good posture while also being soft enough to be comfortable. The perfection of a bed is the character that it has in virtue of these perfecting elements. A blender on the other hand is perfect if it can quickly and effectively liquefy anything one might have reason to liquefy without causing too much noise. The perfection of a blender is the character that it has in virtue of *these* perfecting elements. The perfecting elements for a bed are different in kind from the perfecting elements for a blender, and therefore the resultant perfect character for a bed is different in kind from the resultant perfect character of a blender. An activity of seeing is perfect if one's capacity for sight is in a good condition and one engages with a fine visible object, whereas an activity of smelling is perfect if one's capacity for smell is in a good condition and one engages with a fine olfactory object. These sense modalities and the objects they engage with are different in kind, and

---

9 This argument is also discussed in section 4 of Strohl, "Pleasure as Perfection."

so it follows that the perfect characters that emerge when there is the right kind of fit between them are also different in kind.

The covariance thesis, then, is a natural extension of Aristotle's view that pleasure is the perfection of a perfect activity. Every kind of activity has its own kind of perfection, and so the pleasure arising in connection with different kinds of activities will accordingly differ in kind. This understanding of pleasure may seem unduly formal. Pleasure is, after all, something that one experiences. It seems to me that this worry is ultimately unfounded. The covariance thesis entails that there will be no particular phenomenal element that is common to all pleasant experiences, but I will argue in what follows that Aristotle's theory entails a *phenomenal structure* that all pleasant experiences have in common. The subsequent two arguments that Aristotle gives for the covariance thesis in NE 10.5 provide the best basis we have for understanding this phenomenal structure. I will examine them in turn.

3. The "Increasing" Structure of Pleasant Experiences

Aristotle writes:

[That pleasures differ in kind] is also apparent from the way each pleasure is proper to [συνῳκειῶσθαι] the activity that it perfects. For the proper [οἰκεία] pleasure increases [συναύξει] the activity; for we judge each thing better and more exactly when our activity involves pleasure. If, for instance, we enjoy doing geometry, we become better geometers, and understand each question better; and similarly lovers of music, building, and so on improve at their proper characteristic activity when they enjoy it. Each pleasure increases the activity, and what increases it is proper to it; and since the activities are different in kind, what is proper to them is also different in kind. (NE 1175a29–b1)

The word translated as "proper," οἰκεία, has the connotations of "akin to" and "intimately connected with." In support of the claim that pleasure is proper to activity in a way that entails their covariance in kind, Aristotle points to the phenomenon of pleasure "increasing" the activity that it arises in connection with. All else being equal, when one takes pleasure in performing an activity, this leads one to perform it for a longer period of time, more adeptly, with more enthusiasm, and so on. If one enjoys thinking about a math problem, one will think about it with greater focus and persistence than if one did not enjoy thinking about it.

Aristotle gives a somewhat elliptical argument for the covariance thesis on the basis of this phenomenon: "each pleasure increases the activity, and what increases it is proper to it; and since the activities are different in kind, what is proper to them is also different in kind." The idea here, I take it, is that the fact that pleasure increases the particular activity that it arises in connection with indicates that it bears a special relation to this activity, which he calls "being proper to it." This relation entails that the pleasure differs in kind from pleasures that are connected with activities that differ in kind. That is, the relation is such that if A bears it to B, and C bears it to D, and B and D differ in kind, it follows that A and C differ in kind.

I take it that in claiming that pleasure is proper to activity, Aristotle is again drawing a corollary of his view that pleasure is the perfection of perfect activity and using this corollary to support the covariance thesis. The pleasure of listening to music is the perfect character that the activity of listening has in virtue of the interplay between the fineness of the music being listened to and the good condition of one's capacity for listening. Aristotle is claiming that the perfect character of an activity stands in the relation of *being proper to* the activity itself. This makes sense, as this relation is aptly described as "intimate" and there is a clear sense in which the perfect character of an activity is "akin to" the activity itself. Pleasure is the aspect of a perfect activity that differentiates it from a nonperfect activity of the same type. For example, there is a mountain visible from my office window. I see it all the time, and so I don't tend to focus my attention on it enough to appreciate its beauty. It is a fine object, but my usual activity of seeing it is not pleasant, because I am not in a condition to fully engage the relevant faculties when I see it. On some days, however, circumstances collide such that I stop and notice the mountain's beauty and take pleasure in it. I may be in an appreciative mood where I am more inclined to focus my attention on the ruggedness of the landscape around me, and the mountain might be bathed in particularly stunning golden light, so that I suddenly see it *perfectly*, which is to say that the condition of my faculties and the appearance of the mountain fit together on this occasion. Aristotle identifies the pleasure I experience with the aspect of this experience that differentiates it from my ordinary, nonpleasant experience of seeing the mountain. Pleasure is the character that my activity gains in virtue of the relevant perfecting contributions. It is "intimately related" to the activity in that it is an aspect of that very activity. It is "akin" to the activity in that its character derives from the character of the activity. A perfect activity of mountain-seeing gives rise to a pleasure that is an aspect of such mountain-seeing, and this pleasure will differ in kind from a pleasure that is an aspect of music-listening or fruit-tasting in a way that reflects the difference in kind between activities of seeing on the one hand and listening or tasting on the other.

This story helps us see why pleasure, understood as the perfection of a perfect activity, "increases" the activity it arises in connection with. Take a case where I have just had my morning coffee and am feeling prepared to concentrate and in the mood to read. I pick up a good book and start to take pleasure in reading it. The fit between the — condition of my capacity for reading and the quality of the book causes me to become increasingly focused as I read and therefore to read more quickly and with greater attention to detail. In the course of reading the book in this focused way, I come to a realization about something I had not understood previously, and I begin to think about the book in a deeper way than I was capable of when I began to read. The condition of my capacity for reading is now in a better condition, and I begin to enjoy the book even more and thus read it with even greater focus, thus putting myself in an even better condition for reading (and so on). In this indirect manner, performing the activity with pleasure improves the condition of my capacity and thereby makes it possible to perform the activity even more pleasantly.[10] The improvement of my condition involves an increase in my focus on the object, and may involve other changes as well. For instance, when I enjoy reading, my mood may shift so that I am more open to being emotionally affected by what I am reading, which increases my enjoyment and thus further increases my openness to being emotionally affected, and so on. This strikes me as a very plausible way of explaining the phenomena surrounding the pleasure of reading. The same basic story can be told about even, for example, the pleasure of sitting in the sun. The warm feeling of the sun leads us to continue to sit in the sun and to focus on the pleasant sensation of the sun's warmth more attentively.

Aristotle's argument, then, is that the fact that pleasure increases activity in this manner reveals that it is "proper to" activity so as to entail the covariance thesis. In order for the pleasure of reading to put one in a better condition for reading and not for, say, fruit-tasting, it must bear a particular relation to the activity of reading that it does not bear to other activities. It must be the kind of thing that puts one in a better condition for reading in particular, whereas the pleasure of fruit-tasting must be the kind of thing that puts one in a better condition for fruit-tasting in particular. The two pleasures are therefore different in kind. Aristotle develops this argument further in his third argument for the covariance thesis, which I turn to in section 4, by considering what happens when we engage in two activities at once.

---

10 The notion of "improvement" here is not that the capacity is improved *simpliciter* but rather that it becomes more apt to fit with the object at hand. When I am taking pleasure in a cheap diner breakfast, it does not put me in a condition where I would suddenly prefer fine cuisine, but rather puts me in a condition where I am better able to enjoy the cheap diner breakfast.

Aristotle does not think that there is a general phenomenal characterization of all pleasure, since the phenomenal character of any given kind of pleasure is specific to the activity it arises in connection with. We can now see that he *does* think that there is *structural* similarity between the phenomenal characters of all pleasures. Every pleasant experience has the structural feature of *increasing* due to its pleasant character. This means that *ceteris paribus* all pleasant experiences have the structure of the subject's focus on the object of experience increasing (and perhaps the subject's condition for engaging with the object improving in other ways), thereby leading the subject to continue to perform the activity and to do so with increasing perfection and thus increasing pleasure. This will eventually reach a limit where either the subject has exhausted the object such that it is no longer apt to fully engage the relevant faculties (e.g., I look at a painting with increasing focus until I stop noticing anything new and thus my pleasure and focus wane) or other aspects of the subject's condition interfere (e.g., I study Aristotle with increasing pleasure and focus until I become tired for physiological reasons and my faculties are no longer in a good condition for studying Aristotle and thus my pleasure and focus wane). The way this process of "increasing" proceeds will differ for different kinds of activities, and so it does not entail any particular phenomenal character, but it *does* entail a phenomenal structure that any pleasant experience will have.

4. INTERRELATIONS BETWEEN PLEASURES

Aristotle's third argument for the covariance thesis is closely related to the second:

> This is even more apparent from the way some activities are impeded by pleasures from other activities. For lovers of flutes, for instance, cannot pay attention to a conversation if they catch the sound of

someone playing the flute, because they enjoy flute playing more than their present activity; and so the pleasure proper to flute playing destroys the activity of conversation. The same is true in other cases also, whenever we are engaged in two activities at once. For the more pleasant activity pushes out the other one, all the more if it is much more pleasant, so that we no longer even engage in the other activity. Hence if we are enjoying one thing intensely, we do not do another very much. It is when we are only mildly pleased that we do something else; for instance, people who eat nuts in theaters do this most when the actors are bad. Since, then, the proper pleasure makes an activity more exact, longer, and better, whereas an alien pleasure damages it, clearly the two pleasures differ widely. For an alien pleasure does virtually what a proper pain does. The proper pain destroys activity, so that if, for instance, writing or rational calculation has no pleasure and is in fact painful for us, we do not write or calculate, since the action is painful. Hence the proper pleasures and pains have contrary effects on an activity; and the proper ones are those that arise in connection with [ἐπὶ] the activity in its own right. And as we have said, the effect of alien pleasures is similar to the effect of pain, since they ruin the activity, though not in the same way as pain. (NE 1175b1–24)

This is not an entirely new line of argument. It is meant to support the claim that pleasures are proper to the activities they are connected with in a way that entails their covariance in kind. Aristotle points to a case where a lover of flute music is engaged in a conversation, but then hears flute music. As she begins to take pleasure in listening to the music, this pleasure increases her activity of listening so that she starts focusing on it more and more intensely. Meanwhile, she is increasingly distracted from the conversation, to the point where her capacity for conversing comes to be in an outright bad condition and she stops taking pleasure in connection with the conversation. Eventually, she stops participating in the conversation altogether.[11] Aristotle's point is that there must be something about the character of the pleasure she takes in listening to flute music that increases the activity of listening but impedes the activity of conversing. Both activities are going on at the same time, and she initially experiences pleasure in connection with both. If the pleasures connected with the two activities were the same in kind (as would be the case if, e.g., pleasure were a single type of feeling), there would be no explanation as to why the pleasure connected with the activity of listening increases that activity but impedes the activity of conversing. The pleasure of listening must be the kind of thing that increases the activity of listening but impedes the activity of conversing, and so must be different in kind from the pleasure of conversing, which is the kind of thing that increases the activity of conversing.

This case supports the claim that pleasures are proper to the activities they arise in connection with because it reveals that pleasures stand in very different causal relationships with these activities than they do with other activities that the subject is engaging in at the same time. The pleasure of listening to flute music increases the activity of listening to flute music while destroying the activity of conversation. If the pleasures attending the two activities were the same, then there would be no reason that the pleasure of music-listening would not increase the activity of conversation as well as the activity of music-listening. The fact that it increases the one activity while destroying the

---

11 Aristotle says in the passage under discussion that an alien pleasure does virtually what a proper pain does. He does not give an account of pain in NE 10.1–5, but one might reasonably infer that just as pleasure is the character an activity has when there is a good fit between capacity and object, pain is the character an activity has when there is a poor fit between capacity and object. Take, for instance, someone who has been working on a philosophy article for twelve hours and decides to stop and rest. The person is mentally exhausted, and so if she is later compelled to think about a philosophical problem to answer an email from a student, she will have difficulty focusing, and her activity of thinking about the problem will be impeded in various ways. The impeded condition of her activity of thinking, on the suggestion being considered, counts as pain. The pain the person experiences will cause her to do a progressively worse job thinking about the problem and may lead her to abandon the task altogether and leave the email for the next morning; it will do virtually the same thing an alien pleasure has been seen to do.

other indicates that it is proper to the activity it arises in connection with and different in kind from the pleasure associated with the other activity.

Aristotle may seem to have neglected an alternative explanation of this phenomenon. If one thinks that pleasure is a single type of feeling, one might think that instances of this feeling bear certain causal relations exclusively to the activities they are connected with. On this view, if I am enjoying listening to flute music and conversing at the same time, I experience two instances of the same type of feeling that have distinct sets of causal relations. The pleasure connected with listening to flute music may be related to the activity of listening in such a way that it increases it, but be related to the activity of conversation in such a way that it impedes it. It does not seem right, however, to think that when I take pleasure in two different activities simultaneously I experience two instances of the same type of feeling. I don't even understand what it would be to experience two instances of the same type of feeling at the same time. For instance, if I am nervous both about giving a talk and getting the results of a blood test, I simply feel nervous. It seems bizarre to say that I feel two instances of nervousness at once. The cognitive aspect of my nervousness might be twofold, but not the affective aspect.

Aristotle's empirical observation that the pleasure associated with a given activity impedes other activities may seem false, especially insofar as we think that some pleasant activities synergize with other activities. For instance, one may find that one enjoys having music on while one reads. Aristotle does not address this worry, but it does seem that there is at least one plausible story for him to tell in response. If I think about why listening to music increases my enjoyment of reading, it seems that it is because it creates more suitable background conditions for reading. It is easier for me to split my attention between certain pieces of music (generally less dynamic ones) and reading than it is to read while coping with the more chaotic ambient sounds that the music drowns out. Also, the music may relax me and help me stop thinking about all the things I need to do the next day and thereby enable me to attend to my reading with greater focus. One of the conditions that must be in place for an activity to be pleasant is that the capacity being activated must be in a good condition. In this case, listening to music actually improves the condition of my capacity for reading by drowning out ambient sounds and relaxing me and thus removing various factors that would otherwise impede my capacity for reading. Aristotle could say, then, that the synergy between the two activities exists not because the pleasure of listening to music directly increases the activity of reading, but rather because the activity of listening to music incidentally creates conditions that are conducive to the good performance of the activity of reading. If I were to enjoy the music too much, it would presumably destroy my activity of reading because I would shift my focus away from reading. It seems, then, that this particular phenomenon is not a counterexample to Aristotle's view.

A connected concern is that it is not clear how Aristotle can explain the pleasure of complex activities like watching a play. Watching a play involves (at least) activities of seeing, hearing, and thinking. If he were really committed to the strong claim that the pleasure of one activity always destroys other activities that are different in kind, it would be very difficult for him to explain the phenomena surrounding complex activities that involve the activation of more than one capacity for thought or perception. For his theory to be at all plausible, he must allow for complex activities to constitute a single, unified activity. After all, one of the activities he uses as an example in this very passage is watching a play, which is clearly a complex activity. If he allows for complex activities to count as a single activity, then the claim he is making is considerably weaker than it may seem, and it becomes possible to make sense of various apparent cases of synergy between pleasant activities as cases where the subject in fact undertakes a single complex activity.

5. Is the Covariance Thesis Compatible with the Possibility of Comparing Pleasures with Respect to Pleasantness?

Finally, I will consider the ramifications of Aristotle's acceptance of the covariance thesis for the question of how it is possible to compare pleasures in pleasantness. For Aristotle's theory to be plausible, it must be possible to compare pleasures of different kinds in pleasantness. We frequently make decisions about how to act on the basis of such comparisons. For instance, I might pass on a concert in order to spend the evening reading a novel for the sole reason that I expect to enjoy the novel more than I would the concert. Or I might eat a peanut butter sandwich instead of going out for a more expensive lunch because I think I would reap more enjoyment overall if I saved my money to go to the movies the next day. Considerations beyond pleasantness often come into play in such decisions, but it would be prohibitively counterintuitive to deny that legitimate comparisons of pleasantness can play a role.

On the other hand, it seems wrong to allow that pleasures can always be compared on a *quantitative* basis, as Bentham's influential theory of the hedonic calculus suggests. Bentham thinks that pleasantness can be quantified in terms of intensity and duration and that we can use this quantity to make comparisons in pleasantness. This would have counterintuitive consequences if it were true. Suppose (assuming Bentham's theory) that I enjoy eating a hot dog about a third as much as I enjoy attending a ballet. If someone offers to trade me four hot dogs for my ballet ticket and my goal is to have as pleasant an evening as possible then I should take the deal (assuming I have room in my stomach for four hot dogs). But this seems bizarre. Regardless of how many hot dogs I will get to eat and how much I will enjoy each of them, I may simply prefer the pleasure of the ballet over the pleasure of eating any number of hot dogs (even bracketing considerations such as the diminishing returns of eating so many hot dogs). This need not be because there are reasons aside from pleasantness for preferring the ballet; I might prefer the one kind of pleasure over the other for purely hedonic reasons. I might not be after the largest quantity of pleasure, but rather the highest quality pleasure.

Aristotle's theory seems to me to successfully find the middle ground between on the one hand denying that pleasures can be compared in pleasantness and on the other hand making comparisons between pleasures a purely quantitative matter. He clearly commits himself to the possibility of comparing pleasures in pleasantness: "hence for each capacity the best activity is the activity of the subject in the best condition in relation to the best object of the capacity. This activity will be the most perfect *and the most pleasant*. For every perceptual capacity and every sort of thought and study has its pleasure; the most pleasant activity is the most perfect; and the most perfect is the activity of the subject in good condition in relation to the most excellent object of the capacity" (NE 1174b18–20). In this passage, Aristotle states what it is for an activity to be the most perfect of its kind (i.e., the most perfect way of exercising the relevant capacity) and then states without further explanation or argument that such an activity will also be the most pleasant of its kind. His view appears to be that an activity's degree of pleasantness consists in its degree of perfection. This interpretation renders the inference in question unproblematic, and moreover makes very good sense if Aristotle identifies pleasure with the perfection of a perfect activity. But how can Aristotle maintain a ranking of pleasures in terms of degree of perfection without the notion of degree of perfection ultimately collapsing into a Benthamite notion of quantity?

I take it that the answer to this question can be found by tracing the influence of Plato's *Philebus*. Plato has Socrates state a general account of purity that grounds his understanding of the way pleasures can be compared in pleasantness, using whiteness as an example:

> SOCRATES: Let us take whiteness first, if you have no objection.
> PROTARCHUS: That is fine with me.

SOCRATES: Now, how can there be purity in the case of whiteness, and what sort of thing is it? Is it the greatest quantity or amount, or is it rather the complete lack of any admixture, that is, where there is not the slightest part of any other kind contained in this color?

PROTARCHUS: It will obviously be the perfectly unadulterated color.

SOCRATES: Right. But shall we not also agree that this is the truest and most beautiful of all instances of white, rather than what is greatest in quantity or amount?

PROTARCHUS: Certainly.

SOCRATES: So we are perfectly justified if we say that a small portion of pure white is to be regarded as whiter than a larger quantity of an impure whiteness, and at the same time more beautiful and possessed of more truth?

PROTARCHUS: Perfectly justified.

SOCRATES: Well, now, we don't need to run through many more examples to justify our account of pleasure, too, every small and insignificant pleasure that is unadulterated by pain will turn out to be pleasanter, truer, and more beautiful than a greater quantity and amount of the impure kind. (53a–c)[12]

"Pure" is used here to mean lack of admixture. Socrates says in this passage that pure pleasures are ones that are not mixed with any pain. I do not think that Aristotle takes up this view of what it is for a pleasure to be pure, since he does not accept the theory of pleasure that underlies it, but this passage from the *Philebus* is nevertheless very helpful.

I suggest that when Aristotle makes comparisons between pleasures, he is invoking a notion related to Plato's notion of "purity." Just as

12 Translated by Dorothea Frede, in *Plato: Complete Works*, ed. John M. Cooper and D. S. Hutchinson (Indianapolis: Hackett, 1997)

the whitest white is the purest white, and not the largest quantity of white, the most pleasant pleasure is the purest one, and not the one that maximizes some quantity. Aristotle explicitly links degree of pleasantness with degree of purity in NE 10.7: "besides, we think pleasure must be mixed into happiness; and it is agreed that the activity in accord with wisdom is the most pleasant of the activities in accord with virtue. Certainly, philosophy seems to have remarkably pure [καθαρειότητι] and firm pleasures, and it is reasonable for those who have knowledge to spend their lives more pleasantly than those who seek it" (NE 1177a22–27). I propose that Aristotle's notion of purity tracks degree of perfection—lack of admixture with imperfection. An important piece of evidence for this idea is found in NE 10.5: "sight differs from touch in purity, as hearing and smell do from taste; hence the pleasures also differ in the same way. So also do the pleasures of thought differ from these [pleasures of sense]; and both sorts have different kinds within them" (NE 1175b36–a3). Peter Hadreas has persuasively argued that this ranking of capacities in purity depends on the extent to which each capacity is capable of apprehending order.[13] As I discussed in section 1, a capacity in a better condition is thereby *more capacious* and so requires a more demanding object to be fully activated. We can make the same sort of comparison between different faculties as we can between more and less perfect ways of activating the same faculty. Thought apprehends order to a greater extent than sight, which apprehends order to a greater extent than smell, which apprehends order to a greater extent than touch, and so on. A perfect activity of a purer capacity (i.e., one that apprehends order to a greater extent) is more pleasant than a perfect activity of a less pure one, because the purer capacity is more capacious in the same basic way that a capacity in better condition is more capacious than the same capacity in a worse condition. If perfecting an activity is a matter of fully

---

13 Peter Hadreas, "The Functions of Pleasure in NE X 4–5," *Ancient Philosophy* 24 (2004): 155–167.

utilizing the relevant capacity so as to fully realize its nature, then a capacity that is more capable of apprehending order has more room for perfection than a capacity that is less capable of apprehending order.[14] Fully utilizing a purer capacity is more demanding than fully utilizing a less pure capacity. All it might take to perfect an activity of touch is a smooth surface (which requires a minimal amount of order), while an activity of sight may require a beautiful landscape (which requires much more order), and an activity of thought may require a literary masterwork (which requires a tremendous amount of order).

Aristotle can say, then, that comparisons in pleasantness should be made in terms of which of two pleasures has the highest degree of perfection, and that this has nothing to do with Benthamite quantification. Any amount of experiencing a pleasure of touch, no matter how vast, would be less pleasant than even a few minutes of virtuous theoretical study. To say that the one is more pleasant than the other is to say that one is more perfect than the other. Duration and intensity are irrelevant to comparisons in pleasantness, except insofar as they are integral to a given activity's perfection (e.g., a certain duration would be required for a perfect activity of listening to a certain piece of music). This aspect of Aristotle's theory seems to me to be extremely attractive and intuitive. When we choose one activity over another simply because we expect it to last longer, we are choosing on the basis of a practical consideration about how best to utilize our available time rather than on the basis of pleasantness. Determinations about pleasantness depend on the intrinsic character of the activities themselves.

---

14 Francisco Gonzalez, "Aristotle on Pleasure and Perfection," *Phronesis* 36 (1991): 141–159, has made the interesting suggestion that Aristotle's ranking of capacities in purity is based on the extent to which a given capacity can assimilate to its object. I take this suggestion to be a promising way to explain more precisely why the extent to which an activity involves an apprehension of order is directly proportionate to its degree of perfection. Because touch cannot assimilate to its object as fully as thought, the capacity cannot be as fully utilized by a given activity. There will always be indefiniteness and fluctuation, and the possibility of an even more intense pleasure. I suspect there is a fruitful connection between this idea and Plato's classification of certain pleasures in the *Philebus* as belonging to the class of the "unlimited," but exploring this connection is outside the scope of this piece.

6. CONCLUSION

My aim in this chapter has been to give an interpretation of Aristotle's series of arguments for the covariance thesis, and in so doing to explore the significance of the thesis and of these arguments. I have made the case that, for Aristotle, pleasure is as phenomenally heterogeneous as mental activity is, but that he does think that the phenomenal character of any pleasant activity will have a certain structure. Namely, he thinks that *ceteris paribus* when one takes pleasure in performing an activity, one will perform the activity with progressively greater aptitude, focus, enthusiasm, and so on. This is due, I have argued, to the manner in which a perfect activity improves the conditions for its own performance. I have also considered the prospects for comparing heterogeneous pleasures in pleasantness, and I have argued that Aristotle's theory has the resources to allow for an intuitively attractive account of how such comparison is possible.

CHAPTER FOUR

This So Sullied Flesh? Islamic
Approaches to Human Pleasures

Sajjad Rizvi

The philosophers in the mainstream Islamic philosophical tradition struggled with a basic dilemma of how to reconcile their dualistic approach to human nature, influenced by Aristotelian virtue ethics—distinguishing between the soul as the true self and bearer of identity through time and into the afterlife and the body that was merely the outward "clothing" and vehicle of the soul—with the scriptural accounts that conceived of the human in more holistic terms as a singular embodied reality. The anthropology of the scriptures was deeply concerned with the human as animated by the divine breath or spirit (*rūḥ*) but constituted by a body that feels pains and pleasures both in this world and in the hereafter; the disciplining of the body in this world in accordance with the will of God that would at times include both channeling of pleasures and their sublimation would lead to the true pleasures of the afterlife, which were described in material terms

and as infinite (Qur'an 2:207, 3:162, 3:15, 9:38). This divergence, between the soul and the flesh, lies at the heart of any attempt to make
sense of the category of pleasure in Islamic thought. Beginning with the
philosophical tradition, I will move on to suggest that the privileging
of the spirit over the flesh, of the intellectual over the material, over
the course of Islamic intellectual history was more complicated than
we expect. I will then present an alternative view of embodiment that
ultimately derives from scriptural reflection but was a critical key to
Sufi and Shi'i conceptions of embodied existence in this world. Along
the way a number of key terms were debated about the nature of the
human, the person, the soul, the body, the actions and passions of the
body and the soul, and the nature of their interaction, all in pursuit of
making sense of a philosophical life.

Before beginning with the classical Islamic tradition, it is worth
remembering that the Hellenic inheritance did not have a monolithic
approach to the question of pleasure.[1] Hedonists privileged pleasures
over other pursuits. The Aristotelian tradition put forward a certain
view of the human and his practical wisdom and search for pleasure
and the good within the context of a philosophical way of life geared
toward the understanding of the higher causes of existence, but the
Platonic "platonopolis" model stressed that the pursuit of intellectual
pleasure and the good took place within the framework of philosophy
as *theosis*, becoming divine, following Plato's *Timaeus* and *Theaetetus*.[2]
Above all, one ought to be bear in mind that it was the Arabic Aristotle
and the various texts transmitted in his name and others that informed
the classical debate. Al-Kindī (d. 866) is the first author to mention the
Nicomachean Ethics, in his short treatise on the works of Aristotle, and
al-Fārābī (d. 950) wrote a commentary that is not extant; clearly the

---

1 David Wolfsdorf, *Pleasure in Ancient Greek Philosophy* (Cambridge: Cambridge University
Press, 2013).

2 J. M. Armstrong, "After the Ascent: Plato on Becoming God," *Oxford Studies in Ancient Philosophy*
26 (2004): 171–183, and David Sedley, "The Idea of Godlikeness," in *Plato 2: Ethics, Politics, Religion*,
ed. Gail Fine (Oxford: Oxford University Press, 1999): 309–328.

text—and the whole of Aristotle's ethical and political corpus—was known in the classical period to Muslim thinkers.[3] Al-Kindī's position, filtered from the *Nicomachean Ethics*, was to argue that the bodily pleasures were fleeting, "unclean," and led to harm, while the intellectual pleasures were "divine, spiritual, and heavenly, leading to great nobility."[4] The Arabic text contains an additional chapter, and one suspects that other ethical writings—either from Aristotle directly, from Porphyry's commentary, or from the manual translated from Arabic into Latin as the *Summa Alexandrinorum*—were incorporated. The goal of a successful human life is the attainment of happiness, which is sought for itself, while honor, pleasure, and other virtues and good may be ends in themselves or a means to happiness (NE 1, 1097b5).[5] Pleasures are processes, acts of coming-to-be and not ends; therefore they cannot be goods in themselves (NE 7, 1152b).[6] Goods are of three kinds: those pertaining to the soul, those pertaining to the body, and those external to the human. The first category is privileged—these are "the most worthy and entitled of them to be goods" (NE 1, 1098b).[7] Happiness is ultimately a moral disposition in the soul, an activity in accordance with perfect virtue (NE 1, 1098b–1099a):[8] "Happiness (*saʿāda*) then is the best and most excellent of things, and in it is absolute pleasure (*al-ladhādha*). These are not distinguished and separated. . . . All these things exist for the actions of virtue. We say that happiness is either all these, or one of them and that the best. Yet it appears that happiness needs the external goods. . . . It is impossible, or not easy, to do noble actions so long as there is no assistance from

3 Aristotle, *The Arabic Version of the Nicomachean Ethics*, ed. Anna Akasoy and Alexander Fidora, trans. D. M. Dunlop (Leiden: Brill, 2005).

4 Kindī, *The Philosophical Works of al-Kindī*, trans. Peter Pormann and Peter Adamson (Karachi: Oxford University Press, 2012), 116; see J. Aufderheide, "Processes as Pleasures in *EN* vii 11–14: *Ethics* Book VII," *Ancient Philosophy* 33 (2013): 135–157.

5 Aristotle, *Arabic Version of the Nicomachean Ethics*, 130–131.

6 Aristotle, *Arabic Version of the Nicomachean Ethics*, 408–409.

7 Aristotle, *Arabic Version of the Nicomachean Ethics*, 136–137.

8 Aristotle, *Arabic Version of the Nicomachean Ethics*, 138.

the outside" (NE 1, 1099a–1099b).[9] While the question of assistance is embraced, virtue, pleasure, and happiness can all be acquired through learning. In book 2, Aristotle continues with a discussion on virtues and how their acquisition is both learned through habitual practice, and bodily pleasures—or passions—need to be overcome and controlled for the soul to be virtuous. Virtue must be deliberated and chosen. The "big-souled" individual is the one who seeks the pleasures and virtues of the soul, of which justice is the supreme one (NE 5). In the apocryphal chapter 7, Aristotle's language about pleasure (and it is clear he means corporeal pleasure) is negative: it is not a good in itself, it can be a hindrance to reflection, and foremost it is a process and not an end in itself.[10] But pleasure can pertain to the immaterial, and at the end of chapter 7, the example of divine pleasure as simple and atemporal is posited (NE 7, 1054b26).[11] For God is at rest, not in motion nor susceptible to change, and so his pleasure is the greatest. The most extensive discussion of pleasure comes in book 10, starting with the negative aspects of corporeal pleasures as passions that are often sought in youth—after all pleasure is related to life and movement (NE 10, 1175a).[12] Happiness as the end of life is not a state but the ultimate virtue of the soul, and existing with intelligence it is pleasurable (NE 10, 1177a–1077b).[13] The most perfect pleasure is therefore what is associated with the soul, what is most separated from the embodied human condition, and what is most at rest and changeless, which lies in the perfection of the intellect (see *Metaphysics Lambda* 1071b5).[14]

The *theosis* tradition took this further. From at least al-Kindī onward, pleasure related to the quest for the good and the beautiful. One

---

9 Aristotle, *Arabic Version of the Nicomachean Ethics*, 140–143.

10 Aristotle, *Arabic Version of the Nicomachean Ethics*, 408–409.

11 Aristotle, *Arabic Version of the Nicomachean Ethics*, 422–423.

12 Aristotle, *Arabic Version of the Nicomachean Ethics*, 544–545.

13 Aristotle, *Arabic Version of the Nicomachean Ethics*, 556–559.

14 Aristotle, *Metaphysics Lambda*, in *Arisṭū ʿind al-ʿArab*, ed. ʿAbd al-Raḥmān al-Badawī (Kuwait: Wikālat al-maṭbūʿāt, 1978), 3.

experienced pleasure in the pursuit of the good and through grasping
the beautiful as actions. These were ethical acts through which the
virtues that one acquired and activated achieved closeness to God, the
Good, and the Beautiful. In the Islamic tradition, this was expressed
through a number of famous sayings: "Acquire the character traits of
the divine" (*Takhallaqū bi-akhlāq allāh*), that is, through the cultiva-
tion of virtue and *theosis* inculcate within the self the divine names,
and "God is beautiful and loves beauty" (*Allāhu jamīl wa-yuḥibbu-l-
jamāl*), that is, aesthetics as *theosis* as well—seeking God and seeking
to imitate the divine. The ultimate pleasure was in God and in being
like God, who is beyond materiality, change, space, or time. A pivotal
passage that brought this forth was the doffing metaphor of Plotinus's
Enneads 4.8.1, which was translated into Arabic and widely cited;[15] the
path to perfection and the ultimate pleasure in the One lay in doffing
the body and allowing the true self or soul to rise up.

1. The Aristotelian Legacy—al-Rāzī (d. 925), Miskawayh (d. 1030), and Beyond

The classical Islamic tradition therefore privileged the intellectual and
spiritual over the corporeal. Living the philosophical life was about
pursuing spiritual pleasure and avoiding pains of the soul, and not of
the body (i.e., the *Spiritual Physick* of al-Rāzī). Life was a pursuit of
knowledge and justice (linked to ethical virtue) through which "lib-
eration from this world" could be attained. The pleasures and pains
of this world and of the flesh were finite, satiable, and temporal, while
spiritual pleasures were infinite and eternal in this world and afterlife.
Therefore, the pursuit of pleasure had to be in line with the dictates
of reason. Pleasure itself was defined as a natural human state to be
restored. Rāzī said:

---

15 Plotinus, *Theologia Aristoteles* [Uthūlūjiyā], ed. ʿAbd al-Raḥman al-Badawī (Cairo: L'Institut
français, 1947), 23.

Pleasure consists simply of the restoration of that condition which was expelled by the element of pain, while passing from one's actual condition until one returns to the state formerly experienced. An example is provided by the man who leaves a restful, shady spot to go out into the desert; there he proceeds under the summer sun until he is affected by the heat; then he returns to his former place. He continues to feel pleasure in that place, until his body returns to its original state. . . . The intensity of his pleasure on coming home is in proportion to the degree of the intensity of the heat, and the speed of his cooling-off in that place. Hence the philosophers have defined pleasure as a return to the state of nature.[16]

Contrary to some of the texts that I shall discuss later, he is particularly damning of the concupiscence of the body, and of sexual desire in particular as a distraction from the pursuits of the soul.[17] The disembodied life—in the hereafter—is the perfect life.[18]

Miskawayh took this further with his development of the dualistic notion of the human and the contrast between the desires of the body and the soul. "The fact that the soul longs for that which is not bodily, is concerned to know the realities of the divine, desires and prefers what is superior to the bodily, and turns away from the pleasures of the body to seek those of the intellect—all this demonstrates to us clearly that its substance is much higher and nobler than that of bodily things, for it is impossible for anything to desire what does not pertain to its nature or to turn away from what perfects its essence and sustains its substance."[19] Pleasure seeks and responds to the good. "The soul's desire for its own actions—I mean for the sciences and the forms of

---

16 Abū Bakr Rāzī, *The Spiritual Physick* [al-Ṭibb al-rūḥānī], trans. A. J. Arberry (London: John Murray).

17 Rāzī, *Spiritual Physick*, 81–85.

18 Rāzī, *Spiritual Physick*, 106.

19 Miskawayh, *Tahdhīb al-akhlāq* [The refinement of character], trans. C. Zurayk (Beirut: Maktabat al-Lubnān, 1968), 8.

knowledge—as well as its flight away from the actions proper to the body, constitute its virtue. A person's excellence is measured by the extent to which he seeks this virtue and cares for it. It is enhanced as he pays greater attention to his soul and strives in all his power and capacity to renounce the things which hinder him from achieving this attribute."[20] The soul seeks pleasures that are good and virtuous, which are disembodied. Happiness, as the end of life, is directed in relation to the intellecting faculty of the human soul.

> The happiness of man consists in the performance of his properly human actions in accordance with discernment and reflection. It has also become evident that this human happiness is of different grades depending upon the kind of reflection and of what is reflected upon. Thus, it has been said: "The best reflection is reflection upon what is best." Then reflection declines from one grade to another until it reaches the level of the consideration of possible things in the realm of sense. He who considers these things uses his power of reflection and his own distinctive form, through which he may attain happiness and be worthy of the everlasting kingdom and the eternal bliss, in the pursuit of base things which have no real existence. From this discussion, we can see clearly the different kinds of happiness, in general, and the opposite kinds of misery, and [recognize] that goods and evils in voluntary actions consist, respectively, in choosing the best and living up to it or in choosing the lowest and tending towards it.[21]

The pursuit of pleasure is what one seeks in life. Ignorance is pain, knowledge is pleasure—hence one moves from ignorance to knowledge, from pain to pleasure. It is ignorance to focus on fleeting pleasure as a goal—recognizing that it is fleeting is moving toward knowledge,

---

20 Miskawayh, *Tahdhīb al-akhlāq*, 10.
21 Miskawayh, *Tahdhīb al-akhlāq*, 13–14.

and hence actual pleasure. Pleasures are scaled in degrees and begin with the fleeting and end with the infinite. Al-Fārābī (d. 950) similarly in his *On the Perfect State* (Mabādiʾ ārāʾ ahl al-madīna al-fāḍila), described the attachment to sensory pleasures as the signs of an imperfect state and a spiritual sickness.[22]

In another work *On Pleasure and Pain*, Miskawayh suggests that pleasures are perfections, alluding to *Nicomachean Ethics* 10, which defines pleasure as the perfection of natural activity.[23] These perfections are divine because they involve the cessation of motion or change. Pleasure is not therefore a materialist return to nature.[24] The end of the quest for knowledge and the good is the perception of God, which is the ultimate pleasure and end of human life, and, since God is not material, the perception of God must be mediated by an immaterial instrument such as the soul and its faculties.[25]

By the medieval period, the privileging of the pleasures of the soul and the afterlife had become a commonplace. *The Censure of the Pleasures of the World* (Dhamm ladhdhāt al-dunyā) of Fakhr al-Dīn al-Rāzī (d. 1209) rehearses a number of the positions of Miskawayh on the baseness of bodily pleasures, which constitutes the first part of the treatise, and devotes the second part to the self-evident superiority of intellectual pleasures because they are unattached to accidental materiality, nor are they fleeting, and can be heightened through study and reflection.[26] All of these positions are predicated on the dualism of the body and the soul, and the postulation that it is the immaterial human soul that is the true seat of the identity of the human person.

What we can conclude from these texts is that the classical tradition privileged the intellectual pleasures over the corporeal and often

---

22 Abū Naṣr Fārābī, *Al-Farabi on the Perfect State: Abū Naṣr al-Fārābī's Mabādiʾ ārāʾ ahl al-madīna al-fāḍila*, ed. and trans. R. Walzer (Oxford: Clarendon Press, 1985), 255, 269.

23 Peter Adamson, "Miskawayh on Pleasure," *Arabic Sciences and Philosophy* 25 (2015): 211.

24 Adamson, "Miskawayh on Pleasure," 212.

25 Adamson, "Miskawayh on Pleasure," 213.

26 Ayman Shihadeh, *The Teleological Ethics of Fakhr al-Dīn al-Rāzī* (Leiden: Brill, 2006), 212–265.

deferred them to a spiritual and disembodied afterlife. This entailed a dualistic conception of the human as comprising body and soul. To understand how the flourishing of the self involved the separation of the body from the soul we need to turn to how the question of human subjectivity was raised by Avicenna.

2. Subjectivity in Later Philosophical Thinking

The basis for the subjectivity of the person in the later tradition and the means for understanding the nature of pleasure arose from the psychology of the person and the identification of the true self as an immaterial, incorruptible substance through the famous "flying man" thought experiment of Avicenna. While there is a large literature on just how one ought to understand this argument, the basic points seem clear: first, that within the context of defining the soul, it is clear that it is not identical to the body in either substance or agency, and second, that a clear reflection on the faculties of the human and the seat of her selfhood and agency is located within that soul. Avicenna puts forward this famous argument in his *De Anima*:

> So we say: one of us must imagine himself so that he is created all at once and perfect but his sight is veiled from seeing things extrinsic to him, that he is created floating in the air or in a void so that the resistance of the air does not hit him—a hit he would have to sense—and that his limbs are separated from each other so that they do not meet or touch each other. [He must] then consider whether he affirms the existence of his self. He will not hesitate in affirming that his self exists, but he will not thereby affirm any of his limbs, any of his organs, the heart or the brain, or any external thing. Rather, he will affirm his self without affirming for it any dimension. If it were possible for him in that state to imagine a hand or some other limb, he would not imagine it as part of his self or a condition in his self. You know that what is affirmed is different from what is not

affirmed and what is confirmed is different from what is not confirmed. Hence the self whose existence he has affirmed is specific
to him in that it is he himself, different from his body and limbs,
which he has not affirmed. Thus, he who takes heed understands
the existence of the soul to be something different from the body—
indeed, as different from any body—and to know and be aware of
it. (DA 5.7)

The thought experiment comes within the context of trying to define the soul. It is a reminder (*tadhkīr*) designed to provoke intuition
and is not a demonstration. The conclusion that everyone is capable
of intuiting that his true self lies in an immaterial and immortal soul
that is unaffected by the body is a critical one because it is developed
and challenged in the later tradition. But it is still the case that the
human subject has two elements to it—the substance of the soul and
that of the body—and each of them undergoes pleasures and pains.
When one then considers the faculties of the soul and its pleasures,
Avicenna argues that the pleasures of the senses, including sexual
union, are fleeting and limited even when it seems that they cover the
whole body, while the pleasures of the soul encompass the whole body
and therefore as superior (DA 2.3).

Nevertheless, within this world the human cannot dispense with the
body, which is critical for the person's perfection and for the path of the
soul in its reversion to the One, not least because, following Aristotle,
the soul is the perfection of the natural body.

It is thus established that the soul comes to be as corporeal matter
suited to be used by it, and the body that has come to be is its instrument and governed by it. In the substance of the soul that has come
to be with a body—that body necessitates its coming to be from the
first principles—there is a configuration of its natural tendency to
be preoccupied with and use, to be concerned with its states and to
be attracted to it, which is proper to the soul and turns it away from

all other bodies. Thus there is no doubt that when the soul exists as
individuated, the principle of its individuation attaches to it something from the configurations that designates it as an individual.
Those configurations are necessary to make the soul proper to that
body, and they are in accordance with the mutual suitability of one
to the other, even if that state and that accordance were unknown
to us. (DA 5.3)

Each soul has a body proper to it that is necessary for its development,
for its identity, and for its path into the afterlife.

Similarly that individual through its soul has self-awareness that
recognizes itself as a subject and is cognizant of its need to seek its
pleasures, perfections, and felicity as its goal. In his *Notes* (al-Taʿlīqāt),
Avicenna addresses the question of self-awareness in a series of
responses to questions posed by his students on it.

Self-awareness is essential for the soul, it is not externally acquired;
it is as if when the self occurs, awareness of itself obtains immediately. One is not aware of it by means of an instrument, but one
is aware of it by itself and through itself. . . . Apprehension of the
body takes place by means of a sense, such as vision or touch; thus,
he who allows that knowledge of the self is from an indication to
it by means of a sense, has the consequence that he does not know
himself absolutely but knows himself when he perceives his body.
Furthermore, apprehension *by means of* a sense requires that there is
something that is known to apprehend what is sensed by means of
a sense, and which is different from the sense, and it is no doubt the
soul. As regards our being aware that we were aware of ourselves, it
is through an act of the intellect.

He then turns to the individual human case. "My self-apprehension
is something internal to me, not occurring through a consideration
of another thing. Thus, when I say "I did such and such," I consider

my apprehension of myself, even if I do not pay attention to my self-awareness; how else would I know that I did such and such, if I were not first apprehending myself? Thus, I have first considered my self, not its act, and I do not consider anything by means of which I would apprehend myself. Our awareness of our self is our very existence." Therefore, before we can be aware of, perceive, or know anything external to us, we must have apprehended and been aware of ourselves. This is intuitive, and Avicenna refers to this intuition—just as he referred to the flying man—as a reminder or a thought experiment and not a demonstration. The soul cannot fail, therefore, to be aware of itself. "Self-awareness is innate to the self, it is the self's very existence; so nothing external is needed by means of which to apprehend the self—rather, the self is that which apprehends itself. Thus, it is not appropriate for it to exist without there being awareness of it given that what is aware of it is its very self, and none other."[27] Avicenna's follower Naṣīr al-Dīn al-Ṭūsī (d. 1274) in his *Nasirean Ethics* (Akhlāq-i nāṣirī) carries forward not just the dualistic anthropology but also the same Aristotelian inheritance about the superiority of the intellectual pleasures over the sensory. His opening definition of the soul and its faculties, its affirmation as a substance that is simple, not the body, and immaterial, clearly follow Avicenna's *De Anima*.[28] Therefore, intellectual pleasures are essential and active while sensory ones are accidental and passive.[29] Bodily pleasures are restorative and often mutually conflicting.[30] True pleasures pertain to the true self, which is the soul.[31] Ultimately, "anyone attaining the reality of wisdom knows that the pleasure thereof is above all pleasures and hence pays no heed to any other pleasure. Since

27 Avicenna, *al-Taʿlīqāt*, ed. ʿAbd al-Raḥmān al-Badawī (Cairo: al-Hayʾa al-miṣrīya al-ʿāmma li-l-kitāb, 1973), 160–161.

28 Naṣīr al-Dīn Ṭūsī, *The Nasirean Ethics*, trans. G. M. Wickens (London: Allen and Unwin, 1964), 37–41.

29 Ṭūsī, *Nasirean Ethics*, 71–72.

30 Ṭūsī, *Nasirean Ethics*, 171.

31 Ṭūsī, *Nasirean Ethics*, 139.

it be thus, the philosopher whose wisdom is the most of all wisdoms in God almighty, and only the felicitous philosopher among his servants loves him in reality. . . . In this respect, this felicity is the loftiest of all."[32] In that sense, the self, which is the pleasant subject, seeks its ultimate goal in God. That pleasure in God—like all the pleasures of the afterlife—cannot be embodied or sensory.[33]

If we skip a few centuries to the mature philosophical tradition and Mullā Ṣadrā (d. 1636), one finds the question of dualism somewhat qualified. He also starts with his own version of the flying man thought experiment and its intuition that the true self is beyond the body:

> another demonstration that the living thing is not the sensible form is that we say: if an living thing is supposed such that it is created all at once, and is created perfect, but is veiled in its senses from beholding what is external, and that it is floating in a void or in open air so that the air's volume does not collide with it and it does not sense any qualities, and its limbs are separated so that they do not touch each other, then in this state it will apprehend itself and ignore all of its external and internal organs. Or rather, it will affirm itself without affirming a dimension for it, neither length nor breadth nor any direction; even if it imagined a position, a direction or some organ in that state, it would not imagine it to be a part of itself. It is evident that what one is aware of is different from what one ignores; and so its identity differs from all its organs.[34]

Interestingly, he refers to the argument as a demonstration—perhaps used in a loose sense of proof—and not a "reminder" because of the greater role that intuition plays in his philosophical system.

---

32 Ṭūsī, *Nasirean Ethics*, 209.

33 Ṭūsī, *Nasirean Ethics*, 53.

34 Mullā Ṣadrā, *al-Ḥikma al-mutaʿāliya fī-l-asfār al-ʿaqliya al-arbaʿa*, ed. G. Aʿvānī et al. (Tehran: Sadra Islamic Philosophy Research Institute, 2004), VIII, 47.

Self-awareness is affirmed. Furthermore, that true self is a unified entity possessing faculties.

> Each one of us knows intuitively, before resorting to demonstration, that his self and reality is one thing, not many things. Thereby he knows that he understands, apprehends, senses, desires, is angry, prefers, moves, is at rest, and is characterized by a combination of attributes and names, some of which are of the class of the intellect and its states, some of the class of sense-perception and imagination and their states, and some of the class of the body and its accidents and passions. Although this is something intuitive, most people cannot know it with respect to the art of knowledge but deny this unity when they embark on inquiry and scrutiny, except the one whom God assists by a light from Him.[35]

The body acts as a barrier to the pursuit of the soul's pleasure and heightens its sickness.

> We claim that the intoxication of nature and the soul's stupor in this plane of existence—due to its preoccupation with the acts of the body—prevent it from apprehending the harms and pains of the soul that obtain in it and that are acquired as results of its acts and the concomitants of its vices and habits, by a true apprehension which is not spoiled by what the senses convey to it and what they are engaged in, forgetting and ignoring. Thus, when the veil is lifted from the human by death and the cover is removed, on that day his sight falls upon the consequences of his acts and the results of his deeds, so that they then end up—if he is mean in character traits, evil in deeds and destructive in beliefs—in strong pain and great disaster,

---

35 Mullā Ṣadrā, *al-Ḥikma al-mutaʿāliya*, IX, 72–73.

as in His saying, praised be He: *therefore We have now removed your covering, so your sight today is piercing.* (Qur'an 50:22)[36]

The perfection of the pleasures in the afterlife is not conceivable.

One should understand that intellectual and noetic pleasures to be what neither the eye has seen nor the ear has heard nor the heart has experienced.[37]

The pleasures of the afterlife and its pains are not the same category as those of this world especially as its pleasures remove the pains of this world. All worldly pleasures are passions of the soul that enter it from without and are affective in it, contrary to the pleasures of the afterlife. Those are joys for the soul in essence in every sense of their actuality. Action and passion are two distinct categories. Active pleasure is distinct from passive pleasure in both its genus and its differentia; there is no relation between the two, and no comparison. In paradise, all the objects of intellectual pleasure are in their perfect state and even there "sensory" forms of awareness of pleasure are heightened, in a most perfect and noble state. Those pleasures arise from annihilating pleasures of this world, attachment to which transforms them into pains and torments.[38]

Mullā Ṣadrā to an extent moves in a different monistic direction in which it is only the soul—insofar as it is existence as such—that is, and once it reaches its perfection it reproduces the body appropriate to it in the afterlife. All the faculties, including that of sense perception and

---

36 Mullā Ṣadrā, *al-Ḥikma al-mutaʿāliya*, IX, 48–49.
37 Mullā Ṣadrā, *al-Ḥikma al-mutaʿāliya*, IX, 239.
38 Mullā Ṣadrā, *al-Ḥikma al-mutaʿāliya*, IX, 295–296.

indeed of the perception of bodily pleasures, are thus actually those of the soul itself.

Toward the end of that argument, he surmises:

> The soul perceives particulars. There is no doubt that the soul is an individual essence and is connected to the body, which is a connection insofar as it manages the body and deploys it. . . . It is known that a particular soul cannot manage the universal body otherwise it would be an immaterial universal intellect. In which case it would not have the connection with a particular body but would be an entity having its connection with all the bodies. Since the consequent is invalid, so too is the antecedent invalid. Therefore the soul is the manager of a particular body. Now the managing of the individual insofar as it is an individual is impossible except after having the knowledge of it from the aspect of its essence. That is only possible with the presence of its individual form before the soul. This necessitates the soul to be the perceiver of particulars and the perceiver of universals. Thus, in humans there is one essence possessing numerable levels.[39]

While Mullā Ṣadrā affirms the independence of the soul in its path to the One, he also insists that the soul does not exist without the body either in its generation, or once it dies. At death, it produces a body appropriate to it, and again in the afterlife and to a large extent it experiences its pleasures through it. Thus already we see a complication in the soul body relationship that qualifies the hierarchical nature or even binary contrast between the soul's perception and the body's, between the pleasures of the soul and the body. The soul remains embodied in all its states and "lives."

---

39 Mullā Ṣadrā, *al-Ḥikma al-mutaʿāliya*, VIII, 267.

3. PLEASURE AS EMBODIED

The Sufi and Shi'i traditions on sexuality and embodiment represent
a different approach to the question of the monism of the human self
and the carnality and corporeality of pleasure as a means to the ultimate pleasure of the encounter with the divine. The Qur'an suggests
that the believer is primarily an urban householder and posits a holistic
approach to the human. Pleasures are divinely designed to motivate
humans to seek the good, to cooperate with each other both at the
social level and at the level of the family in order to achieve perfection
and felicity in the afterlife. But the material pleasures of this life are
fleeting; true pleasure is in the afterlife ("the pleasures of this worldly
life are few but the pleasures of the afterlife are the true good for
one who fears God"; Qur'an 4:77). Even the philosophical tradition
considered the ultimate felicity to be in the afterlife, although it was
often said to be a spiritual or disembodied one; the scriptural accounts
were clear through their carnality that the pleasures of the afterlife are
certainly material—the infinite orgasm of paradise, in the words of
Bouhdiba, in which the pleasures of sex are privileged over all others.[40]

In the Shi'i *ḥadīth* tradition, one finds a number of narrations
relating to the techniques of the self insofar as it is an embodied person
seeking perfection and pleasure. The twelfth-century manual of texts
on these techniques that is concerned with the two carnal desires of
food and sex, as well as all manner of etiquette relating to concern
for the body, its hair, its depilation, its adornment, and many other
issues, the *Compendium of Virtues* (Makārim al-akhlāq) of al-Ḥasan
al-Ṭabrisī (fl. twelfth century), dedicates a long chapter to sex and
marriage. Beginning with the exhortation to marriage—sexual union
as half of one's faith in the prophetic narration and an "intercession"
and expiation for one's sins and purification of the self in the eyes of
God—it moves onto sections on the virtues and vices of women one

---

40 Abdelwahab Bouhdiba, *Sexuality in Islam* (London: Routledge, Kegan and Paul, 1985), 72–88.

should marry, the etiquette of engagement and the wedding, the mutual duties of the husband and wife (a major one being sexual rights),
and astrological and other timing considerations of when to have sex.[41]
One ought to compose erotic poetry for the beloved to heighten and
increase the attraction and pleasure.[42] These texts put forward a view
of the human as a holistic embodied self, seeking pleasure to attain perfection with God. A similar compendium of the seventeenth century,
the *Adornment of the Pious* (Ḥilyat al-mutaqqīn) of the famous court
scholar Muḥammad Bāqir Majlisī (d. 1699), has similar concerns in its
compilation, but spends as much time on the etiquette of pleasure and
companionship in married life as it does on the questions of seeking
the good wife and the arts of love.[43] The basic approach of these texts
is to deploy scriptural sources to demonstrate that humans live an
embodied existence and they should embrace their material pleasures
within the constraints of the moral law, since it is only within that
context of the moral psychology of the person that true pleasure and
perfection can be achieved. While acknowledging the account of the
human as the microcosmic entity seeking the perfection of the divine,
these texts reject the philosophical account of the immaterial soul that
is separate from the body being the true self. Instead, they posit a holistic anthropology in which the human is the embodied person animated by a spirit that is the life force, the seat of knowledge and eternal
from a transcendent origin and immortal; and yet that spirit is very
much at one with the body and not immaterial.[44] This is also true of
many other texts and of Sufi traditions relating to the importance of
embodied virtue and pleasure as the path to perfection in the One—as

---

41 Al-Ḥasan b. al-Faḍl Ṭabrisī, *Makārim al-akhlāq* (Kuwait: Maktabat al-Alfayn, 1987), 253–282,
300–307.

42 See Scott Kugle, *Sufis and Saints' Bodies: Mysticism, Corporeality and Sacred Power in Islam*
(Chapel Hill: University of North Carolina Press, 2007), 39.

43 Muḥammad Bāqir Majlisī, *Ḥilyat al-muttaqīn* (Qum: Dhawī-l-qurba, 2003).

44 Majlisī, *Biḥār al-anwār al-jāmiʿa li-durar akhbār al-aʾimmat al-aṭhār* (Beirut: Muʾassasat al-
Aʿlamī, 2008), LVII, 274; LVIII, 284, 290.

Bashir puts it, citing Merleau-Ponty: "the experiencing body is situated at the base of any notion of the human self. . . . Once imagined, the body . . . constitutes a primary bounded system that human beings utilize to map other systematic processes in the cosmos."[45] The body, its desires and pleasures, represents the very immanence of God in these traditions.[46]

This is not to suggest that all of these traditions had a positive approach to the body and the animal self—some of the most famous works of the Sufi and ethical traditions, for example, were rather dismissive of the body and motivated by the need to control lusts and channel pleasure toward "higher," spiritual pursuits, as one sees in the *Alchemy of Happiness* (Kīmīyā-yi saʿādat) and the *Revival of the Religious Sciences* (Iḥyāʾ ʿulūm al-dīn) of Ghazālī (d. 1111), which is particularly geared toward disciplining the self through rejecting the desires of the flesh, in particular the two "lusts" of food and sex.[47] Similar concerns with regulating and controlling female sexuality and curbing the lusts of men are found in the highly influential *Nasirean Ethics* of Ṭūsī, which shares with the mainstream Islamic Peripatetic philosophical tradition an approach to pleasure as the goal of intellectual and immaterial pursuits.[48] These traditions are more geared toward considering human corporeality and embodiment as an obstacle to spiritual and intellectual pleasures, because they take Avicennan psychology, which privileges the immaterial soul as the true self, quite

45 Shahzad Bashir, *Sufi Bodies: Religion and Society in Medieval Islam* (New York: Columbia University Press, 2011), 14. A separate whole discussion about how the vagina is a nervous, sensory organ is mentioned in the *Doctrines of Muslim Theologians* (Maqālāt al-islāmiyīn) of Abū-l-Ḥasan al-Ashʿarī (d. 936) and attributed to ʿAbbād b. Sulaymān—see al-Ashʿarī, *Maqālāt al-islāmiyīn wa-ʾkhtilāf al-muṣallīn*, ed. H. Ritter (Istanbul: Maṭbaʿat al-dawla, 1930), I, 339; see Shihadeh, *Teleological Ethics*, 222–223.

46 Kugle, *Sufis and Saints' Bodies*, 4–5.

47 Abū Ḥāmid Ghazālī, *Kīmīyā-yi saʿādat*, ed. Ḥusayn Khadīvjām (Tehran: Intishārāt-i ʿilmī va farhangī, 1975), I, 283–323; II, 1–62, and Abū Ḥāmid Ghazālī, *On Disciplining the Soul and on Breaking the Two Desires: Books XXII and XXIII of the Revival of the Religious Sciences*, trans. Tim Winter (Cambridge: Islamic Texts Society, 1995).

48 Ṭūsī, *Nasirean Ethics*, 161–167.

separate from the body, for granted.[49] The soul as true self seeks its perfection in the Good and in the pleasure that arises out of incorporeality, although it is acknowledged that virtues in this life are embodied and one cannot seek the good without material means.[50] True felicity lies in overcoming the possessions, benefits, and goods of this world, even one's body, and embracing the pure intellectual life.[51]

Nevertheless, the tradition of Ibn ʿArabī (d. 1240) had a rather different approach to embodiment and the pursuit of pleasure. Love mysticism was an established path in classical Islam and, despite some aesthetic claims upon celibacy, was very much concerned with embodied existence.[52] Because, in the words of a famous purported saying of the Prophet, "God is beautiful and loves beauty," love was, in the words of the poet Jāmī (d. 1492), "a means to ascend to the highest beauty of the divine by steps of the ladder of created souls," and through love the human was transformed into a divine person. Another purported saying of the Prophet presented divine desire as the cause of the creation, since God was a hidden treasure who desired to be known; hence it was through the "sexual union" of the divine names that existence was engendered, and therefore human sexual intercourse in the pursuit of pleasure was a means for reciprocating God's love through beauty and desire to effect a reversion to the One, the ultimate happiness.[53] Desire is productive, and just like children fashioned in the womb, imagination is itself a womb, and therefore a means to return to God.[54] Sexual desire was therefore designed within

---

49 Ghazālī, *On Disciplining the Soul*, xlv–lviii.

50 Ṭūsī, *Nāsirean Ethics*, 61–64.

51 Ṭūsī, *Nāsirean Ethics*, 65.

52 Saʿdiyya Shaikh, *Sufi Narratives of Intimacy: Ibn ʿArabī, Gender, and Sexuality* (Chapel Hill: University of North Carolina Press, 2012), 56–59.

53 Shaikh, *Sufi Narratives of Intimacy*, 123, 125; Sachiko Murata, *The Tao of Islam: A Sourcebook on Gender Relationships in Islamic Thought* (Albany: State University of New York Press, 1992), 153–168.

54 Murata, *Tao of Islam*, 149.

the human by God to reflect divine love and desire and to be a means to seek the One.[55]

This Sufi tradition rejected dualistic anthropologies positing a close interconnected relationship between body and spirit in order for the human to manifest the divine and to revert to the One precisely because that holistic person was a microcosm that reflected God to the cosmos and the face of the cosmos back to God.[56] Seeking pleasure through sexual union was an act of witnessing God—gendered of course through the male gaze—in women. As Ibn ʿArabī put it in his gloss on the famous Prophetic saying that expresses his love for three female entities in this world—namely, the delights of perfume, prayer, and women: "When a man witnesses God in woman, this is a witnessing within a locus that receives activity. . . . His witnessing of God [the Real] in the woman is the most complete and most perfect since he witnesses the Real with respect to the fact that he [God] is both active and locus of receiving activity."[57] Sexual union is an absolute correspondence between the male and the female, between annihilation in the One and the survival in it, the full disclosure of God that establishes spiritual realization as pleasure. Ibn ʿArabī sums this up in his *Meccan Disclosures* (al-Futūḥāt al-makkīya):

> The axial saint knows of something of the self-disclosure of God through sexual union, and that incites him to seek it, being passionately enamoured of it. Indeed he, along with others from among that sages, realizes his spiritual state of servanthood through sex more than any other thing, more than eating or drinking or clothing that protect against harm. He does not desire marriage for personal progeny but only for desire and to populate the land with a new generation as a legal obligation. In his case, raising a new generation

---

55 Murata, *Tao of Islam*, 177.

56 Shaikh, *Sufi Narratives of Intimacy*, 135–139.

57 Shaikh, *Sufi Narratives of Intimacy*, 177, citing Murata, *Tao of Islam*, 192.

is a natural matter for preserving the continuation of the species in this world. So sex for the person of this spiritual status is like sex for the people of paradise in that it is only for desire because it is the greatest self-disclosure of God, hidden from the world except for those whom God especially chooses among his servants. Similarly sex among animals happens only for desire [shahwa] . . .

What is it about sex that gives it its complete nobility, indicating the weakness that is demanded by the spiritual state of servanthood? It is nothing but the overpowering nature of pleasure that obliterates him of his strength and his self-importance. It is a delicious overpowering. Being overpowered generally precludes the one overpowered from delighting in the experience. Delight in the overpowering is a quality specific to the one who overpowers rather than the quality specific to one overpowered. The exception is specifically this act. People remain oblivious to this nobility, making sex an animal appetite. They call it an animal appetite in order to keep themselves above it, despite the fact that they name it with the most noble of names when they call it an "animalistic" appetite. This means it is the special quality of animals, who are endowed with life force [ḥayāt]. What is nobler than life? So what people believe according to themselves to be despicable is actually the essence of praiseworthiness in the view of the perfected sage.[58]

This does not, however, mean that Ibn ʿArabī advocates sexual union as the sole means to spiritual realization. Sexual union is pleasure and a means to love that reverts to God. If it merely remains at the level of natural desire, it does not transform into divine love.[59] Embodiment still requires there to be spirit and form and not form alone.

---

58 Shaikh, *Sufi Narratives of Intimacy*, 188–189, citing Ibn ʿArabī, *al-Futūḥāt al-Makkiyya* (Cairo: Būlāq, 1911), II, 274; see Murata, *Tao of Islam*, 187.

59 Murata, *Tao of Islam*, 195–196.

A prevalent example of the Sufi traditions that embraced embodied pleasure was the appropriation by Indo-Persian authors from the thirteenth century onward of the Kokaśāstra literature in Sanskrit and vernaculars, especially the *Ratirahasya* of Kokkoka, who was probably writing in the twelfth century for a royal courtly patron. This was a medieval text that described the pleasures of sex, how best to enhance them and sustain them—it concerned *kāma*, or sexual desire, one of the four main goals of human life alongside *dharma* (religion, morality), *mokṣa* (salvation), and *artha* (way of life).[60] It provides codes, morals, and etiquettes of behavior geared toward the happy life within the context of religious commitments. But in its taxonomies presenting an "anatomy of sex" it, in effect, provides a guide to the perplexed for the man about town.[61] This androcentric approach is critical to the genre.[62] The aim of the author was to write a work on the art of love, honoring the God of love in order that a man might find joy and pleasure, which is the "sole substantial good in a world fugitive as water in a basket, and the capital fulfilment of all desires."[63] The text is then divided into fifteen chapters on physical typologies, the nature of the climes and times, natural dispositions, the arts of love and sex, and the etiquettes required, including in marriage, and culminating with a section on spells to win over the beloved.

The main translation of the text—extant in many copies and varying recensions—is attributed to a Chishtī Sufi Ẓiyāʾ al-Dīn Nakhshābī (d. 1350), who lived in Delhi and was a major literary figure, famous for *Tale of the Parrot* (Ṭūṭīnāma). Interestingly, some works of Indian erotology place the words of wisdom in the mouth of a parrot.[64] The

60 Shalini Shah, *Love, Eroticism and Female Sexuality in Classical Sanskrit Literature: Seventh–Thirteenth Centuries* (New Delhi: Manohar, 2009), 13.

61 Shah, *Love, Eroticism and Female Sexuality*, 107.

62 Shah, *Love, Eroticism and Female Sexuality*, 190–191.

63 Kokkoka, *The Koka Shastra Being the Ratirahasya of Kokkoka*, trans. W. G. Archer (London: Allen and Unwin, 1964), 102.

64 I have consulted four copies of the text: MS British Library India Office Islamic 908, fols. 188v–210v, MS Kitābkhāna-yi Ganjbakhsh in Islamabad 791, MS Ganjbakhsh 3949, and MS Ganjbakhsh

frame story concerns the lore of sex that was attained by a worldly and wise vizier named Koka Pandit, who knew the arts of love necessary to control and pleasure women. As such, it sets up the text as the fruits of an urban, courtly, and sophisticated culture of the pursuit of pleasure narrated by someone in the know. As in much Sufi literature, not only is embodiment at the center of the story but also the need to acquire knowledge from a sage whose experience attests to his ability to guide. The text itself is then broadly divided into four sections comprising ten chapters, which broadly mirror the original Sanskrit, on the nature of women and sex (including astrological aspects and the influences of the climes), the nature of sexual union, the arts of love under the rubric of "taming" women, and medicines for supporting and enhancing sex and curing dysfunctions. Before beginning this discussion, Nakhshābī says that men in this world have three goals in life: worshiping God (*ʿubūdīyat*), deploying the material provisions (*ḥaẓẓ-hā-yi dunyavī*) that one has been given, and love and pleasure in women's company, which is essential for the preservation of life (*ʿulfat va ʿishrat kardan*). Sexual pleasure within marriage thus constitutes a basic foundation for the happy life since without it and motivated by lusts and corruptions, a man cannot worship God sincerely or without distraction or be contented enough to understand the best way to deploy the divine provision of the material gifts that he has.[65] Sexual pleasure thus within the framework of a moral order ensures the sustenance of a happy life and the acquisition of the felicitous hereafter.

While one cannot be sure that Nakhshābī was the author of this work, he did write other similar works on the importance of embodiment and

10958. I am grateful to Susanne Kurz of Bochum University for her advice on this material and for sharing digital copies of the latter three manuscripts with me, as well as sharing with me prior to publication her "Never Just for Fun? Sexual Intercourse in Persophone Medicine, Erotology and Ethics," in *Muslim Bodies: Körper, Sexualität und Medizin in muslimischen Gesellschaften*, ed. Susanne Kurz et al. (Munster: LIT Verlag, 2016), 97–130.

65 Żiyāʾ al-Dīn Nakhshābī, *Ladhdhat al-nisāʾ*, MS Ganjbakhsh Islamabad 3949, fol. 3v–4r.

the pursuit of pleasure, including *Spiritual Wayfaring* (Silk al-sulūk) and *Parts and Wholes* (Juz'īyat va kullīyāt), on the parts of the body and their significance. In the latter text, he presents the human body as the image of God, and the perfect microcosm that bears a homology to the divine.[66] It is through one's reflection upon one's embodied self that one acquires the pleasure of recognizing the divine, because of the perfect form in which God has created humans—referring to the Qur'anic verse on this and on the dignity of the human created in the divine image.[67] It is only the human who in the entire cosmos is worthy of taking on the qualities and colors of the divine.[68] In his Sufi manual *Spiritual Wayfaring*, he considers the technical terms for stages on the path, mixed with narratives and anecdotes to demonstrate that the spiritual path to God is rooted in human nature and in embodiment.[69]

The Kokaśāstra texts seem to have been particularly popular in the Deccan. One poetic translation made by Muḥammad Qulī Jāmī for the Quṭbshāhī ruler 'Abdullāh (d. 1672) and completed in 1627 was sometimes also given the title *Pleasures of Women* (Ladhdhat al-nisā').[70] It follows the standard albeit abbreviated order of the text and has a similar frame story of the text as advice to a man seeking the pleasure and delights of women in a courtly setting—with some illustrations. *The Key to Bliss for 'Ādil-Shāh* (Miftāḥ al-surūr-i 'Ādilshāhī) begins with the created complementarity thesis that all creatures are produced in pairs and hence humans need to understand that their perfection and pleasure can only be obtained in a pair (*zawj*). In ornate Persian, the

---

66 Żiyā' al-Dīn Nakhshābī, *Juz'īyāt va kullīyāt*, MS British Library India Office Islamic 905, dated 1595, fols. 2r–6r; see Kugle, *Saints and Sufis' Bodies*, 24–29, Aditya Behl, *Love's Subtle Magic: An Indian Islamic Literary Tradition, 1379–1545* (New York: Oxford University Press, 2012), 73–74.

67 Nakhshābī, *Juz'īyāt va kullīyāt*, fol. 5r.

68 Nakhshābī, *Juz'īyāt va kullīyāt*, fol. 5v.

69 Żiyā' al-Dīn Nakhshābī, *Silk al-sulūk* (Delhi: Maṭba'-yi mujtabā'ī, 1895).

70 I consulted Muḥammad Qulī Jāmī, *Kūk shāstra yā ladhdhat al-nisā'*, MS British Museum Add 17489, fol. 41, dated 1211/1797.

author Maḥmūd Ayāz dedicated it to the ruler in 1516 and set out in a prose text a work of sexology that draws heavily on the medical tradition, not just on anatomical and curative approaches to sex and sexual dysfunction but also ways of enhancing pleasure.[71] It also like the other texts has a typology of women to seek for pleasure. He presents himself as a physician fleeing conflict in the north Deccan and seeking a royal patron. The introduction sets out the idea, already encountered, that sexual union and pleasure is the very essence of the animal life force that humans possess and one ought to know how best and when best to harness and deploy it.[72] This text, however, seems quite independent, on the face of it, from the Kokaśāstra texts. From the same period, another independent miscellany on matters sexual, drawing upon poetry, medical texts, the Sanskritic traditions, and the Prophetic ones, is *Bon Mots for the King* (Laṭā'if-i Shāhī).[73] It contains more poetry and scriptural sources than other texts and has a far more advanced occult flavor regarding the determination of times and places. It also betrays a greater concern with the Hellenic tradition, both Galenic and Platonic (e.g., fol. 204v).

It is not just texts of sexology that betrays such an approach to pleasure in embodied sexual union. A number of anthologies, including ones of a theological bent, expressed similar ideas. One example is the eighteenth-century *Garden of Ṣādiq* (Ḥadīqa-i ḥādiq-i ganjīna-yi Ṣādiq), a large compendium on ethics and theology that contains a considerable fifty-page chapter on sexual pleasure. The chapter lies within a section on the courtly virtues that is preceded by a section on service to the king and on courtly love poetry. It follows the Arabic erotological

---

71 Maḥmūd Ayāz, *Miftāḥ al-surūr-i ʿĀdilshāhī*, MS British Library India Office Islamic 2473, dated 1738, fol. iv.

72 Ayāz, *Miftāḥ al-surūr-i ʿĀdilshāhī*, fols. 4r–8r.

73 I consulted MS British Library India Office Islamic 1330, fols. 104–223, which is extant in a codex of mixed, primarily literary texts.

literature (*'ilm al-bāh*) more closely and puts forward the therapeutic nature of sexual pleasure as a way of alleviating the "illness of love."[74] The formulation here is somewhat different—the pursuit of pleasure is wholly embodied insofar as even love, often conceived as a mental or spiritual pleasure, is considered to be a disease of the brain, which requires a cure. Humans are attracted to their partner through physical beauty, and our carnality, directed toward pleasure, just needs to be directed within a moral and legal framework (the laws of marriage).[75] Other anthologies talk about the pleasures and leisures of the self as a means to nourish the human self and to fortify it on its path to perfection—and this often involves the telling of jokes of a sexual nature.[76]

While we usually think of Islamic thought as broadly receiving, modifying to an extent, but perpetuating key notions of Greek thought, the trend in later Islamic thought was to move away from the concerns and assumptions of the classical period. While few denied hylomorphism, category theory, the dualism of the body and the soul, and the hierarchy of the pleasures and the pains of the body and soul, the exigencies of later thought and also of the Sufi traditions (partly explained by their monism) were quite different. The anthropology of these works was therefore more monistic, and hence the pleasures of the body were central to the development of the human and the positive features of his becoming. The ultimate pleasure was the beatific vision and the encounter with God that was often said to be disembodied; and yet the body was a key vehicle to take the person along that path. In this, the religious commitments of the Muslim thinkers that I have discussed should not be underestimated. Philosophy could

---

74 Shākir Khān b. Ṣādiq, *Ḥadīqa-yi ḥādiq-i ganjīna-yi Ṣādiq*, MS British Library India Office Islamic 1781, dated 1716, fol. 183v.

75 Shākir Khān, *Ḥadīqa-yi ḥādiq-i ganjīna-yi Ṣādiq*, fols. 184v–185r.

76 Sajjad H. Rizvi, "Sayyid Niʿmat Allāh al-Jazāʾirī and His Anthologies: Anti-Sufism, Shiʿism and Jokes in the Safavid world," *Die Welt des Islams* 50 (2010): 224–242.

rarely be divorced in the thought of these thinkers from theological concerns and their commitment to the nature of reality as an unfolding of the One and the role of human agency as a ladder of reversion to the One. The pursuit of pleasure was thus one of the key motivations to drive the human to ascend that ladder.

Reflection

ENGRAVING PLEASURE IN PHILOSOPHY TEACHING AIDS

Susanna Berger

In the early modern era, sensual pleasures were crucial to theories surrounding both the creation and the viewing of visual art. Leon Battista Alberti (1404–1472) famously introduced Narcissus, the beautiful youth who rejected all lovers and fell for his own image in a pool, as the inventor of painting. In book 2 of his treatise *On Painting*, written in Italian and Latin versions in the 1430s, Alberti asks in reference to the story of the mythological boy: "What is painting but the act of embracing by means of art the surface of the pool?"[1] This narrative of the origins of painting frames the artist as a tragic lover, who, like Narcissus, seeks what can never be grasped. While the desires of the painter/Narcissus are inevitably frustrated, Alberti also celebrates the capacity of certain artworks to please viewers. He writes: "a 'historia' you can justifiably praise and admire will be one that reveals itself to be so charming and attractive as to hold the eye of the learned and unlearned spectator for a long while with a certain sense of pleasure and emotion."[2] The origins

---

1 Alberti, *On Painting and On Sculpture*, ed. and trans. Cecil Grayson (New York: Phaidon: 1972), 61–63: "Quid est enim aliud pingere quam arte superficiem illam fontis amplecti?"

2 Alberti, *On Painting and On Sculpture*, 78–79: "Historia vero, quam merito possis et laudare et admirari, eiusmodi erit quae illecebris quibusdam sese ita amenam et ornatam exhibeat, ut oculos docti atque indocti spectatoris diutius quadam cum voluptate et animi motu detineat."

of painting continued to be located in a desire for pleasure in the sixteenth century, when the Italian writer, critic, and dramatist Ludovico Dolce (1508–1568) wrote in his *Dialogo della pittura* (*Dialogue on painting*) of 1557: "Painting was invented primarily in order to give pleasure."[3]

By the seventeenth century, it became common for professors to collaborate with artists to employ art's capacity to delight toward pedagogical ends.[4] The refinement of techniques of printing and copperplate engraving in particular made it possible for the first time for professors, artists, and publishers to work together to capture large terrains of knowledge in highly detailed, sophisticated images that could be distributed at once to thousands of students. At this moment a novel category of broadside emerged that combined text and image in prints that often displayed a high level of artistic sophistication. Works in this genre represent entire systems of logic, natural philosophy, metaphysics, and moral philosophy in a comprehensive manner and coherent format, by showing, on a single page, how individual elements of the system relate to the whole. These broadsides inspired viewers to explore philosophical topics through visually appealing works of art. In other words, they functioned to make the activity of learning philosophy and investigating philosophical notions pleasurable and entertaining.[5] In this Reflection, I examine details in two broadsides that present pictorial interpretations of the notion of pleasure and its dangers, in order to show the equivocal attitudes toward sensual pleasures implicit in what was taught in the convent schools associated with the University of Paris in the early seventeenth century.

---

3 Mark W. Roskill, *Dolce's "Aretino" and Venetian Art Theory of the Cinquecento* (Toronto: University of Toronto Press, 2000), 148–149: "Percioche essendo la Pittura trovata principalmente per dilettare."

4 On visual representations in early modern philosophy classrooms, see Susanna Berger, *The Art of Philosophy: Visual Thinking in Europe from the Late Renaissance to the Early Enlightenment* (Princeton: Princeton University Press, 2017).

5 For a detailed discussion of comparisons between philosophical broadsides and the *theatrum naturae*, which was also aimed at teaching and providing pleasure, see Berger, "Martin Meurisse's Theater of Natural Philosophy," *Art Bulletin* 95.2 (2013): 269–293.

Some of the most intriguing philosophical broadsides were made
in Paris in the second decade of the seventeenth century by the
engraver Léonard Gaultier (1560/61–1635/40), the philosophy
professors Martin Meurisse (1584–1644) and Jean Chéron
(1596–1673), and the publisher Jean Messager (1572–1649). The
philosophical engravings produced by these figures were all thesis
prints, or broadsides containing propositions—known as theses—to
be discussed in oral examinations called disputations. These intricate
images show figures and animals exploring and circumnavigating
landscapes, vegetation, and buildings in pursuit of wisdom. Over
the course of the seventeenth century, the imagery of thesis prints
became so luxurious that these broadsides came to be valued as
works of art. In act 2, scene 6 of Molière's *Le Malade imaginaire*
(1673), Toinette tells Thomas Diafoirus that his thesis print could
be hung as a decoration in their bedroom.[6] The most elaborate
thesis prints were designed for lavish public defenses, usually
held at the conclusion of the academic year, that were staged to
strengthen a school's reputation and win the support of a patron.
Professors would select only the best students to act in these oral
exercises in front of parents, friends, and important individuals.
Some disputations were lavish events for which poetry and music
were written. For these more opulent disputations two or three
impressions of thesis prints would be printed on special materials,
such as silk, satin, or vellum.[7] The Houghton Library of Harvard
University owns an impression of a thesis print by Meurisse and
Gaultier titled *Artificiosa totius logices descriptio* (*Artful Description
of Logic in Its Entirety*, hereafter *Descriptio*), that was printed on

6 Molière, *Le Malade imaginaire*, ed. L. Aimé-Martin (Paris: Lefèvre, 1837), vol. 4, 545: "Donnez,
donnez. Elle est toujours bonne à prendre pour l'image: cela servira à parer notre chambre" ("Give it,
give it. It [i.e., the thesis print] is still worth keeping for the image: this will serve to adorn our room");
cited by Jean-François Delmas, "Estampes et textes imprimés sur tissus de soie. Catalogue raisonné de
thèses et d'exercices publics XVIIe–XIXe siècle," *Bulletin du bibliophile* 1 (2005): 91.

7 Véronique Meyer, *L'illustration des thèses à Paris dans la seconde moitié du XVIIe siècle: peintres,
graveurs, éditeurs* (Paris: Commission des travaux historiques de la ville de Paris, 2002), 55.

vellum and hand-colored and decorated with a painted border of
laurel leaves (plate. 1). In view of its fine parchment and decorations,
it is likely that this copy was hung on the walls of Meurisse's
Franciscan monastery, the Grand Couvent des Cordeliers in Paris,
for the audience to appreciate during disputations.[8]

The *Descriptio* inspired the design of another logic thesis print,
titled *Typus necessitatis logicae ad alias scientias capessendas* (*Scheme
of Logical Necessity for the Purpose of Grasping the Other Branches of
Knowledge*; hereafter *Typus*), which was created in 1622 by Chéron,
Gaultier, and Messager for students at Chéron's Carmelite monastery
in Paris.[9] On the right side of the print, a man flees a blindfolded
siren, whose breasts are exposed (plate 2). He quotes Proverbs 3:13,
saying: "blessed is the man who findeth wisdom" (beatus homo
qui invenit sapientiam). The man runs from the siren, because she
represents sensuous pleasures that are antithetical to wisdom.[10]

The dangers of delighting in carnal desires are also symbolized
by a siren in a thesis print titled *Tableau industrieux de toute la
philosophie morale* (*Artful Table of Moral Philosophy in Its Entirety*;
hereafter *Tableau*), made in 1618 by Meurisse, Gaultier, and Messager
for students at the Grand Couvent. A "Siren of concupiscence"
(Syrene de concupiscence), labeled "4.G," brushes her hair and
admires herself in a mirror, as she swims through turbulent waters
(plate 3). In the same engraving, another female sea-creature, labeled

---

8 For an analysis of this thesis print, see Berger, "Martin Meurisse's Garden of Logic," *Journal of the
Warburg and Courtauld Institutes* 76.2 (2013): 203–249.

9 On the *Typus*, see Berger, "The Invention of Wisdom in Jean Chéron's Illustrated Thesis Print,"
Intellectual History Review 24.3 (2014): 343–366.

10 The association between sirens and dangerous sensuous pleasures is already apparent in book
12 of Homer's *Odyssey*. Homer, . . . *Odysseae libri XXIIII* (Cologne, 1534), 90v–91r. In the opening
of Boethius's *Consolation of Philosophy*, sirens are likewise tied to moral and intellectual destruction. Lady Philosophy expels the monsters and comments on their pernicious effects: "Get out, you
Sirens, beguiling men straight to their destruction! Leave him to *my* Muses to care for and restore to
health." Boethius, *De consolatione philosophiae, libri V* (Leiden, 1590), 7; translation from Boethius,
The Consolation of Philosophy, trans. S. J. Tester, Loeb Classical Library (Cambridge, MA: Harvard
University Press, 1973), 134–135: "Sed abite potius Sirenes usque in exitium dulces meisque eum Musis
curandum, sanandumque relinquite." Also cited in Berger, "Invention of Wisdom in Jean Chéron's
Illustrated Thesis Print," 21 n. 33.

"6.G," is identified as a "monster of ignorance" (*monstre d'ignorance*) (plate 4). Like the siren in the *Typus*, she wears a blindfold. Although Meurisse, Chéron, Gaultier, and Messager valued the capacity of art to please viewers, these details illustrating the temptations of beautiful sea nymphs suggest that they were also intent on warning students of the dangers of sensuous pleasures that could distract them from the path to wisdom.

In addition to the siren and the monster of ignorance, the *Tableau* shows the gods Venus and Mars seated at the center of a staircase. They personify the concupiscible and irascible sensitive appetites, or the desires, passions, and wishes that result from sensations (plate 5). Venus displays her golden apple, and Mars wears a helmet and carries a sword and shield. Personifications of the following individual Sensitive Appetites are positioned nearby: Joy, Sadness, Love, Hate, Desire, Flight, Hope, Despair, Audacity, Fear, and Anger. These Appetites and Mars and Venus are bound in chains that are held by Moral Virtues above (not shown), in order to imply that the Moral Virtues direct the Sensitive Appetites. In this manner, the engraving interprets how our sensitive appetites should be controlled. Although Meurisse, Chéron, Gaultier, and Messager make use of the power of visual art to satisfy the sensitive appetites of their students, they also simultaneously warn them of the dangers of succumbing to desires resulting from sensation.[11]

---

11 This ambivalent attitude toward sensuous pleasure is also apparent in Renaissance art theory. Alberti, for instance, while promoting the pleasures resulting from the contemplation of visual art, also urges artists to conform to standards of propriety: "let us always observe decency and modesty. The obscene parts of the body and all those that are not very pleasing to look at, should be covered with clothing or leaves or the hand"; *On Painting and On Sculpture*, 78–79: "pudori semper et verecundiae inserviamus. Obscoenae quidem corporis et hae omnes partes quae parum gratiae habent, panno aut frondibus aut manu operiantur."

CHAPTER FIVE

Pleasure in Later Medieval Latin Philosophy

THE CASE OF THOMAS AQUINAS

Martin Pickavé

Pleasure is a tricky phenomenon. Not only are there many different things in which we take pleasure—food and drink, taking a walk, listening to music, a hot bath on a cold winter day, spending time with friends, solving a mathematic puzzle, to name but a few examples— there also seem to be many different types of hedonic affect: joy, excitement, cheerfulness, elation, contentment, enjoyment, rejoicing, gaiety, and the like. What, if anything, is common to all these experiences? And given this variety how can there be such a thing as a unified account of pleasure? Or is pleasure merely a particular form of hedonic affect? In this chapter I shall examine what philosophers in the later Middle Ages thought about the nature of pleasure. I will mostly follow Thomas Aquinas's lead. For although Aquinas's teachings are often—mistakenly—considered the canonical medieval views on any given topic, his discussion of pleasure is still a good entry point into medieval philosophical thought on this particular topic.

Typically, medieval thinkers consider pleasure as one of the emotions or, to use the medieval term, "passions of the soul." Aquinas's treatment of the emotions in what is known as the *Prima Secundae* of the *Summa Theologiae* (qq. 22–48) is one of the most comprehensive philosophical explorations of the emotions until the early modern period. Four entire questions (qq. 31–34) of this section of the *Summa* are dedicated to pleasure (*delectatio*). These are the main focus of this chapter. In section 1, I shall discuss why Aquinas considers pleasure a passion of the soul and what results from this for his understanding of pleasure. Moreover, in the history of philosophy pleasure is often thought of as a perfection. Aquinas is no exception to this line of thought, so in section 2 I explore what he means by associating pleasure and perfection. In section 3 I will raise an objection against Aquinas's account, for it seems as if in his account of pleasure Aquinas is forgetting that pleasure is a feeling. Moreover, it has been common, at least since Plato, to distinguish between lower and higher pleasures. In section 4, I will show not only that medieval authors adopt this distinction, but also that it motivates some of them to locate all the human emotions, pleasure included, in the will. There I will also talk about different types of pleasure. Finally, by way of concluding, I shall give in section 5 some brief indications as to how other later medieval philosophers further develop or react to the views we can find in Aquinas's works.

1. PLEASURE AS A PASSION OF THE SOUL

The term "emotion" is of course a modern coinage. Ancient and medieval authors refer with many different terms to psychic states such as love, anger, hate, hope, sadness, and pleasure, and some of these terms are decidedly pejorative, such as "perturbances" (*perturbationes*) or "sicknesses of the soul" (*morbi animae*). Aquinas's favorite expression for the class of psychic phenomena, including states such as love, anger, hate, hope, pleasure, and the like, is "passions of the soul" (*passiones animae*).[1] Although this terminological choice has historical antecedents, Aquinas also maintains that "passions of the soul" is a very apt term, since the states in question all involve one and the same type of passivity. While we are passive in many of our psychic states, not all passivity is of the same kind. Just think of perceptual acts. In having them we are receptive with respect to perceptible objects—the objects play an active role and our sensory capacities are the patient— but those capacities are not precluded from being active in some other way. According to Aquinas, receptivity, the passivity applying to perceptions and other cognitive activities, is passivity only in some weak sense, whereas the emotions admit of a passivity in a stronger sense. He holds that there are actually two related ways in which emotions involve passivity.

First, when we experience an emotion we experience that we are drawn toward the object of our emotion or repelled by it. And in being drawn, rather than drawing ourselves, we are somewhat at a loss of active control and thus passive. The emotions of love or hope provide obvious examples of this. But also when we are angry and experience hate we do not just experience ourselves recording the objects of anger and hatred; we are drawn to the objects in a negative way.[2]

Second, it is fairly uncontroversial that some emotions involve bodily changes: people who are ashamed blush, the angry person's heartbeat goes up, and so on. But Aquinas subscribes to a much stronger view: every emotion is essentially connected with a bodily change,

1 Aquinas discusses these various expressions in ST I–II, q. 24, a. 2. These particular expressions come from Cicero's survey of ancient theories of the emotions in *Tusculan Disputations*, 4.5. Note that I use Aquinas's works as in the *Opera omnia*, Editio Leonina (Rome: Commissio Leonina, 1888–1906). For Aquinas's commentary on the *Sentences* I use *Scriptum super Sententiis*, ed. P. Mandonnet and M. F. Moos, 4 vols. (Paris: Lethielleux, 1927–1947). All translations are my own.

2 ST I–II, q. 22, a. 2 and q. 23, a. 4. For Aquinas's general account of the emotions see, e.g., Peter King, "Aquinas on the Passions," in *Thomas Aquinas: Contemporary Philosophical Perspectives*, ed. Brian Davies (New York: Oxford University Press, 2002), 353–384; Robert Miner, *Thomas Aquinas on the Passions: A Study of Summa Theologiae 1a2ae 22–48* (Cambridge: Cambridge University Press, 2011).

even if sometimes these changes are so minor that we do not become aware of them.[3]

These two considerations regarding the passivity involved in love, hate, anger, hope, pleasure, sadness, and the like point, for Aquinas, to the psychological powers that are responsible for our emotions, namely the appetitive faculties of the sensory soul; for it is through them that we are drawn to the things themselves and they are intimately tied to the whole body as their organ. But these considerations have not yet led us to a clear-cut definition of emotions. Pressed to present a definition of what an emotion or passion is, Aquinas usually responds like this: a passion of the soul is a movement (*motus*) of the sensitive appetite, caused by an antecedent cognition of something as good or bad. Here is how he applies this general formula to pleasure: "So it is clear that pleasure [*delectatio*] is a passion of the soul, because pleasure is a movement [*motus*] in the animal appetite [*in appetitu animali*] following the apprehension of the senses [*consequens apprehensionem sensus*]" (ST I–II, q. 31, a. 1). Let me for now highlight two issues concerning the general account of passion or emotion contained in this passage. (1) Human passions belong to the "animal" or sensitive appetite, that is, the appetitive powers we share with nonrational animals. For Aquinas we also possess a so-called rational appetite, also known as the will, but emotions do strictly speaking not belong to that higher power. As a result, Aquinas is happy to admit that animals too experience emotions. (2) Although Aquinas employs the expression "following," the idea is obviously that passions are caused, in some sense, by cognitive acts. As appetitive movements, passions are not acts of one of our sensory powers. Yet passions are partially individuated according to the sensory cognitions that trigger them. Desire, for instance, is an appetitive movement for a good that I do not yet possess; when I thus apprehend something as a good that I do not yet possess,

---

3 ST I–II, q. 22, a. 2 ad 3. See also q. 22, a. 1; ST III, q. 15, a. 4; *In III Sententiarum*, dist. 15, q. 2, a. 1, qua. 2; *Disputed Questions on Truth*, q. 26, aa. 1–2.

then this brings about in me the emotion of desire. In a similar way all other emotions are individuated by their formal objects.

It is not immediately obvious why pleasure should be a passion of the soul, and so it is no surprise that the question opening Aquinas's discussion of pleasure (*delectatio*) is precisely whether pleasure is a passion. One reason to be skeptical is that the expression "passion," in Latin even more than in English, brings with it the connotation of suffering or at least that something happens to something where what is happening is somewhat contrary to the nature of the thing in which the passion occurs. Yet in experiencing pleasure we experience exactly the opposite; we don't experience anything contrary to our nature, but rather something in tune with it. Pleasure thus seems less like a passion; and if passion is opposed to activity, pleasure seems more like an activity.[4]

And even if pleasure were not exactly an activity, it looks as if it consists in some sort of perfection. When I solve a difficult math formula and experience the pleasure both of successfully doing so and, later, of having done so, the pleasure is somewhat a complement of the activity. This idea is, for instance, in the background of Aristotle's discussion of pleasure in the tenth book of the *Nicomachean Ethics*, where pleasure is spoken of as something that perfects an activity. But how can pleasure be a perfection, if it is a passion, something we merely undergo?[5]

Aquinas's responses to these objections will hopefully become clearer in what follows. With respect to the first objection, we have already seen that Aquinas distinguishes different kinds of passion (*passio*), that is, what it means to undergo (*pati*) something. The passivity characteristic of the movements of the sensitive appetite does not for Aquinas necessarily involve experiencing something contrary to our nature, so this is not a good objection to considering pleasure a

---

4 Aquinas raises this as the first objection in ST I–II, q. 31, a. 1.

5 See the third objection in ST I–II, q. 31, a. 1, and NE 10.4, 1174b23–25.

passion of the soul.[6] Moreover, even if Aquinas prefers the expression "passion" (*passio*) because of the characteristic features emotions have in common, emotions are for him strictly speaking movements of the sensitive appetite, as is obvious from the text quoted above: movements that are at the same time passions insofar as they are accompanied by bodily changes.

It is difficult to deny that satisfaction of desires leads to pleasure and their frustration to sadness. When I have a desire to eat chocolate and get some of it in my mouth, I will experience pleasure; when I hope to win a promotion at work and I get it, that too will cause me pleasure. Why, however, does it follow that pleasure itself belongs to the appetitive power, the power through which we desire? Aquinas thinks this is easier to understand when we realize that pleasure is somewhat a state of rest, which we achieve once the appetitive movement toward the desired object ceases naturally. In fact, there are three ways in which our sensory appetite relates to objects that we perceive as good for ourselves. First the perception of such an object will lead to the emotion of love (*amor*), which in turn leads to desire (*desiderium*), if the object perceived is not yet in our possession. But once we are united with the desired object and become aware of this union, the appetite changes from desire to a state of rest.[7] It should not be controversial that love and desire are appetitive acts of the soul directed at objects considered to be good. But if we accept that there can be these two different types of affective attitudes, why not also allow for a third affective attitude that results from the fulfillment of desire?

---

6 Although this might sometimes be the case. When we experience sadness, for instance, we experience both the passivity common to all the emotions and we experience something contrary to our nature. For this reason, Aquinas adds, "sadness is more properly a passion than pleasure" (ST I–II, q. 22, a. 1).

7 See ST I–II, q. 23, a. 2 and q. 25; *In IV Sententiarum*, dist. 49, q. 3, a. 1, qua. 1. Hate, aversion, and sadness, the opposites of love, desire, and pleasure, stand in a similar relationship. The idea that pleasure is a state of rest can also be found in Augustine, *On the Trinity*, 10.10.13, an important source for later medieval psychology. See Augustine, *On the Trinity*, ed. W. J. Mountain and F. Glorie, 2 vols. (Turnhout: Corpus Christianorum, 1968), 327.

Maintaining, as Aquinas does, that pleasure belongs primarily to the sensitive appetite does not mean to deny the importance of sensory cognition in pleasure. As Aquinas says elsewhere in response to an objection, "two things are involved in pleasure [*delectatio*], namely, the perception of what is suitable [*perceptio convenientis*], and this belongs to the apprehensive power [of the soul]; and the act of pleasing [*complacentia*] in that which is offered as suitable; and this belongs to the appetitive power, in which the formal account of pleasure [*ratio delectationis*] finds its completion" (ST I–II, q. 11, a. 1 ad 3). In this passage it almost seems as if he considers pleasure to be an aggregate of an act of perception and an appetitive act of the soul. However, the dialectical context makes clear that Aquinas here wants to emphasize the role of perception, without rejecting the view he holds in other parts of the *Summa*, including the passage containing the "definition" of pleasure quoted above, namely that pleasure strictly speaking consists in a movement of the appetite that follows an act of sensory perception. Yet the consequential relationship between perception/apprehension and emotion/passion in general and pleasure in particular is very tight, and that is why Aquinas emphasizes it, depending on the context, in varying degrees.

Moreover, the talk of pleasure as some sort of rest should not be taken to contradict the idea that pleasure is a "movement" (*motus*) of the sensitive appetite. There is indeed one movement that ceases once the animal has attained what it desires, namely, the movement toward the desired end. Yet this does not mean that when experiencing pleasure the sensitive appetite and the soul are no longer active at all. The attainment of the object leads to another activity in the subject attaining it. Think of what happens when you manage to receive what you were longing for; once you possess this object you now turn to enjoying it, which is another sort of activity, connected with other activities in the body. However, there is another reason why we might resist the idea of pleasure as a sort of movement. Movement is usually thought of as successive. Pleasure, on the contrary, is instantaneous.

For sure, certain pleasure experiences span a fair amount of time or even change over time, but the temporal extension is not essential to pleasure; it is merely accidental to this or that particular experience. Pleasure is complete at any given moment, just as an act of seeing is complete at any given moment. Aquinas points in this context to Aristotle's distinction between *kinesis* and *energeia* (Lat. *motus* and *operatio*). The sense in which pleasure is a movement is as "the act of something perfect, that is, of something existing in act," in the same way in which acts of understanding and perceiving are movements (*motus*) of the soul (ST I–II, q. 31, a. 2).[8]

2. PLEASURE, DESIRE, AND PERFECTION

Insofar as Aquinas emphasizes the role of desire in his account of pleasure he could be taken to come close to endorsing what is now often called the "motivational theory of pleasure." But there is an important difference. The aim of motivational theories of pleasure is to provide a reductive account of pleasure in terms of perceptions and desires directed at these perceptions.[9] On Aquinas's view, however, pleasure cannot be reduced to desires plus something else, for desires are relevant not in the account of what pleasure strictly speaking is, but as something that temporally precedes pleasure. Rather than endorsing a motivational theory of pleasure, Aquinas holds a theory according to which desire satisfaction is a necessary condition for pleasure.

The desire satisfaction view of pleasure is not immune from criticism. It seems that we enjoy things that are completely new to us, so we could not have desired them before, since in order to desire something you have to have some grasp of what you desire. I don't think

---

8 See also *Sententia libri Ethicorum*, 10.5.

9 For a detailed recent defense of the motivational theory of pleasure see Chris Heathwood, "The Reduction of Sensory Pleasure to Desire," *Philosophical Studies* 133 (2007): 23–44.

this objection would trouble Aquinas much. Imagine I eat a completely unknown fruit tonight and enjoy it. Presumably I feel pleasure about it, because the fruit fulfills many of the desires I have: it is sweet and I find sweet things desirable, it has a certain texture I find desirable in food and so on. So even on the desire satisfaction view it is not required that I have a desire for precisely this fruit (which I do not yet know) to explain my pleasure in it; we can construct similar accounts for other pleasure experiences of previously unknown objects. Moreover, we may allow for unconscious desires, at least in the case of some basic desires. Sensory perception is usually required to explain the directedness of our desires. But it might be possible that some objects of our desires are internally represented by the organism without our being conscious of those representations. This idea is particularly plausible given Aquinas's view that everything that exists has appetites, even entities that are not endowed with sensation. When Aquinas describes the difference between natural and animal appetites, he locates it not in the animal's conscious awareness of its appetites or of the appetite's object, but rather in the animal's sensory awareness of the fulfillment of the appetite. Beings without perception have no such awareness: "but this is the difference between animals and other natural things: when the latter are put in a state that is naturally suitable to them, they do not perceive this fact, whereas animals do. And this sensory perception causes a certain movement of the soul in the sensitive appetite; and this movement is called pleasure" (ST I–II, q. 31, a. 1). That at times human beings seem not to enjoy things they desire is also not a counterargument to a desire satisfaction account of pleasure. The account does not rule out that the object desired might have other features, which in turn arouse other emotions canceling out our pleasure. All this is to say that conceiving of pleasures as consequent upon desires is not obviously misguided.

I expect that some will want to resist my reading of Aquinas as proposing a desire satisfaction account of pleasure on textual

grounds.[10] When Aquinas talks about the causes of pleasure he usually does not talk about the union with a desired good or about satisfaction of desire. He uses expression such as acquiring a "suitable
good" (*bonum conveniens*) or the "presence of the connatural good"
(*praesentia connaturalis boni*).[11] This way of talking seems to indicate
either that a desire and its satisfaction are not enough for pleasure: the
object of pleasure also has to be of a certain kind, namely "suitable" and
"connatural"; or that for Aquinas thinking of pleasure in terms of desire satisfaction is misguided. This objection, however, can be resisted
easily. Note that for Aquinas, as for Aristotle, creatures owe their natural desires or tendencies to what they are, that is, their natures. Due
to the makeup of their organism, animals desire certain things; and
the objects of their natural desires can be called connatural goods and
goods that are suitable to the animal, while of course different kind
of animals desire different kinds of objects. Thus, the motive behind
linking pleasures with connaturalness and suitedness is not to deny the
importance of desires, but to point to where pleasures ultimately stem
from, because desires are themselves not fundamental.

Besides, it is not clear that the talk of "suitable" and "connatural" is
meant to restrict the range of objectively pleasure-providing objects.
Obviously, different human beings find different things pleasing. In
line with the general framework according to which the nature explains
the desire, which in turn explains the pleasure, it is plausible to assume
that differences in what people find pleasing are due to differences in
their individual natures. Maybe some aspects of our natures are difficult to change. But it is implausible to assume that our nature is so
fixed that certain things cannot become natural and suitable for us that

---

10 Despite there being passages suggesting such an account, see, e.g., ST I, q. 5, a. 6: "Id autem quod
terminat motum appetitus ut quies in re desiderata, est delectatio."

11 See, for instance, ST I–II, q. 31, a. 1 and q. 32, a. 1. See also ST I–II, q. 11, a. 1 ad 3, quoted above on
page 105. There are, however, also passages in which Aquinas characterizes pleasure explicitly in terms
of desire satisfaction. See, e.g., ST I–II, q. 31, a. 1 ad 2, where he says that pleasure is "a state of rest of
the appetite, when the presence of the pleasing good is perceived, which satisfies the appetite" (*quies
quaedam appetitus, considerata praesentia boni delectantis, quod appetitus satisfacit*).

weren't before, regardless of whether these things are really good for us in an absolute sense.

Aquinas's account is actually fairly simple: because of our nature we are attuned to certain things; if we become aware that what we are attuned to has been acquired by us, pleasure immediately follows; if not, we experience sadness or pain. Note that in order to be aware of a *bonum conveniens* it is not necessary that we perceive it as convenient. Although this might be a condition for having higher-level intellectual pleasures, it is not necessary for having pleasure tout court. Just think about the pleasure associated with taste and touch. I feel pleasure eating chocolate if I perceive certain qualities of the substance in my mouth. When I later learn that eating chocolate is also good for me because of chocolate's healthy properties I might experience new pleasures, but that latter consideration didn't play any role in my original experience.

I already mentioned that according to the common sense understanding of pleasure, we think about pleasure as related to perfection and even as some sort of perfection. Understanding pleasure in relation to desires and their fulfillment provides one explanation why this is so. First, pleasures are related to something that is perfected in the sense of being fulfilled and coming to an end. Yet pleasures are also perfecting since they add something over and above the activity by which we satisfy our desire. The pleasure of eating chocolate is linked to the endpoint of my desire for chocolate and perfects the activity of eating chocolate by adding something to it. And since all human beings desire happiness and the attainment of happiness will lead to pleasure, pleasure is related not only to any sort of perfection but also to the highest perfection. Moreover, pleasure is also perfecting in a further sense or, as Aquinas says, on the "side of the agent cause." The idea is that the pleasure arising from an activity will make the agent more attentive to his or her activity and thereby make the activity even more perfect.[12]

---

12 ST I–II, q. 33, a. 4.

The idea that pleasure is connected to the perfection of an activity is also very prominent in Aristotle's treatment of pleasure in book 10 of the *Nicomachean Ethics*.[13] In his commentary on this work, Aquinas endorses Aristotle's view and makes it even sound as if the phrase "pleasure is the perfection of an activity" (*delectatio est perfectio operationis*) expresses the *quid est* of pleasure, that is, the essence of pleasure.[14] This leads to a problem: at least on the face of it, it is less than clear how the view of pleasure as the perfection of an activity can be compatible with the account of pleasure as a movement of the sensitive appetite or even with the idea that pleasure comes about when desires are satisfied. Moreover, is it really true that pleasure is necessarily the perfection of an activity? When I receive a note indicating a salary increase I presumably enjoy this. But there doesn't seem to be an activity involved that pleasure could perfect, at least no activity on my part.

We can respond to these questions by looking closer at what triggers pleasure. On the one hand there is the union with the desired good, on the other hand there is the perception of this union; the latter is the immediate cause of pleasure. Beings lacking a sensitive soul (e.g., plants) might be able to be united with the good they naturally desire (e.g., sunlight), but they cannot have pleasure (or pain) because they cannot perceive this. The act of perception is of course an activity, but pleasure obviously does not consist in the perfection of this perception. When I experience pleasure about being united with a friend I haven't seen for a very long time, my pleasure is not in the first instance a matter of my perceiving my union with my friend, but it perfects my actual union with the friend, for it is the latter that I find primarily pleasing. But Aquinas is adamant that the union with which the desired good

---

13 See Matthew Strohl, chapter 3 here.

14 See *Sententia libri Ethicorum*, 10.6. For more details on Aquinas's reading of Aristotle's account of pleasure in the *Nicomachean Ethics* see Kevin White, "Pleasure, a Supervenient End," in *Aquinas and the Nicomachean Ethics*, ed. Tobias Hoffmann et al. (Cambridge: Cambridge University Press, 2013), 220–238.

is joined to the subject is also always an activity. Going back to the chocolate example this means that I am united with the chocolate in my mouth by activities such as sensory perception or activities of the nutritive power of the soul. Even in the case of the pay raise is there an activity. For what is strictly speaking responsible for my pleasure in this case is my new possession of money, but possessing something is nothing else than a way of making use of it, and using something is an activity.[15]

From all this it follows that Aquinas can easily incorporate Aristotle's formula into his general account of pleasure. Pleasure is strictly speaking a movement of the sensitive appetite, but insofar as this movement is caused by an activity and perfects this activity, at least by adding something extrinsic to it, pleasure can also be called the perfection of an activity. Aristotle's formula, in other words, makes reference both to the cause of pleasure and to its effects, but other formulas are more appropriate when it comes to delineate pleasure's exact nature.[16]

3. A PROBLEM FOR AQUINAS'S ACCOUNT OF PLEASURE?

At the beginning of this chapter I mentioned that there are many different kinds of pleasure and that a unified account of pleasure has to explain what they have in common. Aquinas's account of pleasure as a movement of the sensitive appetite that follows upon a (sensory) perception that we are united with a desired good provides a response to this challenge. Insofar as pleasure is a specific movement of the sensory appetite connected with a specific bodily change (as opposed to the movements characteristic of other emotions, for instance, those characteristic of anger or despair) all these pleasure experiences have something in common. But of course the pleasure experienced in food and

---

15 See ST I–II, q. 32, a. 1 ad 1.

16 This can also be gathered from how Aquinas discusses the two parts of Aristotle's formula in the *Summa*.

drink is also different from the one experienced in taking a walk and so on. The difference can presumably be accounted for by other factors including the antecedent perception of the different desired goods.

However, not everyone will be convinced by Aquinas's approach to the emotions and to pleasure in particular. Maybe anger and hope are primarily appetitive states, but isn't pleasure rather a special kind of perception, that is, a feeling or an evaluative perception? But if pleasure is a perception, then it cannot, according to Aquinas's psychology, belong to the appetitive powers of the soul. It must belong to one of the cognitive powers: the senses or the intellect. Aquinas never seriously considers the question whether pleasures are perceptions, although he does deny that emotions in general are perceptions.[17] Maybe pleasure is different from the other emotions; maybe pleasure isn't actually an emotion?

To respond to this worry and to appreciate Aquinas's perspective it is helpful to contrast his view with Peter Goldie's contention that an emotion is "complex in that it will typically involve many different elements: it involves episodes of emotional experience, including perceptions, thoughts, and feelings of various kinds, and bodily changes of various kinds; and it involves dispositions, including dispositions to experience further emotional episodes, to have further thoughts and feelings, and to behave in certain ways."[18] Aquinas would no doubt reject this view of the emotions as complex entities. For him, an emotion is strictly speaking only one element of such a series of items, namely, an embodied motivational attitude (a disposition, in Goldie's words); the other elements are items preceding emotions or following them. How a certain behavior is a consequence of an emotion is not hard to understand. Moreover, that emotions in the strict sense dispose the subject to have further thoughts and feelings does not indicate that emotions themselves are cognitions. Since the sensitive appetite is intimately

---

17 See ST I–II, q. 22, a. 2.

18 Peter Goldie, *The Emotions: A Philosophical Exploration* (Oxford: Clarendon Press, 2000), 12–13.

PLATE I Gaultier, after Meurisse, Descriptio, Houghton Library, Harvard University, *FB6.M5718614a (artwork in the public domain; photograph provided by Houghton Library)

PLATE 2 Gaultier, after Chéron, Typus (detail showing man fleeing from a blindfolded siren), Princeton University Library, Broadside 120 (artwork in the public domain; photograph provided by Princeton University Library)

PLATE 3 Gaultier, after Meurisse, Tableau (detail showing a "Siren of concupiscence"), Bibliothèque nationale de France, Paris, Cabinet des Estampes, Réserve QB-201 (21) (artwork in the public domain; photograph provided by Bibliothèque nationale de France)

PLATE 4 Gaultier, after Meurisse, Tableau (detail showing a "monster of ignorance"), Bibliothèque nationale de France, Paris, Cabinet des Estampes, Réserve QB-201 (21) (artwork in the public domain; photograph provided by Bibliothèque nationale de France)

PLATE 5 Gaultier, after Meurisse, Tableau (detail showing Venus, Mars, and the individual Sensitive Appetites), Bibliothèque nationale de France, Paris, Cabinet des Estampes, Réserve QB-201 (21) (artwork in the public domain; photograph provided by Bibliothèque nationale de France)

connected with the body as its organ, every movement of the appetite immediately affects the body. The perceptions of an angry person (and also the beliefs arising from such perceptions) thus differ from those of a calm person because the body of the latter is in an equilibrium that allows the agent a better functioning of her perceptual apparatus than the angry one.[19] We can expect Aquinas to give a similar explanation of the feeling, a kind of perception, experienced when we are in an emotional state. Strong emotional responses change the body, and this affects our sensory powers (mostly our tactile sense), so that the result is a particular feeling, a particular phenomenal state.[20] Whereas the cognition leading to the emotion is antecedent to the emotion itself, this self-perception is consequent to the emotion. I take Aquinas's talk of passions of the soul following upon or being caused by antecedent cognitions to mean that these cognitions are not themselves part of the emotions, but that they play a double role: triggering the emotion and providing the emotion with its intentional content.[21]

We can find all the elements of the picture just outlined in Aquinas's treatment of pleasure. Pleasures follow upon or are caused by the perception of the desired good. And pleasures can interact with our beliefs in many ways. First, they can reinforce agents in their beliefs and in their actions, because the agent performing an action or entertaining a belief is, "through taking pleasure in his action, more eagerly intent on it" (ST I–II, q. 33, a. 4). And pleasure can interfere with our beliefs in multiple ways, either by shifting our attention, by being in opposition to other beliefs, or by affecting the body to such an extent that the use of reason is partly impeded. Maybe some of these ways coincide. When I am enjoying my drink in the bar, my attention is somewhat focused

---

19 See, for instance, ST I–II, q. 9, a. 2 and q. 10, a. 3.

20 *Disputed Questions on Truth*, q. 26, a. 3.

21 I have defended this view in "Emotion and Cognition in Later Medieval Philosophy: The Case of Adam Wodeham," in *Emotion and Cognitive Life in Medieval and Early Modern Philosophy*, ed. Martin Pickavé and Lisa Shapiro (Oxford: Oxford University Press, 2012), 94–115; and "On the Intentionality of the Emotions (and of Other Appetitive Acts)," *Quaestio* 10 (2010): 45–63.

on the object of pleasure, and since my pleasure reinforces in me the judgment that, say, my drink is good, it will be more difficult for me to form the opposing belief that drinking at this time is bad for me. And depending on the amount of pleasure I take in my drink, my perceptual capacities will be restricted, not only by the amount of alcohol in the drink.

And of course pleasure has certain effects on the basis of which we have come up with different names for pleasure: "These other names pertaining to pleasure [*delectatio*] are derived from the effects of pleasure; for 'laetitia' [*gladness*] is derived from the 'dilation' of the heart, as if one were to say 'latitia' [*width*]; 'exultation' [*exultatio*] is derived from the exterior signs of the pleasure inside, which appear outwardly insofar as the inward joy [*gaudium*] breaks forth from its bounds; and 'cheerfulness' [*iocunditas*] is so called from certain special signs and effects of gladness" (ST I–II, q. 31, a. 3 ad 3).[22] It doesn't matter whether the point about *laetitia* and its etymology is correct or not; this passage shows that for Aquinas certain further bodily changes and the perception of these changes, leading to the imposition of specific expressions, are posterior to pleasure itself. I think this point is confirmed by what Aquinas says about the relative strength of pleasures. He notes that sensory pleasures are stronger than pleasures we experience with respect to intellectual objects; stronger, not in themselves, but with respect to us, because they are better known to us.[23] This indicates that for Aquinas pleasures can, in some sense, become objects of sensation.[24] The differences in the phenomenal experiences of pleasures, in how it feels to experience a given pleasure, is then presumably due to a mix of three factors: the differences in (1) the antecedent perceptions of the different desired goods leading to pleasure, (2) the

---

22 See also *In IV Sententiarum*, dist. 49, q. 3, a. 1, qua. 4; *Disputed Questions on Truth*, q. 26, a. 4.

23 ST I–II, q. 31, a. 5; *In IV Sententiarum*, dist. 49, q. 3, a. 5.

24 In ST I–II, q. 38, a. 8 ad 2, Aquinas says that we can perceive the state of rest (*quies*) constitutive of pleasure. I take this to mean that we can become aware of when our desires cease and come to rest. These perceptions will vary in accordance with the strength of the antecedent desire.

perceptions of the bodily change typical for the movement of the sensitive appetite that constitutes pleasure, and (3) the perceptions of the bodily changes involved in the coming to rest of the desires leading up to the pleasure. This is why the pleasure in taking a hot shower feels different from the pleasure of eating chocolate, and why sometimes the same type of activity feels more pleasurable in some circumstances than others. However, Aquinas never explicitly addresses the phenomenal character of pleasure. It is obviously not important to him when it comes to determining the exact nature of pleasure. This he has in common with other medieval philosophers.

4. Varieties of Pleasure

As we have seen , according to Aquinas, pleasures essentially belong to an appetitive power of the soul. Now Aquinas also holds that human beings have different appetitive powers: the sensitive appetite, which is part of the sensitive soul, and the rational appetite, also known as the will, which belongs to the intellective part of the soul. Pleasure (*delectatio*) belongs to the lower part of the soul we share with nonrational animals. But the distinction of appetites raises the questions of whether there can also be pleasures or pleasure-like phenomena pertaining to the will. Aquinas's answer is yes. Aquinas calls these "pleasures" of the will "joy" (*gaudium*).

Joy is a strange phenomenon in Aquinas's moral psychology. Unlike pleasure, which follows on sensory cognition, joy is triggered by intellectual cognition, and it seems to be some sort of emotion, yet not a passion of the soul. Aquinas calls it a "simple movement of the will" (*simplex motus voluntatis*)[25] and an "affect" (*affectus*).[26] And since

---

25 ST I–II, q. 31, a. 4.

26 See ST I, q. 82, a. 5 ad 1; I–II, q. 22, a. 3 ad 3; I–II, q. 31, a. 4. There is not only passionless joy, there are also passionless love and other analogues of embodied passions in the will. See also Peter King, "Dispassionate Passions," in Pickavé and Shapiro, *Emotion and Cognitive Life in Medieval and Early Modern Philosophy*, 9–31.

the will does not have a bodily organ, joy, taken by itself, does not involve a bodily change. Thus there also doesn't seem to be a particular ensuing feeling proper to joy. Pleasure and joy don't seem to have much in common other than being structurally similar kinds of appetitive movements.[27] However, the powers of the soul are not unconnected, so just as a strong rational desire, a wish, will "flow over" and induce a bodily desire in the sensitive appetite, so joy will "flow over" into the sensitive appetite, and via the bodily changes accompanying the movements of the sensitive appetite we can experience joy together with pleasure.[28]

Unsurprisingly, there is a hierarchy of "pleasures" in Aquinas. At the top of this list are the joys we have in spiritual goods, above all the joy we possess when we see God face to face in the afterlife. Below joy come the pleasures we have in the exercise of reason, including those we have when we act in accordance with reason, for instance, when we act virtuously. At the bottom of the scale are the bodily or carnal pleasures, such as sexual pleasures or the pleasures of food and drink.[29] Other kinds of pleasures, for instance the pleasures arising from entertainment and play, come somewhere between the pleasures of reason and carnal pleasures.[30] Note that for Aquinas, pleasures are not by themselves good or bad, but only to the extent to which they are according to or opposed to reason. Taking pleasure in food, for instance, is good, if food is taken in moderation, but bad in the case of gluttony.

Although joy is for Aquinas a species of pleasure (*delectatio*), insofar as "pleasure" can be taken as a generic term,[31] his treatment in the *Summa Theologiae* is primarily concerned with pleasures as passions of the soul. This may come as a surprise if you think that a Christian author

---

27 *In IV Sententiarum*, dist. 49, q. 3, a. 1, qua. 2 ad 3; ST I–II, q. 31, a. 4 ad 3.
28 ST I–II, q. 24, a. 3 ad 1; *Disputed Questions on Truth*, q. 25, a. 4; q. 26, a. 3 ad 13.
29 ST I–II, q. 31, a. 5; II–II, q. 180, a. 7; *In Psalmos*, 18, n. 7.
30 Aquinas discusses ludic pleasures in ST II–II, q. 168.
31 ST I–II, q. 31, a. 3.

should be more concerned with the lofty joys we have in common with God and the angels. But even if we have such elevated capacities as the will and the intellect, human nature is still essentially embodied. For this reason, the (embodied) passions of the soul are more relevant to the moral psychology outlined in the second part of Aquinas's *Summa*, for passions are principles of human action and are what our moral virtues are supposed to be concerned with and to moderate. Although Aquinas speaks about joy at various places in the *Summa*, he does not provide a systematic treatment of joy as he does with pleasure.

Note, however, that for Aquinas the emotional life of human beings does not only distinguish itself from that of nonrational animals by the ability to have joy. There is also an important difference between how we human beings have emotions and how animals do. Some emotions, such as pleasure, might be triggered by simple sensory cognition, but most require some higher-level processing. Information processing in humans is different from that in nonhuman animals, since we have an intellect and we can thus, at least in principle, achieve some cognitive penetration of our emotions. So even if nonrational animals and human beings both experience pleasure, their pleasures will in some cases be radically different.

Not all of Aquinas's contemporaries agreed with him that human emotions are primarily of the embodied kind. John Duns Scotus, for instance, concurs with Aquinas that there are passions in the sensitive soul (including pleasure as a passion), but he does not think that it is correct to consider them as the proper human passions. For him, proper human passions, the true passions of the soul, only exist in the rational appetite, the will.[32] Scotus's reasons for locating emotions (including pleasure) in the will are many. One reason has to do with the

---

32 For Scotus's account of the emotions see Olivier Boulnois, "Duns Scot: Existe-t-il des passions de la volonté?," in *Les passions antiques et médiévales: Théories et critiques des passions I*, ed. B. Besnier et al. (Paris: Presses Universitaires de France, 2003), 281–295; Ian Drummond, "John Duns Scotus on the Passions of the Will," in Pickavé and Shapiro, *Emotion and Cognitive Life in Medieval and Early Modern Philosophy*, 53–74.

seat of moral virtues. Scotus argues that moral virtues, as dispositions of choice, must be located in the will, since the latter is our faculty of choice; and since moral virtues moderate our passions—courage moderates fear and confidence, temperance pleasures, etc.—the passions too have to be located in the will.[33] However, as we usually imagine the will as an active human potency, it is hard to see how there could be passions in the will, and this leads Scotus to reinterpret the notion of a passion.[34]

To go back to what triggers pleasure in us and other animals: we have already seen that the immediate causes of pleasure are (1) the union with a desired good, through which the pleasurable object is present to us, and (2) the perception of that union. Aquinas succinctly describes these two elements in saying that "pleasure is caused by the presence of a suitable good, insofar as the presence is perceived" (ST I–II, q. 32, a. 3). But can this be correct? It seems that this does not do justice to a lot of pleasures. Take my state of mind before my last vacation. In anticipation of some time off in the mountains I felt pleasure, yet clearly neither the mountains nor my being on a vacation in the mountains were present to me at the moment. Or think about friends: one thing friends do is to have pleasure in each other's exploits. Yet many of my friends' exploits are not obviously present or united to me.

Aquinas himself raises these apparent objections to his account of pleasure. In his response he points out that something can be present or united in different ways: either it is really the case that the desired good is present, or the desired good is only present and united to me as something known by the mind, that is, by means of a mental representation. But because both are genuine ways of being present, pleasure can follow from both.[35] I am able to experience

---

33 See, e.g., John Duns Scotus, *Ordinatio* III, dist. 33, q. 1, *Opera Omnia*, vol. 10 (Vatican City: Typis Polyglottis Vaticanis, 2007), 157–158, n. 34.

34 He does this, among other places, in *Ordinatio* III, dist. 15, q. un., *Opera Omnia*, vol. 9 (Vatican City: Typis Polyglottis Vaticanis, 2006), 477–534.

35 ST I–II, q. 32, a. 3.

pleasure in anticipating my future vacation because I think of my-self being on holiday in this or that spot of the world. Whether or not the presence is real or not matters, but mostly for the pleasure's intensity. As Aquinas writes: "therefore the greatest pleasure [*maxima delectatio*] is the one arising from a sensory perception, which requires the presence of the sensible object. The pleasure of hope [*delectatio spei*] holds the second place; here there is a pleasur-able conjunction, not only according to an apprehension but also according to the faculty or power of obtaining the pleasurable ob-ject. The third place belongs to the pleasure of memory [*delectatio memoriae*], where there is only a conjunction of apprehension" (ST I–II, q. 32, a. 3).

The idea that representational presence alone is sufficient for pleasure can also be exploited in explaining why we take pleasure in the exploits of our friends. For such exploits may just remind us of the presence of our friends or of the presence of some other good associated with our friendships, and thinking about these things will trigger pleasure. There are, however, other ways in which the actions of others can cause us pleasure. Naturally, we can always find pleasure in the acts of someone else if these acts contribute to our obtaining a new desired good for ourselves. Some people might feel pleasure in their partner winning the lottery simply because it means that they too now possess financial means they didn't have before. Yet this case is not strictly speaking an experience of pleasure in someone else's good. More typical of friendship is that we experience pleasure in the actions of our friend and the good things coming from them be-cause they are in a sense our own actions and our own goods. For the love of friendship makes it the case that a human being "regards his or her friend as identical with him or herself" (ST I–II, q. 32, a. 5). Friendship expands our personality and with it our opportunities for pleasure (and sadness).

Aquinas's remarks about the different forms of being present show not only that pleasures differ on account of their object and their intensity but also that he admits of more than just one type of hedonic affect. To a certain extent the distinction between pleasure (*delectatio*) and joy (*gaudium*) already suggests this conclusion. But, as we have seen, now he is also willing to distinguish between the pleasure of hope (*delectatio spei*) and the pleasure of memory (*delectatio memoriae*). It is possible to read his remarks about the various names of pleasure and joy as an indication of his willingness to distinguish between various types. One type of pleasure I haven't yet mentioned and that seems to corroborate that Aquinas is comfortable distinguishing between different hedonic affects, is "enjoyment" (*fruitio*). That there is a difference between enjoyment and pleasure can already be gathered from the way we speak. I can take pleasure in the anticipation of my vacation, but I cannot enjoy my vacation in anticipating it. Enjoyment seems to include that what I take pleasure in is actually present to me. Aquinas maintains that enjoyment has other characteristics: he also thinks that enjoyment strictly speaking can only be had of an end.[36] Not surprisingly, enjoyment plays a huge role in Aquinas's theology, since it is one of the elements of the beatific vision, in which we see God face to face in the afterlife.

5. Epilogue: Pleasure after Aquinas

I hope this brief chapter demonstrates that we can find in Aquinas's writings an elaborate theory of the nature of pleasure. Some elements of his theory may strike us at first as opaque, such as his "definition" of pleasure as a movement of the sensitive appetite following on the perception of a union with a desired good; but Aquinas's theory can account for the different types of pleasures and pleasure experiences

---

36 For Aquinas's treatment of enjoyment see ST I–II, q. 11, and *In I Sententiarum*, dist. 1, q. 1, a. 1. Later authors engage in heated debates about the nature of beatific enjoyment, including whether enjoyment is identical with pleasure or not. These debates are instructive for later medieval views on pleasure. See Severin Valentinov Kitanov, *Beatific Enjoyment in Medieval Scholastic Debates: The Complex Legacy of Saint Augustine and Peter Lombard* (Lanham, MD: Lexington Books, 2014).

and is thus fully capable of explaining, in a nuanced way, the various aspects of our hedonic life.

However, Aquinas is not the only late medieval Latin philosopher thinking about pleasure. So let me conclude by briefly mentioning how two authors writing after Aquinas develop some of the themes I have discussed so far. Because it is impossible to do justice to the rich discussions regarding all sorts of issues in moral psychology that we can find in late thirteenth- and early fourteenth-century philosophers, I have to be highly selective.

I have already mentioned that some authors, such as John Duns Scotus, react to Aquinas by challenging him on the issue of the location of our emotions, including pleasure. They argue that human emotions are rather to be located in the will, a capacity that separates us from nonrational animals. But medieval philosophers all seem to agree that pleasure and the other emotions belong to the appetitive powers of the soul, instead of the sensory powers and the intellect. As a result, they deny that emotions are sensory or intellectual "cognitions" (*cognitiones*), although they are related to such cognitions as that which causes emotions to occur. There is, however, at least one medieval author challenging this orthodoxy: Adam Wodeham, a student of William of Ockham. In his commentary on Peter Lombard's *Sentences* he writes: "second, I say—not by way of expressing an assertion, but by way of expressing an opinion—that every act of desiring [*actus appetendi*] and hating [*odiendi*], and so enjoyment [*frui*], is a cognition of some sort [*quaedam cognitio*] and an apprehension of some sort [*quaedam apprehensio*], because every experience of some object is also a cognition [*cognitio*] of that same object. But every appetitive act [*actus appetitivus*] is an experience of some sort of its object; that is, it is that by which such an object is experienced, because every vital act is some sort of experience."[37] Although his remarks focus on very specific

37 Adam Wodeham, *Lectura secunda in librum primum Sententiarum*, dist. 1, q. 5, n. 4, ed. Rega Wood and Gedeon Gál (St. Bonaventure, NY: Franciscan Institute, 1990), 278. For a more detailed

appetitive acts (namely, desire, hate, enjoyment), Wodeham's "opinion" is clearly about all appetitive acts, for all such acts are "experiences of some sort" and thus cognitions and apprehensions "of some sort." Since he, as everyone else, considers pleasures to be appetitive acts, his conclusion also covers pleasures.

The reasoning behind Wodeham's opinion seems plausible. Appetitive acts are caused by cognitions. My current craving for cookies, for instance, is the result of my seeing them on my desk, and so on. But the desire following upon a cognitive act is in itself not "blind"; it is about something, and it represents its object, and this it has in common with ordinary cognitive acts. The same seems to apply to pleasure. When I take pleasure in something my pleasure is about that thing, or in Wodeham's words, is a certain experience of that thing (as pleasurable), similarly to how ordinary cognitive acts are experiences of their objects. Wodeham does not reject the common view that emotions such as pleasure are appetitive acts. What he rejects is that being an appetitive act rules out being a cognition. For Wodeham, appetitive cognitions are very different from ordinary cognitions, and the challenge facing him is to say more about their nature. His critics, including Gregory of Rimini, think he fails to do so.

Peter Auriol is another fourteenth-century philosopher with interesting things to say about pleasure. He criticizes Aquinas for distinguishing between three "affirmative" appetitive acts: love (*amor*), desire (*desiderium*), and pleasure (*delectatio*). For him, there are only two, because "every instance of love is either an instance of desire or an instance of pleasure."[38] "Love" is just a generic term comprising two basic forms, one of which is an active tendency of the appetite (desire) and the other a state of resting (pleasure). In other words, pleasure

---

analysis of Wodeham's view and reactions it elicited see Pickavé, "Emotion and Cognition in Later Medieval Philosophy."

38 Peter Auriol, *In III Sententiarum*, dist. 15, a. 2 (Rome, 1605), 443b. See also *Scriptum super primum Sententiarum*, dist. 1, q. 8, ed. E. M. Buytaert (St. Bonaventure, NY: Franciscan Institute, 1952), 395; dist. 46, q. 73, a. 2.

is simply a kind of love, and not, as for Aquinas, something resulting from love. Auriol applies the same reasoning to Aquinas's three "negative" appetitive acts. According to Auriol, aversion (*fuga*) and sadness (*tristitia*) are similarly just two forms of hatred (*odium*). Moreover, Auriol defends the surprising thesis that only acts of pleasure are formally free, which leads him also to endorse the view that nonhuman animals and infants are free, because they experience pleasure.[39]

Adam Wodeham and Peter Auriol are just two examples of the many authors who further developed the type of approach to pleasure that we can find in Aquinas. They illustrate the importance that the inquiry into the nature of pleasure had for philosophers of the later Middle Ages.

---

39 *Scriptum super primum Sententiarum*, dist. 1, q. 8, a. 3, ed. Buytaert, 449–451.

CHAPTER SIX

Malebranche on Pleasure and Awareness in Sensory Perception

Lisa Shapiro

Malebranche's story of the Fall of Man in the *Search after Truth* foregrounds neither of the usual cast of characters—a deceiving reptile, a gullible and treacherous woman—nor is the Fall framed as a tale of temptation (though temptation is not wholly absent). Rather, the spotlight falls on Adam, and the difference in how Adam thinks about—both perceives and desires—the apple before and after the Fall. Although, no doubt, there is much of theological interest here, this chapter concerns the difference in the way Malebranche positions pleasure in Adam's pre- and postlapsarian cognition of the apple. Through this story of original sin, Malebranche provides the core of his account of our distinctively human perception, and its distinction

My attention to Malebranche's account of original sin derives directly from the pleasures of the discussions of a Malebranche reading group that included Rosalind Chaplin, Emily Hodges, Katie Creel, and Nicholas Dunn. This chapter itself has benefited greatly from comments from Tad Schmaltz, Alison Simmons, and Colin Chamberlain.

from the Vision in God that Adam experienced before the Fall and to which we human beings aspire now in our search after truth.

Malebranche's positioning of pleasure as centrally involved in cognition is of particular philosophical interest, as it highlights an often neglected way of addressing the problem of sensory representation in the seventeenth century.[1] Contemporary discussions of this problem typically focus on the distinction between primary and secondary qualities and our ideas of them, most commonly identified with Locke. On Locke's account, primary qualities (shape, size, motion) are real properties of things with causal efficacy in producing our ideas of them. Our sensory perceptions (ideas) of primary qualities are caused by their objects, which they resemble and so represent. Secondary qualities on the other hand are more elusive. Our ideas of secondary qualities (color, taste, sound, smell, texture) do not resemble qualities of bodies, and so it seems that they do not represent those bodies. Nonetheless, it is not clear whether these ideas, these sensory perceptions, are wholly internally caused, and so mere epiphenomenal experiences, or are caused by something in bodies that can be considered the representational object of our sensory perceptions. The discussion thus becomes a debate about whether there is something of epistemic value about our sensory perception of colors, smells, tastes, and so on, and the question of the representationality of sensory perceptions is tied to epistemic concerns. Little about this way of discussing sensory perception involves pain or pleasure. And indeed, if pain and pleasure are considered, they are taken to be uncontroversial examples of mere experiences; they are taken not to have any epistemic value and so not to have any representational content.

Recently, however, interpretative focus has shifted to a different strand in seventeenth-century discussions: the relation between

---

[1] Malebranche's retelling of the story also gives pleasure a role in self-knowledge, but my focus here will be on its place in our sensory knowledge.

sensory perception and self-preservation. In making this shift, commentators effectively take up a side in the initial debate about the status of our ideas of secondary qualities and reframe the question. Sensory perceptions, on this line, be they of primary or secondary qualities, are not epiphenomenal and are caused by things in the world. Nonetheless, sensory perceptions do not resemble their objects, and so the question becomes one of *how* sensory perceptions represent, of *how* our experiences tell us about the material world.[2] The answer holds that sensory perceptions do not represent the natures of bodies but rather represent the relations between the bodies surrounding us and ourselves, that is, they represent bodies insofar as they benefit or harm us as fully embodied human beings. Pleasure and pain figure in this account of sensory representation, but it is unclear just how they do so. Are pleasure and pain modalities of sense perception, akin to taste, color, smell, hunger, thirst, and so some of the various ways in which we represent the beneficial and harmful relations between things in our environment and ourselves?[3] In this case, we can ask how we ought to distinguish those benefits and harms proper to pleasure and pain. On this line, pleasure and pain would themselves be representational. Alternatively, we might think that our representations of the relationships of things to us are intrinsically pleasant or painful, and so that pleasure and pain are an aspect or element of every sensory

---

2 This strand of the discussion is typically taken to begin with Descartes, who, in the Sixth Meditation, addresses the skeptical worries raised at the outset of the *Meditations*. As is now widely acknowledged, part of the project of the *Meditations* is the rejection of a resemblance account of sensory representation. In the Sixth Meditation, Descartes is clear that our sensory experiences are caused by bodies and so are, in some sense, about those bodies: in this sense, they are intentional states. However, he also maintains that sensations need not resemble their causes, but that nonetheless we systematically experience the sensations we do in a way that "is most frequently conducive to the preservation of a healthy man" (AT 7:87; CSM 2:60). See Alison Simmons, "Are Cartesian Sensations Representational?," *Noûs* 33.3 (1999): 347–369; Raffaella De Rosa, *Descartes and the Puzzle of Sensory Representation* (Oxford: Oxford University Press, 2010); Lisa Shapiro, "How We Experience the World: Passionate Perception in Descartes and Spinoza," in *Emotion and Cognitive Life in Medieval and Early Modern Philosophy*, ed. Martin Pickavé and Lisa Shapiro (Oxford: Oxford University Press, 2012), 193–216.

3 In chapter 7, Melissa Frankel considers the way Berkeley addresses this question, and in chapter 10, Murat Aydede brings this set of concerns into contemporary philosophical discussion.

perception we experience, the feelings marking our experience of benefit and harm. On this alternative line, there are again two ways to go. On one line, pleasure and pain themselves are not about anything at all but rather merely qualitative aspects of our sensory experiences, aspects of experiencing color, smell, taste, and the like, without content. On another line, pleasure and pain are qualitative aspects of sensory experiences, but ones that nonetheless contribute to the representational content of the perception in some way. Articulating the way in which qualitative aspects of perception figure in content is a challenge.[4]

Malebranche's account of the Fall of Man engages with that strand of discussion concerning the place of pain and pleasure in sensory perception. I begin by laying out his account of original sin, and I argue that pleasure, for Malebranche, is intimately tied to phenomenal consciousness.[5] It is properly understood to be neither representational nor epiphenomenal but rather a structural feature of our representations. I then turn to consider an interpretive puzzle regarding Malebranche's account of sense perception, and I argue that considering pleasure as tied to consciousness can resolve this puzzle.

1. MALEBRANCHE ON THE FALL OF MAN

Malebranche consistently maintains that before the Fall, Adam "was alerted [*averti*] by prevenient sensations [*sentiments prévenants*], and not by clear knowledge, as to whether he should join himself to, or separate himself from, the bodies surrounding him" (OC III 72–73;

---

4 Interestingly, Lisa Feldman Barrett's recent work suggests that a debate exists along similar lines within contemporary psychology. See Barrett, *How Emotions Are Made: The Secret Life of the Brain* (New York: Houghton Mifflin Harcourt, 2017). Ann M. Kring and Amy H. Sanchez, "Reflection: Pleasure Experience in Schizophrenia" in this volume, touches on this debate.

5 I will not here consider the place of pleasure in intellectual perception, though Malebranche's remarks regarding the pleasure taken in considering perfections, both one's own and of God, suggest that intellection is similarly pleasurable.

ST Elucidation 8; LO 580).[6] It is not wholly clear how to understand these prevenient sensory perceptions. However, there is a clear parallel with the way Malebranche discusses pleasure and pain. Prevenient sensations are contrasted with clear knowledge, but insofar as they are anticipatory of future events, they advise us just about what is good or bad for us. Similarly, "pleasure and pain are the natural and indubitable characteristics of good and evil: but this holds only for those things that, being neither good nor bad by themselves, cannot also be recognized as such through clear and evident knowledge" (OC I 72–73; ST 1.5; LO 21). Moreover, Malebranche explicitly assimilates prevenient sensations and pleasure and pain. "Adam, then, had the same senses as we do, by which he was advised of what was necessary for his body, but without being distracted from God. Like us, he sensed pleasures and even pains, or involuntary and prevenient displeasure. But these pleasures and pains could neither enslave him nor make him unhappy, as they do us, because as absolute master of the motions generated in his body, he stopped them, if he so wished, as soon as they had performed their advisory function (and no doubt he always wished to do so with regard to pain)" (OC I 75; ST 1.5; LO 22). I will return to this passage, but it is worth highlighting here that Adam's senses are prevenient insofar as they advise him about his bodily needs, and this advice is here identified with Adam's pleasures and pains, for it is the pleasure and pain that performs the "advisory function." Adam's experiences, Malebranche asserts, involve pleasure and pain toward things that "do not merit the mind's attention" (OC I 73; ST 1.5; LO 21). Thus, insofar as they are prevenient they involve pleasure and pain in some way.

It is somewhat striking that Adam is taken to experience pleasure and pain in the first place, for the Edenic state is meant to be one of

---

6 Adam also experienced a sensation of joy, which is distinct from pleasure as involving a kind of reflection, "as a consequence of the perception of his perfections. . . . This sensation was able to lead him to consider his own perfections and to be pleased with himself if he forgot or in some way lost sight of Him whose operations cannot be perceived" (OC III 48; ST Elucidation 4; LO 564–565).

perfection, in which Adam lacks nothing. What then could be the cause of pain? And in a perfect state what could cause him to feel pleasure? Malebranche, however, takes Adam's feelings of pleasure and pain to be a basic premise shared even by those who understand the Fall in a different way. All accounts of the Edenic state maintain that since Adam had a body to preserve, "God must also have made him experience pleasures through the senses like those we enjoy in the use of things conducive to the preservation of life" (OC I 70; ST 1.5; LO 19). Malebranche takes it that prelapsarian Adam felt pleasure and pain in connection with the way things around him impacted his bodily condition, and he felt joy in considering his own perfections.

However, Malebranche wants to take issue with an account of the Fall premised on the principle that "pleasure is a natural instinct, or to speak more clearly, an impression from God himself directing us toward some good, which impression must be proportionately stronger as the good is greater" (OC I 70; ST 1.5; LO 19). On this view, again, which Malebranche rejects, upon Adam's partaking of the forbidden fruit, God withdraws himself from Adam, "no longer will[ing] to be his good, or rather, no longer made him feel the pleasure that indicated that He was his good" (OC I 71; ST 1.5; LO 20). Adam thus loses the strong feeling of pleasure of God as his good, and feels only the pleasure of bodily goods: "the sensible pleasures, which lead only to the goods of the body, were left isolated, no longer counterbalanced by those that heretofore had led him to his true good" (OC I 71; ST 1.5; LO 20). Significantly, on this account, what changes is Adam's ability to take pleasure in God as his good; nothing much changes in the way Adam experiences sensual pleasures.[7]

On the account of the Fall Malebranche proposes in its stead, pleasure is not that through which we are directed toward our good. Rather, pleasure is but one way in which we can apprehend our good.

---

7 "At bottom the change cannot be said to have been very great on the side of the senses" (OC I 71; ST 1.5; LO 20).

As just noted, it is a way reserved for "for those things that, being neither good nor bad by themselves, cannot also be recognized as such through clear and evident knowledge" (OC I 72–73; ST 1.5; LO 21) and so "do not merit the mind's attention" (OC I 73; ST 1.5; LO 21). Insofar as pleasure and pain allow us to pursue those goods that allow for our self-preservation *instinctively*, without examination or otherwise attending to them, they are necessary: "for in the final analysis, had it been necessary for him [Adam] to examine the configurations of the parts of some fruit, then those of the parts of his body, and then the resultant relation between them, in order to judge whether, with the present temperature of his blood and the thousand other dispositions of his body, the fruit was nourishing, then clearly things unworthy of its attention would have exhausted the mind's capacity; to do so would have even been useless enough because he would not have preserved himself for long by this means alone" (OC I 74; ST 1.5; LO 22).[8] Without pleasure and pain, the amount of effort Adam would have had to direct to matters of his own survival would have undermined the aim of those very efforts. Moreover, in his Edenic state, Adam directed his mind as it was designed to be: he was focused entirely on his true good, God, of which he had "clear and evident knowledge" (OC I 73; ST 1.5; LO 21). While Adam, in attending to God, loved him, this love was a love of choice, one that did not involve pleasure or instinct.[9]

For Malebranche, original sin does not result in God forsaking Adam, and so taking away one source of pleasure, his enjoyment of his true good. It consists rather in the misdirection of Adam's mind. Adam's original sin consists in his mind turning toward those very things that

---

8 See also OC III 72–73; ST Elucidation 8; LO 580. Knowing clearly that a fruit is nourishing would involve cluttering the mind with "so many things" and reasons, which would overly occupy the mind.

9 "One has only to see Him as He is to be brought to love Him and He need not avail Himself of the instinct of pleasure as a kind of stratagem to attract our love without deserving it" (OC I 73; ST 1.5; LO 21).

do not merit attention, thereby leaving him unable to attend fully to his proper good: God. Returning to the passage I appealed to earlier, here is how Malebranche sums things up:

Adam [before the Fall], then, had the same senses as we do, by which he was advised of what was necessary for his body, but without being distracted from God. Like us, he sensed pleasures and even pains, or involuntary and prevenient displeasure. But these pleasures and pains could neither enslave him nor make him unhappy, as they do us, because as absolute master of the motions generated in his body, he stopped them, if he so wished, as soon as they had performed their advisory function (and no doubt he always wished to do so with regard to pain). Happy would he, and we, have been had he done the same thing with regard to pleasure, and had he not voluntarily turned himself away from the presence of his God by allowing his mind's capacity to be exhausted by the beauty and anticipated sweetness of the forbidden fruit, or perhaps by the rash joy excited in his soul by the contemplation of his natural perfections, or finally by his natural fondness for his wife and the inordinate fear of displeasing her, all of which apparently contributed to his disobedience. (OC I 75; ST I.5; LO 22)

According to Malebranche, Adam's fateful error involves a shift in the way in which he perceives or cognizes the apple. In his prelapsarian state, Adam perceives the apple in a way that involves a prevenient pleasure, a kind of pleasure that Malebranche later contrasts with the pleasure proper to joy, which comes from reason or knowledge;[10] it is through this sensation of prevenient pleasure that Adam is advised of the nourishment the fruit provides to his body. This sort of perception of pleasure or pain allows Adam simply to

---

10 See OC III 47; ST Elucidation 4; LO 564.

respond to his environment in a way that involves a minimal amount of attention. He does not need to examine his situation, to make calculations, inferences, and conclusions; he simply responds appropriately and moves on. Moreover, he simply erases the perceptions from his mind once they have served their purpose.[11] Then something changes. Adam errs in failing to have "erased from his mind all sensations that divided it and that placed it in some danger of being distracted" from God (OC III 76; ST Elucidation 8; LO 582). He focuses attention on the apple, on its "beauty and anticipated sweetness." His feeling of pleasure (and pain) is somehow different, and insofar as he feels pleasure differently, he *cognizes* the apple differently, in a way that now captures and distracts his mind from his true good.

There are a number of points of philosophical interest in Malebranche's reworking of Adam's original sin. First, on his view, there is no change in what constitutes the good of a human being—whether we achieve perfection or err in imperfection, we have the twin goods of preserving ourselves in existence and perceiving the truth in ideas in God. Second, whether we achieve perfection, that is, attend properly to God, is tied to the epistemic status of sense perception. In attending properly to God, we grasp our true good and think of bodies instinctively. In losing sight of God, and our true good, we ascribe properties to bodies—in the case of the apple, beauty and sweetness—falsely. And for my purposes here, what is of philosophical interest is that the epistemic status of sense perception is tied to a difference in the place of pleasure in our sensory experience. What epistemic role does pleasure play in Malebranche's account our sensory perception of bodies?

---

11 OC III 73; ST Elucidation 8, LO 580: "although the first man was warned through prevenient sensations as to whether or not he should make use of the bodies surrounding him, he was not excited by involuntary or rebellious impulses. He even erased from his mind the ideas of sensible things when he so wished."

2. MALEBRANCHE ON SENSATIONS
AND *JUGEMENTS NATURELS*

To address the question of role of pleasure in the sensory perception of bodies for Malebranche we need to look a bit more closely at his account of sensation. For Malebranche, it is hardly the case that our sensations are the source of knowledge. Rather, we are to search after truth, and so arrive at knowledge, by turning our mind to God and seeing all things through God's ideas. This doctrine, understandably often referred to as Vision in God, holds that only ideas in the mind of God represent things and so that we can only arrive at the truth by seeing all things in God. Vision in God is achieved by the pure intellect, the mind alone, and not by the mind as joined with the body. It is thus not surprising that Malebranche seems to deny that sense perceptions have any epistemic role to play. Malebranche maintains repeatedly that sense perceptions are nothing but modifications of the soul. For instance, "all the sensations of which we are capable could subsist without there being any object outside us. Their being contains no necessary relation to the bodies that seem to cause them, as will be proved elsewhere, and they are nothing other than the soul modified in this or that fashion; consequently, they are properly *modifications* of the soul" (OC I 42–43; ST 1.1; LO 3).[12] For this reason, Malebranche has been read by many to hold that sensations are purely subjective states, mere feelings that refer to no "object outside us" and so are about nothing at all.[13] Moreover, Malebranche goes on to maintain, it seems,

---

12 See also OC I 128; ST 1.10; LO 52, OC I 140; ST 1.12; LO 59, OC I 433; ST 3.2.5; LO 228, OC I 452; ST 3.2.7; LO 238, OC II 259; ST 6.1.3; LO 416.

13 See Ferdinand Aliquié, *Le cartésianisme de Malebranche* (Paris: Vrin, 1974); Nicholas Jolley, "Sensation, Intentionality, and Animal Consciousness in Malebranche's Theory of the Mind," *Ratio* 8 (1995): 129–135; Andrew Pyle, *Malebranche* (New York: Routledge, 2003); Thomas Lennon, "Malebranche's Argument for Ideas and its Systematic Importance," in *Minds, Ideas, and Objects: Essays on the Theory of Representation in Modern Philosophy*, ed. Phillip Cummins and Guenter Zoeller (Atascadero, CA: Ridgeview, 1992), 57–71; Steven Nadler, "Malebranche's Theory of Perception," in *The Great Arnauld and Some of His Philosophical Correspondents*, ed. E. Kremer (Toronto: University of Toronto Press, 1994), 108–128; Steven Nadler, *Malebranche and Ideas* (Oxford: Oxford University Press, 1992); Daisy Radner, *Malebranche: A Study of the Cartesian System* (Amsterdam: Van Gorcum,

that our sensory perceptions, that is, perceptions of sensible things, consist of sensation and pure idea. The idea seems to be that sensation is a modification of our soul, or what we feel, in perceiving an idea in God.[14] A sensation might well feel a certain way, but it seems to do no cognitive or epistemic work to get us to the truth. Indeed, the feelings that constitute our sensations, insofar as they lead us to believe how things appear to us, might well be thought a distraction from focusing on ideas in the mind of God. Now, Malebranche here is discussing *all* sensory perceptions, and not simply pleasures and pains, but surely if more standard sensations of color, smell, taste, and so on are mere feelings signifying nothing, then pleasures and pains would be as well. Nothing about pleasure or pain is particularly distinctive as far as sensory perception goes, on this view.

This standard reading has typically focused on Malebranche's remarks on sensation in book 3 of the *Search after Truth*, where he explains that only vision in God can get us to the truth, and it neglects to consider the very rich and textured account of human sense perception developed in book 1. Recently, however, Alison Simmons and Lawrence Nolan have each turned to the book 1 account in defending alternative interpretations of Malebranche's account of our sense perception.[15] Both these interpretations aim to rehabilitate sensations as

---

1978); Tad Schmaltz, *Malebranche's Theory of the Soul: A Cartesian Interpretation* (Oxford: Oxford University Press, 2003); Tad Schmaltz, "Malebranche on Ideas and the Vision in God," in *The Cambridge Companion to Malebranche*, ed. S. Nadler (Cambridge: Cambridge University Press, 2000), 59–86.

14 See for instance: "but although I may say that we see material and sensible things in God, it must be carefully noted that I am not saying we have sensations of them in God, but only that it is God who acts in us; for God surely knows sensible things, but He does not sense them. When we perceive something sensible two things are found in our perception: *sensation* and *pure* idea. The sensation is a modification of our soul, and it is God that causes it in us. He can cause this modification even though He does not have it Himself, because He sees in the idea He has of our soul that it is capable of it. As for the idea found in conjunction with the sensation, it is in God, and we see it because it pleases God to reveal it to us. God joins the sensation to the idea when objects are present so that we may believe them to be present and that we may have all the feelings and passions that we should have in relation to them" (OC I 445; ST III–II.6; LO 234).

15 Alison Simmons, "Sensation in a Malebranchean Mind," in *Topics in Early Modern Philosophy of Mind*, ed. J. Miller, Studies in the History of Philosophy of Mind 9 (Dordrecht: Springer, 2009),

being something more than mere empty feelings waiting to be affixed to an idea in God. Simmons maintains that for Malebranche sensory perceptions, just like intellectual perceptions, are intentional states. Sensory perceptions are not mere feelings but rather are directed to or about intelligible extension, just as our intellectual perceptions of bodies are directed to or about intelligible extension.[16] On Simmons's interpretation of Malebranche, sensory perceptions differ from intellectual perceptions in their *manner* of perceiving this same object, and as such they are a different kind of act. Malebranche's emphasis on sensations being modifications of the mind is meant to mark this distinctive manner of thinking. Sensory perceptions involve a special kind of consciousness, an inner feeling (*sentiment intérieur*) through which they are brought to our attention, whereas intellectual perceptions, though they must certainly involve some kind of awareness, are directed outward and so do not involve this "inner feeling"; they are thus not at the fore of our consciousness. It is the fact that our sensory perceptions come with this "inner feeling" that makes them less epistemically viable. That "feeling" occludes and confuses our intellectual perception of intelligible extension.

Whereas Simmons is concerned to emphasize Malebranche's concern with the inner feeling of sensory perception, Nolan aims to clarify the content proper to sensory perception. He argues that for Malebranche sensory perceptions ought to be understood as seeings-as, and so as acts of perceiving themselves. This interpretation emerges

---

105–129. Lawrence Nolan, "Malebranche on Sensory Cognition and 'Seeing As,'" *Journal of the History of Philosophy* 50.1 (2012): 21–52.

16 Briefly, intelligible extension is an archetypal ideal representation of the corporeal world, or geometrical extension. One of the interpretive challenges in reading Malebranche is to adduce whether, and if so how, ideas of sensible objects are supposed to be related to intelligible extension. It should be noted that neither our sensations nor our intellectual perceptions represent things on Simmons's reading of Malebranche, for on Malebranche's view, only God's ideas are truly representational. Because sensations fail to be truly representational, commentators, such as those alluded to in note 12, dismiss them as not of particular philosophical interest. However, it is still possible to consider the epistemic value of sensations for human beings, and this ultimately involves understanding the relation of sensations to intelligible extension.

from a consideration of Malebranche's account of natural judgments
(*jugements naturels*). There are two basic elements to Malebranche's
account of natural judgments. First, natural judgments are *judgments*
just insofar as they involve compounds or relations of sensory
perceptions. They are not judgments in the sense of requiring a self-
conscious endorsement. Second, natural judgments consist in our
sensory perceptions of objects *as* possessing the sensible properties
they appear to us as having—for instance, we see the moon as round,
stone-colored, and at a particular distance—that is, they constitute our seeings-as, or otherwise perceivings-as, full-fledged objects.
Malebranche maintains that these judgments are *natural* precisely insofar as they derive from our nature as unions of mind and body and
function to preserve that union in existence.[17] So "we should rely on
the testimony of the sight not in order to judge concerning the truth of
things in themselves but only to discover the relation they have to the
preservation of the body" (OC I 79; ST 1.6; LO 25).

Though, on the face of it, it can appear that Simmons's and Nolan's
interpretations are working at cross purposes, they are in fact complementary. Simmons's reading focuses on the phenomenal aspect of
sensory perception as "inner feeling," while Nolan focuses on *what* we
seem to sense, the objects of our perceptual experiences. It is important, however, to recognize that Nolan and Simmons both understand
Malebranche as holding that our sensory perceptions are directed
to intelligible extension. For Nolan, the objects of our perceptual
experiences are just what we, for instance, see intelligible extension
as. Simmons's account suggests that for Malebranche, what we see intelligible extension as is tied to the "inner feeling," or consciousness,
proper to sensory perception. Further explicating Malebranchean natural judgments will help in better understanding how inner feeling

---

17 See OC I 119–120; ST 1.9; LO 46–47. Alison Simmons develops this aspect of Malebranche's
account in "Guarding the Body: A Cartesian Phenomenology of Perception," in *Contemporary
Perspectives on Early Modern Philosophy: Essays in Honor of Vere Chappell*, ed. P. Hoffman, D. Owen,
and G. Yaffe (Peterborough, Ontario: Broadview Press, 2008), 81–114.

and natural judgment are connected, but it will also shed light on Malebranche's account of the Fall of Man and the role of pleasure in human perception.

Malebranche identifies sensory experiences with natural judgments, and he is clear that they are properly called judgments because they are compound sensory perceptions. He explains what a natural judgment consists in by considering a range of cases, from the quite simple to the more complex. For instance, when we look at a cube, an image is presented on our retina with unequal faces, but that is not what we see. Rather, we see a three-dimensional figure with equal faces (OC I 96; ST 1.7; LO 34). This appearance of the cube in our visual experience is a typical natural judgment: "it is clear that this natural judgment is but a compound sensation that consequently can sometimes be mistaken. I call it compound because it depends on two or more impressions occurring in the eye at the same time" (OC I 96; ST 1.7; LO 34). Similarly, when we see a man walking toward us, we do not experience him as changing size, getting larger and larger as he approaches. Rather, we see the man as having a constant size. Malebranche appeals to increasingly complex cases of natural judgments: our perception of a bell tower to be at varying distances depending on whether other things are in our field of vision; the size of the moon as varying with its position in the sky, either on the horizon or overhead, and the appearance of objects as we are running as either static or moving with us, depending on their relative distance to us. (See OC I 99; ST 1.7; LO 35.) With these examples Malebranche has two aims: first, to illustrate that the changes that intelligible extension occasions in our sense organs (in this case, our eyes) are distinct from what we experience in sensory perception, and second, to demonstrate that what we experience in sensory perception, what we are aware of, is irreducibly complex and is constructed without our being aware that the construction is happening. In this way, we perceive intelligible extension *as* one thing or another and are aware of the world *as* being a particular way in virtue of our compounding how that world affects us.

What Malebranche does not say much about, however, is what *explains* the compound sensation, that is, what explains how sensations come together as compounds. Indeed, it is striking that he does not refer to simple sensations.[18] What he does claim repeatedly is that our sensory experiences—our natural judgments—do not get us to the natures of things but do get us to the relations in which things stand to our continuing existence, as part of our good. Here is a series of passages from *Search after Truth* 1.6, where he defends this claim:

> we should rely on the testimony of the sight not in order to judge concerning the truth of things in themselves but only to discover the relation they have to the preservation of the body. (OC I 79; ST 1.6; LO 25)
>
> Thus it is a groundless prejudice to believe that we see objects as they are in themselves. For our eyes, which were given us only for the preservation of our body, perform their duty quite well by providing us with ideas of objects proportioned to the idea we have of the size of our body, although there are in these objects an infinite number of parts that they do not disclose to us. (OC I 87; ST 1.6; LO 29)
>
> It must not be imagined, however, that our senses correctly inform us of the relation that other bodies have to our own, for exactitude and precision are not essential to sense knowledge, which need serve only for the preservation of life. (OC I 92; ST 1.6; LO 32)

---

18 The one place where he might is toward the end of book 1 of the *Search* where he distinguishes four things that are typically confused in a discussion of sensation: the action of the physical object; the way the sense organ is affected; the "passions, sensation or perception of the soul," or what we feel; and the judgment the soul makes about what it is perceiving (OC I 129–130; ST 1.10; LO 52). The last item presumably includes natural judgments, as Malebranche distinguishes those sensory judgments from the free judgments in which we endorse our perceptions. That would leave the third item to be either the simple sensations or simply the phenomenological "feel" of our natural judgments.

As his discussion of sensory experience proceeds, it is clear that he claims that all our natural judgments—of relative distance, of motion and rest, as well as of sensible qualities of objects—guide us with regard to our self-preservation.

Insofar as our natural judgments provide us with the knowledge requisite to our self-preservation, they must involve pleasure or pain in some way. Our self-preservation is, after all, our bodily good, and pleasure, as Malebranche defines it, is a natural instinct that directs us toward those things that are good relative to us. The question concerns *how* natural judgments involve pleasure or pain. There are at least two options. First, a feeling of pleasure or pain could simply attach to our seeings-as, in accordance with whether they indicate a benefit or harm in our environment. On this view, pleasure and pain are not part of the complex of sensations that form a natural judgment, but rather attach to a natural judgment already formed. Sometimes Malebranche does seem to talk in these terms: "it is clear that vivid, affective sensations must be felt in the pricked finger rather than in the thorn in order to pull it away, and non-affective sensations of colors must be sensed in objects in order to distinguish them from each other" (OC I 133–134; ST 1.11; LO 55). Here Malebranche distinguishes nonaffective sensations that we attribute to objects from the affective sensations—pleasures and pains—that we ascribe to ourselves. This suggests that we first perceive things as objects with properties independently of our feelings of pleasure, and then further compound those perceivings-as with pleasures or pains.

However, there is also another option: pleasure could be that through which our sensations are combined to constitute natural judgments. To see this option, we need to look at another aspect of Malebranche's discussion of pleasure and to return to his account of the Fall of Man. Malebranche distinguishes three kinds of ways in which we sensorily experience things. Some sensory experiences are strong and lively, others are weak and languid, and the third are somewhere in between. What distinguishes each of these experiences is the degree of pleasure intrinsic to them. Strong and lively sensory experiences are either quite pleasant or very unpleasant; weak and languid experiences are neither pleasant nor unpleasant; and intermediate experiences fall somewhere in between. Moreover, Malebranche maintains that it is through these varying intensities of experience, these feelings, that we know our soul to be modified—that is, as perceiving something:

> given that we do not know our soul through an idea, as I shall explain elsewhere, but only by the inner sensation we have of it, we do not know through simple perception but only through reasoning whether brightness, light, color, and the other weak and languid sensations are modifications of our soul. But for lively sensations such as pleasure and pain, we easily judge that they are in us because we perceive that they affect us, and we need not know them through their ideas to know that they belong to us.
>
> As for the intermediate sensations, the soul finds itself puzzled. For on the one hand, it wishes to follow the natural judgments of the senses, and as a result, it denies ownership of these sorts of sensations as much as it can in order to attribute them to objects. But on the other hand, it cannot but perceive within itself that they belong to it, particularly when these sensations approach those I have termed strong and lively. . . . If the sensation sufficiently | affects it, the soul judges it to be in its own body as well as in the object. If the sensation affects it but very little, the soul judges it to be only in the object. (OC I 139–140; ST 1.12; LO 58–59)

It is somewhat hard to understand what Malebranche is getting at here. Simmons suggests that Malebranche is concerned with our consciousness or awareness of ideas: the stronger our sensory experience, the more we recognize the experience as our own, a modification of the mind, the more perceptions are, in a certain sense, conscious. Insofar as our perceptions are more present to consciousness, we are less tempted to ascribe what we are experiencing to objects. The less they are present to consciousness, the less we take our experiences to be ours, modifying our minds, and the more likely we are to project our experience onto something distinct from us. On this reading, it would seem that the more pleasant (or painful) a sensory experience is, the less likely we are to ascribe it to something outside us. On the face of it, this interpretation seems intuitive: the more self-consciously conscious we are, the more room there is to open a gap between our own experiences and what they seem to be about. Nonetheless, this intuition is in tension with what Malebranche takes to be the purpose of sensory experiences and of natural judgments: our self-preservation. On Simmons's interpretation, the natural judgments through which we perceive an object as having properties are only weakly pleasing. Because it is weakly pleasing we do not in the first instance refer the perception to ourselves and so can refer it to an object. However if our natural judgments are to be conducive to our self-preservation, as Malebranche insists that they are, they need to be pleasing. So through our sensory experiences how can we both ascribe properties to objects and perceive in a way conducive to our self-preservation? From another angle: on Simmons's line, a very pleasant experience involves a heightened self-awareness, but this same pleasant experience, in virtue of being pleasant, must also steer us toward our bodily good. How can the awareness that we are simply having experiences be conducive to our self-preservation? From this angle the problem is: How can we both perceive in such a way that we recognize that our sensory perceptions aren't veridical and at the same time recognize that they are conducive to our self-preservation?

It seems clear that Malebranche does align the intensity of our inner feeling with consciousness or awareness. The issue is how to understand that alignment. Returning to the story of the Fall of Man can help us to do so. At the outset of this essay, I suggested that for Malebranche the Fall consists in a shift in some aspect of Adam's consciousness or awareness of the apple. In his prelapsarian state, Adam experiences what Malebranche terms prevenient sensations, sensations that are conducive to his self-preservation. However, Malebranche makes no mention of prelapsarian Adam having natural judgments.[19] That is, before the Fall Adam has an awareness of things in the world insofar as they are conducive to his continued well-being, but he does not perceive these things *as* things with properties. After the Fall, however, Adam becomes conscious of one thing, an apple, *as* a thing, with a particular beauty, a particularly pleasant taste, that is, with properties he ascribes to it. Thus, with the Fall Adam begins to make natural judgments. But these natural judgments, too, are also conducive to Adam's self-preservation, and so too must involve pleasure.

Two dimensions of Adam's thought change with his Fall. First, he perceives the apple differently. He is aware or conscious of the apple in a different way before and after the Fall: before the Fall he is oriented toward the apple so as to be nourished by it; after the Fall he sees it as an object with particular properties. But here it is interesting that Malebranche singles out properties that seem directly related to pleasure: beauty and sweetness. In doing so he highlights the second point of difference. Before the Fall, Adam feels a well-tempered pleasure, such that he can secure his well-being while attending to his proper good, namely God. After the Fall, Adam's experience of pleasure distracts him from God, and his attention is focused on what he sees as an apple with particular properties that produce his pleasure. A weak and languid pleasure thus does involve a lesser presence to consciousness of a worldly thing: Adam's mind is turned to God, and so we might say he is fully conscious or aware of God; however, he also is, in some sense, aware of himself—after all, he preserves himself in existence—and aware of the world around him as beneficial or harmful to him. It is notable here that for Malebranche this intellectual apprehension of God does not involve pleasure, though it does involve an

---

19 He does not ascribe natural judgments to Adam in the *Search after Truth*, though he there does assert that Adam has natural inclinations. I have not comprehensively surveyed Malebranche's other works in a way that can rule out such an ascription. My discussion here, however, is drawn largely on the *Search*.

intellectual joy.[20] After the Fall, Adam feels a strong and lively pleasure, but this pleasure is tied to our attending to things as things, attributing properties to them as aligned with our sensations. While Simmons is right to note that those ascriptions of properties are reflections of the modifications of our mind rather than anything in the world, Adam does not notice that, and indeed that is his mistake, his original sin. The untempered feeling of pleasure then involves *both* a heightened self-awareness, insofar as the pleasure is strongly felt, *and* a heightened awareness—a consciousness—of objects as objects. These two aspects of our consciousness are not opposed to one another, but rather are coordinated and complementary.

I am suggesting that the untempered pleasure that we humans feel in our natural fallen state (Malebranche thinks that even a gestating fetus is a sinner) (OC III 76–78; ST Elucidation 8; LO 582–583) provides a kind of guiding principle that shapes our experience of things *as things*. We have a sense of ourselves in virtue of feeling ourselves as affected in a certain way through pleasure. It is perhaps because of this that pleasure directs us toward our good as embodied; we want to keep having a sense of ourselves, for doing so intimates that we continue to exist. In directing us toward this self-preservation, pleasure can also be under-stood to provide the principles of compounding through which our natural judgments are formed. Through those natural judgments we perceive the world (intelligible extension) as consisting of the things we take it to be, and in so doing we do, for the most part, success-fully navigate through that world. In ordinary contexts, we are con-scious of things as things but unaware that our sensory experiences are self-shaped rather than true representations of the world around us. However, as we come to know God once again, we also come to recognize that our sensory experiences do not tell us about things as they really are, but rather only tell us about how the world affects us. It is tempting to think of this move forward in the search after truth

---

as a heightened self-awareness, but insofar as it involves apprehending ideas in the mind of God, it involves absenting ourselves from our own proper mind, even while we continue to experience sensations and use those sensations as guides to our own preservation.

3. THE NATURE OF PLEASURE

Let me conclude by returning to the place of pleasure in seventeenth-century accounts of sensory representation. Earlier I left dangling a set of questions about how pleasure and pain fit into accounts that hold that sensations represent relational properties of the world with respect to us: Are pleasure and pain species of sensation, so some of the various ways in which we represent the relations between things in our environment and ourselves? If so, what particular benefit or harm do pleasure or pain represent? Or are pleasure and pain the feelings that characterize our experience of benefit and harm? If so, are pleasures and pains themselves not about anything at all but rather some qualitative aspect of our sensory experiences, a way of experiencing color, smell, taste, and the like? On the reading of Malebranche that I have offered here, he presents us with a third alternative, one that draws something from each of those two options. For him, pleasure does track the ways in which the world relates to us, such that it can sustain our continued existence, and in this regard pleasure represents our good. In our postlapsarian state, pleasure is distinct from other sensory qualities, but the objects of our various sensory perceptions are not fully available to us independently of our natural judgments. We are affected sensorily in a variety of ways, and from those ways we form compound sensory perceptions through which we perceive objects as having particular sensible properties. We can analyze those natural judgments to distinguish experiences of various sensible qualities, and pleasure, a good feeling, is among those experiences that we can distinguish. This way of feeling pleasure, however, does not seem to be about objects so much as it is a feeling of self-awareness.

If it represents anything, it is something about us. However, for Malebranche, pleasure also plays another role, for it is through a particularly strong and lively feeling of pleasure that humans do come to make the natural judgments through which we perceive things as things. In this way, pleasure plays a constitutive role in distinctively human perception.

CHAPTER SEVEN

Pleasures, Pains, and Sensible Qualities in Berkeley's Philosophy

Melissa Frankel

There are a number of places in Berkeley's corpus in which he discusses pleasure and pain.[1] In the second Dialogue of *Alciphron*, for instance, in working through some views in moral philosophy, Berkeley considers distinctions between different varieties of pleasure—for instance, bodily pleasures ("pleasures of sense") as opposed to imaginative or intellectual pleasures ("pleasures of imagination" and "pleasures of reason"; ALC 2.14)—and also reflects on possible scalar rankings of pleasures, for example, according to their duration and

---

1 Unlike contemporary theorists, who might give a different account of pleasures than they do of pains (see Murat Aydede, chapter 10 here), Berkeley—like many other early modern philosophers—seems to treat pleasures and pains as on a par with one another, such that, e.g., any analysis he gives of one will also be true of the other. Thus, although in what follows I mainly discuss pleasures, I will discuss passages in which Berkeley explicitly refers to pains as providing textual evidence for his views about pleasures as well.

intensity.[2] But discussions of pleasure also play an important role in the metaphysical and epistemological texts, including in his earliest writings in the *Notebooks*, as well as in his more mature metaphysical and epistemological works, the *Principles of Human Knowledge* and *Three Dialogues between Hylas and Philonous*. In these texts, Berkeley often places pleasures alongside sensible qualities/sensible quality perceptions;[3] in the first Dialogue of DHP, in particular,[4] Berkeley leans heavily on an analogy between pleasures and sensible qualities to support his arguments for idealism, that is, his view that there are no mind-independent material objects, but that all physical objects are constituted of ideas or groups of ideas.

Berkeley is not altogether unambiguous on what relation he takes to hold between pleasures and sensible qualities. In some passages, Berkeley seems to *equate* pleasures with sensible qualities, although it is unclear whether he means us to conclude from this that sensible qualities are just pleasures, or that pleasures are just sensible qualities. As for the former, Berkeley suggests that sensible qualities are just varieties of pleasures, among other places, at DHP 178, where he has his interlocutor Philonous proclaim that "warmth, or a more gentle degree of heat than what causes uneasiness, [is] a pleasure," and at DHP 179–180, where he claims that "a sweet taste [is] a particular kind of pleasure or pleasant sensation."[5] As for the latter, meanwhile, at DHP 177 he seems to claim that pleasures are just sensible qualities:

> PHILONOUS: Or can you frame to yourself an idea of sensible pain or pleasure in general, abstracted from every particular idea of heat, cold, tastes, smells? &c.

---

2 ALC 2.18. Moreover, in his Sermon on Immortality (among other places) Berkeley talks of the transcendent pleasure of the afterlife, as opposed to the determinate pleasure of the present life.

3 Since Berkeley typically equates sensible qualities with sensible quality perceptions, I will often talk of the two as if they are synonymous in what follows.

4 See especially DHP 176–181.

5 See also DHP 176, on heat being a pain, 180 on bitterness as a pain, 180–181 on various odors being merely "pleasing or displeasing sensations," etc.

HYLAS: I do not find that I can.

PHILONOUS: Doth it not therefore follow, that sensible pain is
nothing distinct from those sensations or ideas, in an intense
degree? (DHP 177)

That is, since pleasures and pains cannot be abstracted from sensible qualities, they are arguably reducible to them. In yet other
passages, however, Berkeley simply lists pleasures alongside sensible
qualities, as in NB 136, where he asks: "qu: wt can we see beside
colours, wt can we feel beside, hard, soft cold warm pleasure pain."
This is ambiguous between either of the above views or, indeed, a
slightly weaker one, on which Berkeley merely means to be claiming
that pleasures, pains, and sensible qualities must admit of similar or
parallel metaphysical analyses. The first question that I will address,
then, is what this metaphysical analysis might be. Following this,
I will consider some epistemological implications for Berkeley's
parallel accounts of sensible qualities and pleasures. I will explore
Berkeley's view that we can have knowledge of the existence and
nature of physical objects via our sensible quality perceptions, and
I will consider whether he might or does say the same with respect
to pleasures.

1. PLEASURES, SENSIBLE QUALITIES, SENSATIONS

What is Berkeley's analysis of pleasure, and what is its relationship
to his view of sensible qualities? One prominent interpretation has
it that for Berkeley, pleasures, pains, and sensible quality perceptions
alike are *sensations*,[6] where what is characteristic of sensations is that

---

6 See, e.g., Thomas Reid, *Essays on the Intellectual Powers of Man*, ed. Derek Brooks and Knud
Haakonssen (State College: Pennsylvania State University Press, 2000); more recently, Willis Doney,
"Two Questions about Berkeley," *Philosophical Review* 61 (1952): 382–391, Phillip D. Cummins,
"Berkeley's Ideas of Sense," *Noûs* 9 (1975): 55–72, and Robert G. Muehlmann, *Berkeley's Ontology*
(Indianapolis: Hackett, 1992); perhaps most recently, Samuel Rickless, *Berkeley's Argument for*

they do not admit of an act-object analysis, but rather are merely subjective feels; sometimes this is expressed as the claim that sensations are merely mental states or mental episodes.[7] One reason to think that pleasures are sensations follows from a view on which *to perceive pleasure* is just *to feel pleasure*, and thus that there is no sense in distinguishing a pleasure (the object of perception) from the perceiving of it (the act of perception). That is, to talk of having perceptions *of* pleasure is misleading; strictly speaking, it would be more proper to talk in terms of *pleasurable sensations*. And indeed, Berkeley does seem sometimes to deny that pleasures and pains can be distinguished into act and object. At DHP 197, for instance, he writes that "since you [the materialist] distinguish the *active* and *passive* in every perception, you must do it in that of pain"; the text indicates clearly that this is meant as a kind of modus tollens argument against the materialist, and so implicitly seems to commit Berkeley to the view that we ought *not* to "distinguish the active and passive" in the case of pain or pleasure.[8] In another suggestive passage from DHP 176, Berkeley has his materialist interlocutor Hylas admit that no "unperceiving thing [is] capable of . . . pleasure," which seems prima

---

Idealism (New York: Oxford University Press, 2013). These commentators are among those who suggest that equating (or, more pejoratively, conflating) sensible qualities with sensations is central to Berkeley's case for idealism—Rickless, e.g., argues that Berkeley's case for idealism centers on the passages equating sensible quality perceptions with pains and pleasures, where the latter are sensations. In what follows, I will not explicitly discuss the relationship of Berkeley's analysis of pleasures and sensible qualities to his argument for idealism, although some of what I say may have implications for that relationship.

7 See, e.g., Muehlmann, *Berkeley's Ontology*, 18. For evidence that some early modern philosophers thought that sensations could not be distinguished into act and object, consider Malebranche's claim that sensations are merely modifications of minds, e.g., in ST 1.1, LO 3, and DMR 3.1, JS 31. In what follows, I will typically treat the claims that pleasures are sensations, and that they cannot be distinguished into act and object, as interchangeable.

8 That said, it is possible to read this passage as an ad hominem against the materialist. (Thus, Berkeley might think only that *the materialist* denies the act-object distinction for pleasures/pains, and so that the materialist must do so for all perceptions.—But this on its own is perhaps not enough to suggest that Berkeley himself denies the distinction.) I say more about this in Melissa Frankel, "Acts, Ideas and Objects in Berkeley's Metaphysics," *Canadian Journal of Philosophy* 43 (2013): 475–493.

facie to support the claim that he takes pleasures to be mental states or episodes.[9] Moreover, in his discussion of divine and human pain at DHP 240–241, Berkeley seems to equate human pain perception with suffering. And this, too, seems to indicate that for Berkeley, one cannot distinguish between *the pain* and *the feeling of it*, that is, between the object and the act.

   Given the evidence that Berkeley means to give a parallel analysis of pleasures and sensible qualities, we might extrapolate from the above that Berkeley ought to think of sensible qualities as sensations as well. And indeed, there is some textual evidence that Berkeley takes sensible qualities to be sensations. Take, for example, the passages from the first Dialogue in which Berkeley equates pleasures and sensible qualities, outlined in the introduction. In these passages, Berkeley continuously refers to, and rejects, the materialist's so-called external objects (DHP 176–181), offering as an alternative his own view: that sensible qualities are "passions or sensations in the soul" (DHP 197). Beyond this fairly explicit remark, one might point to a number of other passages where Berkeley similarly refers to sensible quality ideas as sensations, or where he slides easily between referring to them as ideas *or* as sensations, including PHK 1–5, 18, and 87 and DHP 240, among others. Moreover, in the *Notebooks*, Berkeley writes that "the Distinguishing betwixt an Idea and perception of the Idea has been one great cause of Imagining material substances."[10] (The latter, of course, he takes to be one of the great errors of philosophy.) In the published writings, we find similar texts, including a suggestive passage from the *Principles of Human Knowledge*: "light and colours, heat and cold, extension and figures, in a word the things we see and feel, what are they but so many sensations, notions, ideas or impressions on the sense; and is it possible to separate, even in thought, any of these from

9 It *minimally* suggests that pleasures cannot exist in the absence of acts of perception.
10 NB 609; see also NB 572: "I Defy any man to Imagine or conceive perception without an Idea or an Idea without perception."

perception? For my part I might as easily divide a thing from it self" (PHK 5). That dividing a color from the perception of that color is tantamount to "dividing a thing from itself" suggests quite strongly that the color and the perception of it are identical; that this passage follows almost directly on the heels of Berkeley's claim at PHK 3 that "the various sensations or ideas imprinted on the sense . . . cannot exist otherwise than in a mind perceiving them" merely reinforces this point.[11]

2. SENSATIONS AND KNOWLEDGE

Suppose then that Berkeley thinks that pleasures and other sensible qualities alike are sensations. There are epistemological implications that we can draw from this. Specifically, one might think that sensations cannot convey knowledge—or that if they can convey knowledge, that the kind of knowledge they can convey is restricted. Such a view can be found in the writings of the Cartesians; both Descartes and Malebranche, for instance, were arguably committed to it. Consider, for instance, Descartes's famous description of sense perceptions as "obscure and confused," in opposition to the clear and distinct perceptions that play a role in our knowledge of the existence and essential properties of substances.[12] Malebranche echoes this claim about the obscurity of our sensations, proclaiming in his *Dialogues* (via his interlocutor Theodore): "what a difference there is, my dear Aristes, between the light of our ideas and the obscurity

---

11 Note that this is not an uncontroversial reading of Berkeley, especially because of his claims that ideas do not exist in the mind as modes. (See, e.g., PHK 49.) But I think the texts are fairly clear, and other commentators have also seen Berkeley as denying an act-object distinction. Keota Fields, *Berkeley: Ideas, Immaterialism and Objective Presence* (Lanham, MD: Lexington Books, 2011) makes the prolonged case for this.

12 E.g., at *Principles of Philosophy* 4.203 Descartes writes: "all the other notions we have of things that can be perceived by the senses are confused and obscure, and so cannot serve to give us knowledge of anything outside ourselves, but may even stand in the way of such knowledge" (AT 8A 326; CSM 1 288).

of our sensations, between knowing and sensing" (DMR 3.3, JS 32).[13]
Knowing, he thinks, is exclusively concerned with the essences
of things: "to know is to have a clear idea of the nature of the object" (DMR 3.6, JS 34). This can be reasonably seen to follow from
Malebranche's view that sensations are modifications of minds. One
might plausibly think that, in order to know something, one has to
minimally be able to represent that thing. But given that sensations
do not admit of an act-object distinction, one might think that
they cannot represent anything.[14] And it follows quite directly from
this that our sensations cannot represent the essences/properties of
objects outside of ourselves—hence cannot, for Malebranche, convey
knowledge. Another way to see this is to propose that the contents
of knowledge-claims should be capable of being evaluated for truth
or falsity. This, one might think, requires that they be structured
propositionally; otherwise what would we be evaluating? But if
sensations are merely mental states or episodes, then they are *not* so
structured, and so plausibly do *not* have truth-conditions. Indeed,
in line with this, a number of commentators have suggested that the
denial of the act-object distinction is associated with an *adverbialist*
account of sensation;[15] thus, rather than claiming *that I perceive a
pleasure*, it is perhaps more proper to claim that *I pleasurably perceive*,
and similarly, if (say) colors are sensations, then *I perceive red* might
be recast as *I redly perceive*. But then what is it that I am meant to
be evaluating for truth or falsity? Plausibly, the most that I can say is

---

13 And a bit later in the same Dialogue: "in themselves they can find only sensations, often quite
lively but always obscure and confused, only modalities full of darkness" (DMR 3.4, JS 33).

14 There is a significant interpretive debate about whether the Cartesians took sensations to be representational. See Margaret Dauler Wilson, "Descartes on the Representationality of Sensation," in
Ideas and Mechanism: Essays on Early Modern Philosophy (Princeton: Princeton University Press,
1999), 69–83, Alison Simmons, "Are Cartesian Sensations Representational?," *Noûs* 33.3 (1999): 347–
369, among many others.

15 Malebranche, e.g., has been read as an adverbialist in this way; see Walter Ott, "Malebranche and
the Riddle of Sensation," *Philosophy and Phenomenological Research* 88 (2014): 689–712, for a recent
discussion of the literature on Malebranche as an adverbialist. (Note that Ott himself argues against
this reading.)

that I *am* pleasurably perceiving—that I *am* redly perceiving—and not that the pleasure experience or the red experience is true or false, accurate or inaccurate.

So the view that sensations do not admit of an act-object distinction seems to suggest that they cannot convey to us knowledge of things outside of the self (or outside of our own minds). Qua mental states, sensations simply do not have the right kind of structure to convey this kind of knowledge. But this is perhaps consistent with the view that sensations *can* give rise to a kind of knowledge of the *self* (knowledge of our own minds), in the following two ways. First, in feeling a sensation—a pleasure, say—we might know of the *existence* of that experience: we might know *that we are having a sensation*. Second, in feeling that pleasure, we might know the *nature* of that experience— *that it is a pleasurable one*. This is perhaps the sort of thing that Descartes has in mind when he denies that sensations can afford us knowledge "of anything outside ourselves,"[16] but nonetheless concedes that we gain a sort of knowledge via sensation when he writes in the second Meditation: "I certainly *seem* to see, to hear, and to be warmed. This cannot be false."[17] There is something special about our access to our own mental states that makes it the case that we can have knowledge of them—indeed, that this knowledge is *infallible*.[18] Berkeley, too, clearly endorses this claim that our access to our own mental states is infallible at a number of places in his corpus, including for example at PHK 87, where he writes: "colour, figure, motion, extension and the

---

16 See AT 8A 326; CSM 1 288, cited in note 12; also AT 7 29; CSM 2 19.

17 AT 7 29; CSM 2 19. Descartes arguably also expresses this view at *Principles of Philosophy* 1.66, where he writes that sensations (among which he lists pains and pleasures—see 1.48) "may be clearly perceived provided we take great care in our judgments concerning them to include no more than what is strictly contained in our perception—no more than that of which we have inner awareness" (AT 8A 32; CSM 1 216); also 1.68, "pain and colour and so on are clearly and distinctly perceived when they are regarded merely as sensations or thoughts" (AT 8A 33; CSM 1 217).

18 This is sometimes called "the doctrine of privileged access"; see, e.g., Quassim Cassam, "Contemporary Reactions to Descartes's Philosophy of Mind," in *A Companion to Descartes*, ed. Janet Broughton and John Carriero (New York: Wiley-Blackwell, 2008), 482–495.

like, considered only as so many sensations in the mind, *are perfectly known, there being nothing in them which is not perceived.*"[19]

Note that there are two routes we could take here. We could think that these two pieces of knowledge are gained only subsequent to or concurrent with the sensation (that is, that we gain them via some separate act, say, an act of judgment). In this case, pleasures (say) would not themselves be thought of as knowledge-conferring; instead, this separate act would play the cognitive role. But I do not think that this is the right move to make. Instead, I think, it is more plausible to hold that these two pieces of knowledge are gained *in having the pleasure*, and not by means of some separate act; that is, that experiencing a pleasure is on its own sufficient for gaining this knowledge. This arguably follows precisely from denying the act-object distinction for sensations, since given this denial, it is impossible to both have a sensation and not to also simultaneously be aware that one is having that very sensation. So, for instance, if pain were distinct from the feeling of it, then at least in principle it should be possible for us to have a pain but not to feel it; but if, as Berkeley suggests at DHP 241, to have a pain is just *to suffer*, then we cannot simultaneously have a pain and fail to be aware *that we are suffering*. Thus we ought to think that the self-knowledge gained in having sensations is not just infallible, but also immediate and noninferential.

3. BERKELEY'S ANTISKEPTICISM AND ITS IMPLICATIONS

There is a view on the table on which sensations like pleasures, qua mental states, can at best convey knowledge of the self (that is, of states of our own mind), but not knowledge of things outside of the self. And perhaps one might rest contented with this claim. But I think it is important to note at this point that for Berkeley, sensible quality

---

19 My emphasis. Note that in this passage he explicitly links the claim that sensible quality ideas are *sensations* with the view that we have this kind of knowledge of them.

perceptions *do* convey knowledge of things outside of the self. Indeed, he is committed to the rather strong claim that we have intuitive or demonstrative knowledge of the existence and properties of physical objects on the basis of sensible quality perceptions.[20] So, for instance, in his *Notebooks* Berkeley writes: "I know with an intuitive knowledge the existence of other things" (NB 563);[21] in DHP he reiterates: "I am no sceptic with regard to the nature of things, [nor] as to their existence. . . . What a jest is it for a philosopher to question the existence of sensible things . . . or to pretend our knowledge in this point falls short of intuition or demonstration" (DHP 230). This, indeed, is a central element of Berkeley's view, insofar as he insists that external world skepticism is a pernicious doctrine that must be opposed.

But if Berkeley thinks that sensible quality perceptions convey knowledge of things outside of the self, and if he thinks sensible quality perceptions are just sensations, then he ought also to think that sensations—including pleasures!—convey knowledge of things outside of the self. Indeed, he ought to hold the rather strong view that pleasures convey intuitive and demonstrative knowledge of such objects. In what follows, then, I want to first briefly outline one way in which Berkeley might hold that sensible quality perceptions, qua sensations, convey this knowledge; I will then draw out the implications for his account of pleasure.

3a. Sensible Qualities and Knowledge

I claimed in section 2 that there are some reasons to think that sensations cannot convey knowledge of things outside of the self, although they might indeed be thought to convey knowledge of the self,

---

20 "Intuitive knowledge," here, in essence, refers to knowledge that is immediate, noninferential, and indubitable or perhaps infallible. See, e.g., Descartes in *Rules for the Direction of the Mind*, rule 3 (AT 10 366–368; CSM 1 13–14), or John Locke, *Essay Concerning Human Understanding*, ed. P. H. Nidditch (Oxford: Oxford University Press, 1979), 4.2.

21 NB 563; see also NB 547: "we have an intuitive Knowledge of the Existence of other things besides our selves and even praecedaneous to the Knowledge of our own Existence."

insofar as we can know that we are having a sensation, and what the sensation is like. But notice now that this distinction between knowledge of external objects and knowledge of the self makes sense only in the context of a metaphysical distinction between objects and the self; that is, it makes sense within a realist framework, in which there is a real distinction to be made between bodies and minds. Famously, however, Berkeley is no realist. For Berkeley qua idealist, strictly speaking, there *are no* objects external to the mind.[22] Indeed, this is made explicit (among other places) precisely in those passages at DHP 176–181 where he equates sensible quality perceptions with pleasures and pains; his express target in those passages is the unqualified view that external objects exist.

Of course, that external objects do not exist does not, for Berkeley, imply that bodies—physical objects—do not exist. Instead, Berkeley's view is that physical objects are not external objects in the sense that that they do not exist independently of minds. Berkeley is customarily read as holding that physical objects are constituted of ideas or groups of ideas.[23] Typically, he lists sensible quality perceptions as among the ideas that constitute objects, for instance, when he writes that "a certain colour, taste, smell, figure and consistence having been observed to go together, are accounted one distinct thing, signified by the name *apple*" (PHK 1). When we bring on board the view that sensible quality ideas are just sensations—for instance, in light of

---

22 To be sure, Berkeley sometimes *speaks* as if there are external objects—e.g., he talks about the independent existence of objects (e.g., at DHP 195, "this tulip may exist independent of your mind or mine"). But such passages can be accounted for in various ways. For instance, independent existence can be understood in terms of independence from a particular mind, though not from all minds—e.g., suppose the tulip is constituted of x's ideas and y's ideas; then, depending on one's views about constitution, it might exist even if x's ideas did not exist, so it is independent of x's mind (and similarly for y). Alternatively, independent existence can be understood in terms of causal independence; see, e.g., DHP 214. See Frankel, "Acts, Ideas and Objects," for some discussion of such passages.

23 This is ambiguous between an idealist reading on which Berkeley takes objects to be groups of occurrently perceived ideas and a phenomenalist reading on which he takes them to include possibly perceived ideas. I will not broach this issue here.

Berkeley's claim that "colours [etc.] . . . [cannot be] separate[d], even in thought . . . from perception" (PHK 5)—we read him as holding that the apple is constituted of a color-*sensation*, a taste-*sensation*, a smell-*sensation*, and so on.

In light of this consideration of Berkeleyan metaphysics, we might revisit an earlier concern: that sensations are not propositionally structured. In rendering sensible qualities mental acts, and in eliminating the existence of objects external to the mind, it looks like we can never attribute sensed qualities to things, but only express truths about our sensings. That is, we cannot ever express such propositions as *I perceive a red apple* (or: *the [perceived] apple is red*); strictly speaking, we can only make such claims as *I am having a red-apple sensation*, or perhaps *I am redly-applely perceiving*. Indeed, Berkeley explicitly recognizes that, in eliminating material objects, he appears to undermine our ability to attribute experienced properties to such objects. But he suggests that we can nonetheless meaningfully utter sentences in which we seem (grammatically) to attribute properties to objects, so long as we re-interpret these sentences in light of the idealist metaphysics. Thus he writes that "to say a die is hard, extended and square, is not to attribute those qualities to a subject distinct from and supporting them, but only an explication of the meaning of the word *die*" (PHK 49). That is, the word "die" refers, not to a subject independent of minds, to which mind-independent properties are attributed, but to a group of sensible quality-ideas, that is, sensations: a hard-sensation, a square-extended-sensation, and so on, which we group together as being a single object that we call "die." So a die *is* hard, square, and so on—this is the *is of identity* or constitution. (The die is a group of sensings including a hard-sensation, and so on.) But *because* the die is hard and square in this sense, Berkeley says that we may also truthfully say that it *is* hard and square, where what we seem to be using (grammatically) is the *is of predication*. To return to the apple, what one might say on Berkeley's behalf is that when we utter the sentence "the apple is red," what we are expressing is the claim that the thing that we call an "apple" is at least partly constituted of a red-sensing, that is, *that a perceiver P is redly-sensing*. Moreover, the utterance that "the apple exists" expresses the claim that the group of sensings constituting the apple exist, that is, *that P is sensing them*. Thus, Berkeley writes, "the table I write on, *I say, exists, that is, I see and feel it*" (PHK 3, my emphasis).[24] And now we can see that for a perceiver to have sensations is sufficient for the perceiver to establish the truth of both of these kinds of claims—that is, it is sufficient for the perceiver to have knowledge: P's having a red sensation is sufficient for P's knowing that an object (in this case, an apple) is red, and P's having red-sweet-fragrant-crunchy sensations is sufficient for P's knowing that the apple exists.[25]

What we effectively see here, then, is that, for Berkeley, sensations have a dual metaphysical role, both as mental states/episodes and as constituents of physical objects. Because of the former, we may have immediate, noninferential, infallible knowledge of them; because of the latter, it is possible to claim that physical objects exist, and to attribute properties to those physical objects. And when we combine the two points, we see that our knowledge of our own mental states is precisely what enables us to gain immediate, noninferential, infallible knowledge—that is, *intuitive* knowledge—of both the existence and nature of objects: in knowing *that I am having various experiences*, I know that the objects (constituted of those experiences) exist; in knowing *what those experiences are like*, I know what those objects are like, as well.

3b. Implications for the Account of Pleasure

What I have shown is that it is because sensible qualities qua sensations are both mental states and constituents of objects that Berkeley may take himself to be entitled to the claim that we have knowledge of the

---

24 See also DHP 249.

25 Depending on one's views about constitution, having (say) a red sensation alone might in fact be sufficient to establish this.

existence and nature of physical objects. So now we must ask: Does Berkeley give a parallel account of pleasure? That is, is there any evidence that Berkeley also takes pleasures qua sensations to be both mental states and constituents of objects? I have shown evidence for the former, but what of the latter?

As it turns out, there is both indirect and direct evidence that Berkeley does indeed take pleasures to be constituents of physical objects. The indirect evidence comes from simply combining the texts in Dialogue 1 of DHP, where Berkeley equates sensible qualities with pleasures, with the numerous texts in which he claims that sensible qualities are constituents of physical objects. So let us consider again our apple, which may include among its constituents a sweet-sensing and a fragrant-sensing. With respect to the sweet-sensing, it is worth recalling Berkeley's words at DHP 179: "a sweet taste [is] a particular kind of pleasure or pleasant sensation." This immediately gives us license to say that at least one pleasure is a constituent of the apple: the sweet-taste-pleasure. Thus, in knowing that we are having a sweet-pleasure sensation, we know also that the apple is sweet, that is, that it has a particular kind of pleasure in it. With respect to the fragrant-sensing, we may consult DHP 180–181; there Berkeley has Philonous ask "whether what hath been said of tastes doth not exactly agree to [odours]? Are they not so many pleasing or displeasing sensations?" It is clear that he means us to answer in the affirmative (as Hylas immediately does); on the reasonable assumption that we would think of a fragrant-sensing as a pleasing sensation rather than as a displeasing one, we may conclude that another pleasure is a constituent of the apple, namely, the fragrant-odor-pleasure. And we may continue in this vein for any other sensible quality that Berkeley explicitly identifies with pleasure or pain.

That said, it might be nice to see Berkeley stating outright that pleasure or pain can be among the constituents of physical objects. One thing to note at this point is that, unlike his contemporaries, who sometimes argued that while some qualities (the so-called "primary

qualities," which might include shape, size, solidity, and so forth) were
"in" (that is, are correctly attributed to) physical objects, nonetheless
other qualities (the "secondary qualities," including tastes, odors, and
so forth) were "in" minds qua ideas, Berkeley argues at length that the
distinction between primary and secondary qualities is untenable and
even incoherent; he thus often suggests that the secondary qualities are
just as much in objects as the primary ones are, as for instance at NB
392, where he writes: "there are [those] who say the Wall is not white,
the fire is not hot &c. We Irish men cannot attain to these truths."[26]
Berkeley almost certainly has at least Locke in mind here; he might
easily have cited *Essay Concerning Human Understanding* 2.8.17, where
Locke writes: "Light, Heat, Whiteness, or Coldness, are no more really in [bodies], than Sickness or Pain is in Manna."[27] But in fact the
wall *is* white, and the fire hot, insists Berkeley—that is, the whiteness
is in the wall, and the heat in the fire; but then we might *also* plausibly
assert that the sickness and pain *are* in the Manna. After all, to use the
example of the fire: heat is in fire (NB 392); heat is a pleasure (DHP
178); so pleasure is in the fire. This is about as straightforward a bit of
argumentation as one could get. And helpfully, we can find at least one
piece of direct evidence confirming that this is Berkeley's view: at NB
444, he writes: "I may say the pain is in my finger etc according to my

---

26 See also NB 222, where he writes: "men are in the right in judging their simple ideas to be in the
things themselves, certainly Heat & colour is as much without the mind as figure, motion, time etc."
One *could* take this as a modus tollens: if figure, motion, and time are in objects, then so are heat and
color; heat and color are not in objects, so neither are figure, motion, and time. Indeed, Berkeley
sometimes leans in this direction, as, e.g., at PHK 10, where he writes: "in short, extension, figure,
and motion, abstracted from all other qualities, are inconceivable. Where therefore the other sensible qualities are, there must these be also, to wit, in the mind and no where else." But I think that
this is just part and parcel of the view that I am attributing to Berkeley here: sensible qualities, qua
sensations, are *both* in minds (as per PHK 10) *and* in objects (as their constituents) (as per NB 222,
392, etc.).

27 To be fair, Locke vacillates on the question of whether the secondary qualities might be thought to
be in objects, e.g., as powers to produce ideas. But this section in particular seems to lend support to a
reading of Locke on which he takes secondary qualities to be in minds, and certainly this view would
place him in the company of some of his contemporaries. See, e.g., Phillip Cummins, "Perceptual
Relativity and Ideas in the Mind," *Philosophy and Phenomenological Research* 24 (1963): 202–214.

Doctrine." So just as we may say that figure and motion are in an object, so too may we say that color and pleasure are in it. And now we may give the same epistemological account for pleasures as we did for other sensations. I experience a pleasurable sensation; I thereby know (immediately, noninferentially, infallibly—that is, intuitively) of the existence and nature of this pleasure, merely in experiencing it (as is the case for all sensations.) But given that pleasures can be a constituent of physical objects, in having this knowledge I thereby *also* know intuitively of the existence and nature of a physical object of which this pleasure that I experience is a constituent.

One last remark on this matter: given that pleasures are both mental states and constituents of objects, one might reasonably ask whether, for Berkeley, we could ever form sentences like "the apple is pleasure," in the same way that we can form sentences like "the apple is red." After all, I have suggested that for Berkeley, pleasure and redness have equivalent metaphysical status—they both play the dual role of being sensations and being constituents of objects like the apple. Now to be sure, "the apple is red" is grammatical, while "the apple is pleasure" is not—indeed, one might have even thought that the latter involved a kind of category error. But I suggest that it is only ungrammatical, and that we only think that an error is being made here, because the "is" that is being used in these sentences looks like the *is* of predication. And as I showed earlier, it turns out that for the Berkeleyan idealist, what is *really* at play must be the *is* of identity or of constitution. Thus, what we may conclude is that in *both* the case of "the apple is red" *and* the case of "the apple is pleasure," the surface grammar of the sentences is misleading. The grammar of "the apple is red" can mislead us into thinking that there is some subject, apple, to which I am attributing the property of redness, when in reality the redness (red sensation) is a constituent of the apple; and the ungrammatical nature of the sentence "the apple is pleasure" can mislead us into thinking that pleasures *cannot* be in apples, when indeed they can, again qua constituents. In both cases, syntax misleads.

4. Sensible Qualities, Pleasures, and Laws of Nature

So far I have provided evidence that for Berkeley, pleasures, like other sensible qualities, are sensations; I have also made the case that qua sensations, pleasures are for him both mental states and constituents of objects, and so that we can gain intuitive knowledge of the existence and nature of physical objects on the basis of pleasures. But what of Berkeley's claim that we can also gain demonstrative knowledge of objects, that is, knowledge that is not immediate and noninferential, but that involves inferring to a conclusion via "intermediate ideas," each of which is itself intuitively known?[28] In what follows, I will discuss Berkeley's view that we may legitimately draw some inferences from our present sensations, including pleasures, to our future sensations, also including pleasures. (These are the kinds of inferences that are sometimes called "causal" or "inductive" inferences.)

As one might expect, for Berkeley, it is the natural laws that will license any kind of inference from presently experienced sensations to those that we might expect to experience. He writes: "by a diligent observation of the phenomena within our view, we may discover the general laws of Nature, and from them deduce the other phenomena" (PHK 107). Berkeley's account of natural laws, in line with his idealist metaphysics, is one on which those laws are just generalizations on the regular patterns in which our sensations follow one another in experience.[29] So what happens is that we notice various regularities in our experienced sensations; we generalize from these regularities to form the natural laws; and we then use these natural laws to make predictions about our future experiences. But are these predictions licensed? As Hume asks later in the eighteenth

---

28 See Locke, *Essay Concerning Human Understanding* 4.2.1.

29 See, e.g., PHK 30. To acquire knowledge of the natural laws is thus to learn the general rules of which sensations regularly follow which others: see, e.g., PHK 62, 105, 150.

century, what is it that guarantees that the generalizations that we make on our observed experiences will continue to hold in the future: what (if anything) is it that grounds the present regularity of our sensations, and does that same thing ground their continued regularity?

Berkeley does in fact have an explicit answer to this question. For Berkeley, all of our sensations depend on God as their cause. God causes our sensations and, moreover, causes them to follow one another in a regular manner; this, in turn, attests to God's benevolence, because these regularities "[give] us a sort of foresight, which enables us to regulate our actions for the benefit of life" (PHK 31). That is, it is good for us that these regularities exist, because they allow us to navigate through the corporeal world; more on this shortly. Our ability to *continue* to regulate our actions in this way depends on the supposition that God's nature will *remain* eternally benevolent, that is, that God will continue to produce ideas that follow the same patterns—the laws of nature will not change. Thus the current and continued existence of the laws of nature is grounded in the current and continued existence and benevolence of God. Following this, we may say that our inductive inferences are licensed by appeals to the laws of nature; our appeals to the laws of nature, in turn, are licensed by appeals to the existence and nature of God. Note that this indicates that, given that demonstrative knowledge is thought to involve intuitions at each of the intermediate steps, Berkeley is *not* in fact entitled to the view that we can gain demonstrative knowledge via the causal inferences that we make with respect to sensations. Instead, as he himself admits, we should think of the conclusions that we arrive at via such inferences as *deductive*: he writes: "I do not say *demonstrate*; for all deductions of that kind depend on a supposition that the Author of Nature always operates uniformly, and in a constant observance of those rules we take for principles: which we cannot evidently know" (PHK 107). I take it that what he means by this is that we cannot *intuit or demonstrate* that

God exists and is benevolent, which is what might be needed to render the deductions demonstrative.[30]

Now, I have already shown that Berkeley gives a parallel analysis of sensible quality perceptions and pleasures qua sensations and constituents of objects. Hence when Berkeley maintains that the laws of nature are generalizations on the regularities of our sensations that allow us to make inferences about future sensations, he ought to be including pleasures as among those sensations about which we can generalize and make predictions. Indeed, this comes out quite explicitly in Berkeley's claim that the laws of nature allow us to "regulate our actions for the benefit of life" (PHK 31). What Berkeley has in mind here, at least in part, is this: to learn the patterns in which our sensations follow one another is also to learn which human behaviors (constituted of patterns of sensations) regularly lead to pain, and which to pleasure; he calls these "the never enough admired laws of pain and pleasure" (PHK 146).[31] But pains are typically concomitant with bodily damage (that is, with the sensations that constitute bodily damage)—indeed, pains may partly constitute such bodily damage, as per section 4b; recall Berkeley's claim that "I may say the pain is in my finger etc according to my Doctrine" (NB 444). So when we learn the laws of pain and pleasure, we gain the ability to make inferences that are conducive to the preservation of our bodily well-being, insofar as we can make predictions about future pain and pleasure experiences, hence predictions about what courses of action will lead to bodily damage, and so what courses of action to pursue or avoid.[32]

---

30 See Douglas M. Jesseph, "Berkeley, God and Explanation," in *Early Modern Philosophy: Mind, Matter and Metaphysics*, ed. Christia Mercer and Eileen O'Neill (New York: Oxford University Press, 2005), 183–205, for an argument that Berkeley's various arguments for the existence of God take the form of inferences to the best explanation.

31 Of course, on the view on which Berkeley *equates* sensible qualities with pleasures or pains, *all* natural laws are "laws of pain and pleasure"; but I will not belabor the point.

32 A similar story may perhaps be told with respect to the preservation of our *spiritual* well-being; this relates to Berkeley's discussion of different kinds of pleasures, as mentioned in the opening of this essay. See, e.g., ALC 2.12. The point about the preservation of well-being is connected with Berkeley's moral philosophy. Without delving too deeply into the details, in *Passive Obedience* (PO) Berkeley is

Effectively what we have here is a view about pleasures and pains being not only constituents of *presently* experienced objects but also constituents of *future* experienced objects. I have previously shown that when I know that I am having a pleasurable experience, I thereby also know that there is something in the world of which that pleasure is a constituent. Thus, for instance, I am licensed in claiming that there is a pleasure in the apple when I experience that pleasure. And what we see now is that, given some occurrent sensations, and given the right law of pleasure, I can infer that I *will* have a pleasurable experience, hence I can know that there *will* be something in the world of which that pleasure will be a constituent. Thus, for instance, when I have, for instance, a shiny-red visual sensation and a firm-crunchy tangible sensation that constitute an apple, I may be licensed in claiming (on the basis of an inference from the right law of pleasure) that there will be pleasure in the apple (say, when I bite into it). That this is Berkeley's account—that is, that he connects a metaphysical claim about pains and pleasures as constituents of physical objects with his view about our license to make inferences—emerges, among other places, in the *Principles of Human Knowledge*, where he writes: "the mixture of pain or uneasiness which is *in the world*, pursuant to the general laws of Nature . . . is indispensably necessary to our well-being" (PHK 153, my emphasis). Berkeley arguably makes a similar claim in *Notebooks*, where he writes: "we do not properly speaking in a strict philosophical sense make objects more or less pleasant, but the laws of Nature do that" (NB 144).

On a final note: what I have suggested here is that Berkeley offers a unified account of how we make inferences from occurrent sensations

---

sometimes read as upholding a version of rule utilitarianism, on which human happiness or well-being (both bodily [PHK, PO] and spiritual [ALC]) is constitutive of the good, and moral rules are rules about maximizing that good. See, e.g., Paul Olscamp, "Some Suggestions about the Moral Philosophy of George Berkeley," *Journal of the History of Philosophy* 6 (1968): 147–156, and Paul Olscamp, *The Moral Philosophy of George Berkeley* (The Hague: Martinus Nijhoff, 1970). Because avoiding pain allows us to preserve our bodily well-being, acting morally, for Berkeley, involves acting (or intending to act) in accordance with rules that maximize pleasure and minimize pain.

(including pleasures) to future sensations (including pleasures). But although there is a unified account here, nonetheless Berkeley sometimes indicates that he thinks of the laws of pleasure and pain as in some sense the *original or paradigmatic* natural laws (as opposed to simply being a subset of the natural laws). This is because he thinks that the *primary* function of the laws of nature is to allow us to make the sorts of predictions that will enable us to guide our actions. Along these lines, Berkeley writes that "the human mind, naturally furnished with the ideas of things particular and concrete, and being designed, not for the bare intuition of ideas, but for action or operation about them, and pursuing her own happiness therein, stands in need of certain general rules or theorems to direct her operations in this pursuit; the supplying which want is the *true, original, reasonable end* of studying the arts and sciences" (ALC 7.11, my emphasis). The importance of the laws of pleasure and pain for Berkeley thus cannot be overstated—as he says in the *Principles of Human Knowledge*, they are "never enough admired" (PHK 146).

5. Conclusion

It was not unusual for philosophers in the early modern period to take pleasures and pains to be paradigmatic of sensations; it was also not unusual to find philosophers drawing analogies between pleasures, pains, and other sensible quality perceptions—one finds such analogies in Descartes, Malebranche, and Locke, among others. But what I hope to have shown in this essay is that, for Berkeley in particular, this analysis of pleasures as on a par with other sensible quality perceptions has considerable epistemological implications. It follows from Berkeley's view that sensations are constituents of physical objects; that we can have knowledge of the nature and existence of objects by means of our sensations, including pleasures.

CHAPTER EIGHT

Rationally Agential Pleasure?
A Kantian Proposal

Keren Gorodeisky

Reading without enjoyment is stupid.
—JOHN WILLIAMS

What can we learn, if anything, from Kant's view of pleasure? Many, even some of Kant's most faithful advocates, retort: "nothing," for they take this view of his to represent one of the greatest weaknesses in his thought. Here, for example, is Christine Korsgaard: "Kant . . . denies that pleasure and pain tell us anything about anything . . . Kant thinks that pleasure and pain are mere feelings, that they are, to put the point a little bluntly, stupid."[1] In the realm of aesthetics, too, interpreting Kant's understanding of pleasure, perhaps not as "stupid," but none-theless as a "mere sensation"—a passive, nonintentional, opaque, and

This essay greatly benefited from discussions with audiences at Auburn University, the University of Chicago, and Tel Aviv University. Special thanks to Arata Hamawaki and Eric Marcus.

1 Christine M. Korsgaard, "From Duty and for the Sake of the Noble," in *Aristotle, Kant and the Stoics*, ed. S. Engstrom and J. Whiting (Cambridge: Cambridge University Press, 1996), pp. 203–236.

only quantitatively differentiated state—has reigned in the literature until recently.[2]

In this essay, I offer a rebuttal of this line of interpretation by presenting the rational character of the pleasure one takes when making judgments of taste.[3] Kant's account of the pleasures we take in the good and in the beautiful is at odds both with this line of interpretation and with a standard contemporary account of pleasure as either passive, non-object-directed, and opaque or as cognitive *by virtue* of the beliefs or desires that accompany it.[4] Kant's account offers a model for thinking about pleasure as a conscious state that is *itself* capable of

---

2 For Paul Guyer's famous interpretation of aesthetic pleasure as nonintentional and opaque, see his *Kant and the Claims of Taste* (Cambridge: Cambridge University Press, 1979), chap. 3. For criticisms of Guyer's view, see Henry Allison, *Kant's Theory of Taste* (Cambridge: Cambridge University Press, 2001), chaps. 2 and 3, and "Reply to the Comments of Longuenesse and Ginsborg," *Inquiry* 46.2 (2003): 182–194; Hannah Ginsborg, *The Normativity of Nature* (Oxford: Oxford University Press, 2015); Rachel Zuckert, *Kant on Beauty and Biology* (Cambridge: Cambridge University Press, 2007), chap. 6; and Joseph Cannon, "The Intentionality of Judgments of Taste in Kant's *Critique of Judgment,*" *Journal of Aesthetics and Art Criticism* 66.1 (2008): 53–66.

3 For other interpretations that stress the nonpassive, intentional, and even normative nature of aesthetic pleasure but not its peculiar *rational* nature see Allison, *Kant's Theory of Taste*, Ginsborg, *Normativity of Nature*, R. Zuckert, *Kant on Beauty and Biology* (Cambridge: Cambridge University Press, 2007), and Joseph Tinguely, "Kantian Meta-aesthetics and the Neglected Alternative," *British Journal of Aesthetics* 50.2 (2013): 211–235. In addition to this difference regarding the *rationality* of aesthetic pleasure, my view differs from these in the following ways: it differs from Zuckert's in that she denies that either the pleasure or its principle is normative (*Beauty and Biology*, 271–278). While Allison emphasizes the normative nature of the *judgment of taste*, his account seems to foreclose the possibility that the pleasure in the beautiful *itself* is normative. (Ginsborg offers a detailed criticism of Allison's view in this respect in *Normativity of Nature*.) While Ginsborg does regard the pleasure as internal to the judgment and stresses its normativity, as I do, my view differs from hers primarily in that, on my reading, aesthetic judgment and pleasure are (1) about the *beauty of the objects judged*, and (2) explained by the distinctive logical form of aesthetic judgment. The picture I portray here comes closest to Tinguely, especially in stressing the active nature of aesthetic pleasure, but he explains that nature in terms of the pleasure's discriminatory ability while I explain it in terms of its responsiveness to reasons. Moreover, I suspect that, on his picture, the rationality of aesthetic pleasure does not categorically differ from the rationality of belief and action, a difference that is the heart of my view in K. Gorodeisky, *A Matter of Form: The Significance of Kant's Judgment of Taste* (unpublished manuscript).

4 For the sake of simplicity, I call the "pleasure in the beautiful" for the most part of this essay "aesthetic pleasure," even though Kant uses the term "aesthetic" to refer both to judgments of beauty, sublimity, and fine arts *and* to judgments of agreeableness. His technical term for the former is "aesthetic judgment of reflection" and for the latter "aesthetic judgment of sense" (FI, 20:224). Nevertheless, though it is a "pathologically conditioned satisfaction" (CPJ, 5:209), the pleasure in the agreeable is as *practical* as it is aesthetic given its relation to the faculty of desire and to practical reason. This gives

responsiveness to reasons. My main aim in this essay is to articulate the distinctive way in which aesthetic pleasure, on his view, though a felt, affective state, is itself an exercise of rationality.

However aptly the unappealing understanding of pleasure as either "stupid" or, at best, a "mere sensation" might apply to Kant's earlier conception, Kant's 1787 discovery of the new a priori principle of the power of judgment—the power that he identifies as the intellectual part of the faculty of pleasure and displeasure—marks a significant shift in his view. From that time, Kant clearly and explicitly denies that all pleasures and displeasures are "mere sensations."

On my reading, rather than brute, opaque, atomic, and passive, even our sensory pleasures (the ones Kant calls "pleasures in the agreeable") are not merely animal pleasures, but always already *human* pleasures (for they are dependent for their very possibility as pleasures on the determination of practical reason—on the efficacy of the will, which is the faculty for practical cognition).[5] In addition, and much more relevant to my purposes here, Kant insists that certain kinds of pleasure— the pleasure in the good and the pleasure in the beautiful—are *rational* pleasures insofar as they are conscious, complex states that are active not because they are produced "at will," but because they are affectively self-conscious, and capable of *responsiveness to reasons*, albeit they are responsive to categorically different kinds of reasons (moral and aesthetic reasons, respectively).[6] Aesthetic pleasure, particularly, is not

---

me further license to use the term "aesthetic pleasure" to refer to the pleasures of taste alone. While, for Kant, the pleasure in the sublime is as rational as the pleasures in beauty and fine art, it is more complex than the latter. Hence, my discussion in this essay is restricted to the pleasures in beauty and fine art.

5 I expand on this claim in *Matter of Form*. For a fine, detailed explanation of the relation between pleasures of the agreeable and practical reason, see Stephen Engstrom, *The Form of Practical Knowledge: A Study of the Categorical Imperative* (Cambridge, MA: Harvard University Press, 2009).

6 Even though both moral pleasure and aesthetic pleasure are exercises of rational agency, in this essay I focus on the latter. While the rational nature of moral pleasure is, for Kant, closely tied to this pleasure being a motivation for action, the rational nature of aesthetic pleasure is independent

only an intentional and discriminating (*unterscheiden*)[7] state of aware-ness,[8] but also, according to Kant, an exercise of rational agency thanks to its affective self-consciousness and capacity for responsiveness to a distinctive kind of reasons.

While portraying this picture of pleasure, I will suggest that seeing it clearly requires that we divest ourselves of the following disjunc-tion: either feelings are the noncognitive, passive ways through which we are affected by objects; or they are cognitive states by virtue of the theoretical beliefs they necessarily involve. On my reading of Kant, this disjunction is false. Aesthetic pleasure is neither passive, nor either theoretically or practically cognitive, and yet, it is an exer-cise of rational agency by virtue of belonging to a domain of ration-ality that is largely overlooked in the history of philosophy: aesthetic rationality.

My strategy is as follows: in section 1, I explain that aesthetic pleasure is rational and analogous to believing for a reason and acting for a reason. When proper, (1) it is an affective mode of being conscious of its ground (namely, of the reasons for feeling it) and thus of itself as called for, and (2) its self-conscious nature renders its actuality dependent on reflective endorsement: it is constituted and maintained and thus actually felt insofar as it is affectively recognized—however implicitly—as "to be felt." In section 2, I an-swer the objection that my proposal does not do justice either to the receptive nature of pleasures or to Kant's own view by explaining the kind of activity characteristic of aesthetic pleasure and the distinctive nature of aesthetic reasons.

---

of desire and of any motivational structure of action. And yet, its responsiveness to reasons renders it rational and agential in the way I aim to establish and explain below. Aesthetic pleasure, then, is very well suited for explaining and highlighting the possible rational and agential, albeit nonmotivational and nondesirative, nature of pleasure in general.

7 See CPJ, 5:204.

8 E.g., FI, 20:231–232, CPJ, 5:222.

1. The Rationality of Aesthetic Pleasure

The distinction between three kinds of pleasures—the pleasure in the agreeable (*Angenehm*), the pleasure in the good, and the pleasure in the beautiful—is one of the central distinctions in Kant's mature philosophy. Here is one formulation of the difference. The pleasure in the agreeable is a mode of gratification: "Pleasure of this kind, since it comes into the mind through the senses and we are therefore passive with regard to it, can be called pleasure of **enjoyment** [*Lust des Genusses*]" (CPJ, 5:292).[9] The pleasure in the good, a pleasure of "self-activity" (CPJ, 5:292) that is grounded in a "command of an absolutely necessitating law" (CPJ, 5:267), is called either "moral" or "intellectual pleasure" (e.g., CPJ, 5:271, CPJ, 5:292). And the pleasure in the beautiful, which pleases "in the mere judging [*Beurtheilung*]" (CPJ, 5:262), is described as a pleasure of "mere reflection" (CPJ, 5:292; see FI, 20:249).

On that account, the pleasure in the agreeable is passive and grounded in (and wholly explained by) the way an object affects the subject's sensory desires and predilections. The pleasure in the good is active and grounded in (and explained by) concepts, most prominently, the concept of the moral law. Aesthetic pleasure is *not* a pleasure of sensation (e.g., FI, 20:224)—it is not a passive state produced by the way the object sensorily affects the subject. Nor is it a "conceptual pleasure"—a pleasure that is grounded in a concept. What does it mean for it to be a pleasure of "mere reflection" that pleases "in the mere judging"?[10]

---

9 In this chapter, boldface indicates words that Kant emphasized in the original text.

10 Melissa Zinkin holds that pleasure is constitutive of reflection insofar as it is that by which reflection is capable of carrying on its distinctive reflective function, which Kant regards as the "holding together" of various representations or of a representation and a cognitive power (e.g., FI, 20:211). On her view, pleasure enables this function by being a state that maintains the reflected-upon representation in the same state. I agree with her about the necessary relation between pleasure and reflection, but disagree that the reflection at stake is the very same reflection that underlies *all* cognition since Kant is careful to distinguish between the logical act of reflection that underlies all conception and is an exercise of the understanding and the reflection carried on by the power of judgment. Even under the latter, he distinguishes between aesthetic reflection and logical reflection. Thus, Zinkin's view obscures the distinctive nature of the aesthetic kind of rationality and hence the categorical (rather

On the reading I propose here, an essential and central aspect of Kant's way of connecting aesthetic pleasure with reflection and judging concerns its distinctive rationality. I take Kant to suggest that aesthetic pleasure is rational insofar as it is an affective mode of self-consciousness, which is capable of being responsive to reasons for feeling it—reasons that, when the pleasure is proper, both explain why it is felt and justify it.[11] While reconstructive, I believe that this reading of Kant's notion of aesthetic pleasure is well supported by the text and by his overall view.

Kant suggests that aesthetic pleasure is thus rational when he claims that judging a beautiful object aesthetically is "merely repeating its [the object's] own claim to everyone's satisfaction" (CPJ, 5:282). This means that aesthetic pleasure is a mode of responsiveness to what the object *calls for* or *merits*. Beautiful objects are such that call for or figure in reasons for feeling a particular kind of feeling.[12] Not "repeating" beautiful objects' own claims on us would result in a failure of responsiveness to what certain objects merit.

Relatedly, Kant is quoted as claiming that "we give the beautiful, like the good, our approval."[13] The pleasure in beauty is a form of approval because questions about what the object *calls for* and *merits*, not what it elicits from us, are internal to aesthetic pleasure. And these questions show the relevance of the rational "why?" question. Even if you cannot answer it, or think there is no answer, the question "why do you like it (the object that you judge to be beautiful)?" is always applicable to aesthetic pleasures so that if the object you like and judge to be beautiful does not merit aesthetic

---

than merely quantitative) difference between aesthetic reflection and judging on the one hand and cognitive reflection and judging on the other. See Zinkin, "Kant and the Pleasure of Mere Reflection," *Inquiry* 55.5 (2012): 433–453.

11 For two other features that render Kant's notion of aesthetic pleasure a rational state, see my *Matter of Form*.

12 Perhaps, on his view, because of their relation to mindedness in general, namely to the subjective conditions of judging anything at all.

13 Quoted from students' notes of Kant's lectures, edited as *Metaphysik Dohna*, in LM, 28:676.

pleasure, one is under rational pressure to reexperience the object and be ready to change affectively. This sense of approval and the relevance of this "why?" question are at the heart of the rationality of aesthetic pleasure.

Kant also emphasizes that aesthetic pleasure is grounded in a priori grounds. Thus, he claims to "have shown that there are also grounds of satisfaction a priori . . . even though they cannot be grasped in **determinate concepts**" (CPJ, 5:347). On Kant's account, when proper, aesthetic pleasure is grounded in grounds that cannot be articulated by general concepts or principles. But the nongenerality of these grounds makes them no less reasons. Like reasons for believing and reasons for acting, the grounds of aesthetic pleasures are *reasons* since, when the pleasure is proper, these grounds both explain and justify it—they show not only why it is felt but why it *should* be felt, that is, why it is proper, merited, or called for. These grounds thus belong to what Joseph Raz dubbed the "normative-explanatory nexus," a phrase that is meant to explain reasons in terms of the convergence between their explanatory and justificatory functions.[14] In Kant's account, the grounds of aesthetic pleasure are reasons because they are those in light of which aesthetic judgment legitimately and justifiably "determines that pleasure or displeasure **must** be combined with the representation of the object" and does so "a priori by means of [this very same] sensation of pleasure or displeasure" (FI, 20:229).[15]

My reading of aesthetic pleasure as rational in this way receives further support from the discussion of what Kant sometimes regards as the "ground of this pleasure" (e.g., CPJ, 5:218): what he notoriously calls "the free play of the faculties of cognition with a representation through which an object is given" (e.g., CPJ, 5:217) or the "harmony of

---

14 See Joseph Raz, *From Normativity to Responsibility* (Oxford: Oxford University Press, 2011). I will go back to this briefly in section 2.

15 Kant emphasizes that this is done both by means of the feeling and "a priori, through the faculty of cognition (the power of judgment)" (FI, 20:229).

the faculties of cognition" (e.g., CPJ, 5:218) and sometimes refers to as the "judging [*Beurtheilung*] of the object" (e.g., CPJ, 5:216).[16]

While there is a wide disagreement about the grounding relation between the free harmony of the faculties and aesthetic pleasure, I will restrict myself here to a few remarks that reject the temporal and causal reading of this relation and argue for a rational relation of grounding. Though Paul Guyer's understanding of this relation as temporal and causal reigned in the literature for a long while, it has been under heavy attack during the last two decades.[17] And for good reasons. Even though in the notorious section 9 of the third *Critique* Kant thinks of this grounding relation in terms of "precedence," claiming that, insofar as the harmony of the faculties is the ground of the pleasure, it "precedes" it, there are very strong indications that this precedence cannot be understood as temporal and causal.[18]

First, while Kant argues that the relation between the mind's faculties and the beautiful object—"the judging of the object"—is the ground of the pleasure, he also claims that aesthetic pleasure is the "determining ground of a judgment which for that reason is called aesthetic" (FI, 20:224). He argues further that this pleasure is the "determining ground" that animates the "cognitive powers" (CPJ, 5:222; see CPJ, 5:219), implying that the pleasure and the

---

16 Kant may seem inconsistent in his descriptions of the a priori ground that both explains and justifies the necessity and universality of aesthetic pleasure, for he refers to it not only as the harmony of the faculties but also as "the subjective [but a priori principle] of the power of judgment in general" (CPJ, 5:286; see FI, 20:229). I don't think that this is a threatening inconsistency. The air of inconsistency may be resolved by appealing to different levels of grounding and justification. Kant may well be taking the principle of the power of judgment to justify and ground the capacity of aesthetic judgment *in general* to be the source of a legitimate demand for universal agreement in pleasure. This principle explains why a judgment of a singular beautiful object, made through a feeling of pleasure, can in principle make such a legitimate demand, but it does not ground or justify any particular feeling of pleasure taken in any particular object. The free engagement of the faculties of the understanding and the imagination with a particular object is required to rationally ground and justify any specific case of feeling aesthetic pleasure.

17 See Guyer, *Kant and the Claims of Taste*, and, for example, Allison, *Kant's Theory of Taste*, Zuckert, *Beauty and Biology*, Tinguely, "Kantian Meta-aesthetics and the Neglected Alternative," and Ginsborg, *Normativity of Nature*.

18 If causality is restricted to efficient causality.

judging are *reciprocally* grounding and grounded. If they are, neither one can be said to be temporally prior to, or efficiently causing, the other.

Second, in numerous passages, he stresses that the pleasure and the harmony are not separated mental states, but *two sides of the same coin*. This is most explicit in the passages where Kant draws an analogy between moral pleasure and aesthetic pleasure as two kinds of pleasure that are grounded a priori. In these discussions, Kant goes as far as to argue *against* the temporal and causal reading of the relation between aesthetic pleasure and the harmony of the faculties. He emphasizes that, just as the determination of the will to act on the basis of the categorical imperative *can in no way* be regarded as the *efficient cause* of moral feeling, but is rather the other side of the same coin, so the harmony of the faculties *can in no way* be regarded as the efficient cause of aesthetic pleasure, but is rather the other side of the same coin: the two are temporally inseparable aspects of the whole, which is aesthetic judgment:

> in the critique of practical reason ... we did not actually derive this **feeling** [of respect] from the idea of the moral as a cause, rather it was merely the determination of the will that was derived from the latter. The state of mind of a will determined by something, however, is in itself already a feeling of pleasure and is identical with it, thus it does not follow from it as an effect. ...
>
> Now it is similar with the pleasure in the aesthetic judgment, except that here it is merely contemplative and does not produce an interest in the object, while in the moral judgment it is practical. The consciousness of the merely formal purposiveness in the play of the cognitive powers of the subject in the case of a representation through which an object is given *is* the pleasure itself. (CPJ, 5:222; my italics)[19]

_____

19 See also: "Provisionally, it can also be noted that no transition from cognition to the feeling of pleasure and displeasure takes place **through concepts** of objects ... and one thus cannot expect to determine *a priori* the influence that a given representation has on the mind, as we previously noticed

But if it neither temporally precedes it nor efficiently causes it, in what sense is the free engagement of the faculties with a beautiful object nonetheless the ground of aesthetic pleasure? I argue that the free engagement of the faculties with a particular object is the *rational ground* of aesthetic pleasure insofar as it explains and justifies aesthetic pleasure, and insofar as the latter is constituted by being conscious of its fitness to this ground. The free play of the faculties thus "precedes" aesthetic pleasure only in the "rational" order of things.[20]

Consider the whole passage: "The consciousness of the merely formal purposiveness in the play of the cognitive powers of the subject in the case of a representation through which an object is given is the pleasure itself because it contains a determining ground of the activity of the subject with regard to the animation of its cognitive powers, thus an internal causality" (CPJ, 5:222). Here Kant claims that the pleasure in the beautiful constitutes and maintains itself *by* involving *consciousness* of its *ground* ("the free play of the cognitive powers"), consciousness that also maintains this ground (is the animating ground of this play). On my reading, this means that the pleasure in the beautiful involves a specific kind of *rational* causation,[21] or, differently put, rational

---

in the *Critique of Practical Reason*, where the representation of a universal lawfulness of willing must at one and the same time determine the will and thereby also arouse the feeling of respect, as a law contained, and indeed contained a priori, in our moral judgments, even though this feeling could nonetheless not be derived from concepts. In just the same way the resolution of the aesthetic judgment of reflection will display the concept of the formal but subjective purposiveness of the object, resting on an a priori principle, which is fundamentally identical with the feeling of pleasure, but which cannot be derived from concepts" (FI, 20:229).

20 Insofar as aesthetic judging is the rational cause of aesthetic pleasure, and the latter is the consciousness that maintains the former, this judging is also, as Zuckert correctly claims, "transcendentally" prior to it: it is the condition of the possibility of aesthetic pleasure. See Zuckert, *Beauty and Biology*, 308–310.

21 I am using the phrase "rational causation" roughly following Eric Marcus, *Rational Causation* (Cambridge, MA: Harvard University Press, 2012), but I don't insist on it. My main point is that a mental state that is constituted and maintained by being conscious of its fittingness to its ground (consciousness of itself as called for or required) exhibits rational structure, or, put differently, is an exercise of rationality. Notice that the pleasure in the good involves both external causality and consciousness of its ground (of the good as good and as deserving pleasure). It may thus also be an exercise of rational causation, but it is different from aesthetic pleasure insofar as it (1) it is not constituted and maintained *only* by being itself consciousness of its ground, (2) involves the external causality, and

structure: aesthetic pleasure is constituted and self-maintained merely by being aware of itself as fitting to its rational ground (to the reasons for feeling it). In this sense, it is *rationally* caused and maintained—it is an exercise of rationality.

While all pleasures maintain and must, by definition, maintain themselves, as states that are defined by their reproduction (FI, 20:230–231; CPJ, 5:220), the pleasure in the beautiful alone maintains itself merely by being *itself* a mode of awareness of its ground.[22]

Kant contrasts the "internal causality" that in the passage above he attributes to aesthetic pleasure to the "external causality" of the pleasures in the good and in the agreeable (e.g., FI, 20:231–232). Briefly, the pleasure in the good and the pleasure in the agreeable involve "external causality" because, both in order to be constituted and maintained, they require something that is *external* to themselves, the production of either an object (an instance of the same pleasing object) or an action (the action that is required by the concept of either the moral good or the instrumental good) through the efficacy of the will. If I am to continue feeling pleasure in drinking the hot chocolate I am drinking on this cold and crisp winter day, I need to make sure I drink another such cup in similar circumstances. And if I am to continue feeling the pleasure I take in volunteering at the local food bank, I must persist in my endeavor (or perform equivalent virtuous actions).

Aesthetic pleasure *alone* requires nothing other than the mind's engagement with a beautiful object in order to be reproduced. In that sense, it is *independent of desire* (which is roughly what Kant means by its "disinterestedness"). One need neither act in any specific way (say, preserve, curate, etc.) nor consume or produce an

---

exhibits the rationality, of practical reason, and (3) is grounded in different kinds of reasons—*practical* reasons for *acting*. I explain these three differences in more detail below.

22 For Kant, pleasures also maintain the *life* of the feeling subject (whether animal or human), life that is by definition self-maintaining (e.g., CPJ, 5:278, CPpR, 5:9n). I cannot here elaborate on this aspect of pleasure, but only note that I take its explanation to be parallel to the explanation of each pleasure's own self-maintenance that I am proposing.

object in order to feel aesthetic pleasure and in order to maintain it—one needs only to properly judge it and, through this pleasure, be conscious of its ground.

I take it that this way of being constituted and maintained—merely through a state's awareness of its ground and of itself as fitting this ground—is a mark of rationality. Acting and believing for a reason are marked by the same kind of rational structure.

Intentionally acting is a paradigmatic expression of this rational structure of causation since it (say, intending to kick a ball) necessarily involves a consciousness of its ground. A mere bodily movement (say, a reflex action of kicking a ball, which is a jerk of my leg) does not.

If I am in a state of denial of my competitive ambition and temperament, I may "fail" to know that I kicked the ball (intentionally) to score points and win the game. But when no story of denial, self-deception, or alienation is in the offing, intentional actions involve unmediated consciousness of themselves as "to be done," that is, consciousness of the reasons that show the actions to be called for. This way of understanding intentional action does not deny the possibility of intentional actions whose grounds we are unable to articulate. Rather, it means only that our actions are always subject to the question "why?" so that, if the action is shown not to be grounded in a good reason, the agent is under rational pressure to revise her plan or abandon it.

Belief is another manifestation of this rational causation, and, I claim, so is aesthetic pleasure. Believing a proposition for a reason is a manifestation of rational causation insofar as it involves a consciousness of its ground: an awareness of the corresponding proposition as "to be believed": consciousness of the belief as grounded in the reasons that show it to be called for. Even if I am incapable of articulating my reasons for believing, say, that Paris is in France, my belief is always subject to the question "why?" I take it to be true, so that if the belief is shown to be false, or otherwise not properly responsive to reasons, I am under rational pressure to revise or abandon it.

Like believing and acting for a reason,[23] aesthetic pleasure is also a mental attitude that, when proper, is rationally constituted and maintained by its awareness of itself as grounded in reasons that show it to be called for (as grounded in the relation between the cognitive faculties and the object).[24] Although most of us are not attuned enough or practiced enough to articulate, let alone to explain the reasons for our aesthetic pleasures, and although aesthetic reasons serve neither as evidence or proofs (as reasons for beliefs) nor as practical justifications, aesthetic pleasure is always subject to the question "why do you feel that?," a question that requires a justifying explanation. And the applicability of this justificatory-explanatory question is explained by the fact that aesthetic pleasure *itself* is responsive to the question "what is to be felt disinterestedly?"[25] Aesthetic pleasure is a stance that is shaped by responsiveness to reasons.

This means that aesthetic pleasure, just like believing and acting for a reason, does not simply *happen* to be rational: we are not *determined* to take pleasure in beauty (by any external or psychological force). While our own predilections and physical constitution usually cause us to feel (agreeable) pleasure, say, in certain flavors but not in others, no psychological or physical force determines us to appreciate through pleasure beauty and art. Rather, in judging aesthetically we rationally make up our minds about a beautiful object by being responsive to the question "what is to be felt (disinterestedly)?," namely, "what does this object call for or merit?"

---

23 On the important differences between belief, action, and aesthetic pleasure, see section 2.

24 My proposal involves no claim about the empirical, psychological generation of this pleasure, only about its *rational* causation, which is categorically different from efficient causation. (See Marcus, *Rational Causation*, chap. 4.) That's why I am happy to use the phrase "rational structure" or "rational character" instead of "rational causation." And, in any case, while efficient causes are either change-makers or change-preventers, rational causes do not bring about or prevent changes in a similar way, but are the states of awareness that a certain "rational effect" is called for.

25 Briefly, "that which is to be felt disinterestedly" (the answer to this question) is an object that calls for or deserves a disinterested pleasure, i.e., aesthetic pleasure. Disinterested pleasure is independent of interest, and interest is a rule-governed connection between pleasure and desire (MM, 6:212). Accordingly, disinterested pleasure neither is caused by a rule that one formulates on the basis of either a sensory or rational desire, nor causes a desire following a rule that one formulates on the basis of this pleasure.

Kant writes: "in order to decide [*unterscheiden*] whether or not something is beautiful, we do not relate the representation by means of the understanding to the object for cognition, but rather relate it by means of the imagination (perhaps combined with the understanding) to the subject and its feeling of pleasure and displeasure" (CPJ, 5:204), and argues that, while judging aesthetically, we decide "the fittingness of the object (its form) . . . through pleasure" (CPJ, 5:194). I take it that he means that aesthetic pleasure is answerable to the question "what is to be responded to with a (disinterested) feeling?" *in* and *through* the actual feeling of this pleasure. We are not psychologically or physically pushed to feel aesthetic pleasure, but "decide," by means of the shared activity of the free imagination, the understanding and feeling whether the pleasure is deserved by the object.[26] "Aesthetic purposiveness is the lawfulness of the power of judgment in its **freedom**. The satisfaction in the object depends on the relation in which *we* would place the imagination: namely, that it entertain the mind by itself in free activity" (CPJ, 5:270–71; emphasis (bold) in the original; my italics).

This all means that aesthetic pleasure is capable of the reflectively or affectively conscious constitution and self-maintenance that I introduced above (capable of "internal causality") because it involves a future-directed commitment to what its object calls for or merits; a commitment, that is, to always be responsive to this object as that which has a "claim on everyone's satisfaction" (CPJ, 5:280–281).

Now, the pleasure in the good also involves commitment to the value of its corresponding action, as either morally or instrumentally good (in light of a further end) and thus as meriting practical pleasure, and it also involves an affective consciousness of a certain power of the mind (though a different power, the faculty of desire in its intellectual guise as practical reason). Yet, (1) whereas the pleasure in the good is

---

26 Again, I do *not* claim that the mental activity of the faculties efficiently causes the pleasure, but that the pleasure is always an affective consciousness of, and responsiveness to, the relation of the object and the subject.

responsive to the reasons for feeling it through the cognitive awareness of the concept that demands its corresponding pleasing action, aesthetic pleasure is responsive to the reasons for feeling it (and thus constitutes and maintains itself) *merely* through being an affective awareness of them. It thus pleases through "mere reflection." (2) To be reproduced, the pleasure in the good requires the performance of the relevant action: if the action is not performed, there are no reasons to feel the pleasure. Reasons for aesthetic pleasure are reasons for always (positively) evaluating the object through pleasure (whether one engages with it directly *again*—"produces it"—or not). Like belief, but unlike the pleasures in the agreeable and in the good, aesthetic pleasure involves a future-directed commitment, independently of the production of any object or action.

Some might think that the reflective and rational character I attribute to aesthetic pleasure fails to do justice to the phenomenology of aesthetic experience. Are aesthetic pleasures really responsive to the question that I introduced? While I do not claim that we *in fact* ask the question each time we aesthetically like an object, I maintain that we are always subject to this question because, when proper, the pleasure is *itself* a way of being responsive to that which is to be liked disinterestedly. I claim, then, (1) that we are always *subject* to the rational question "why" while aesthetically enjoying a beautiful object, but deny both that aesthetic pleasure is the product of any kind of *explicit* process of reasoning and that we are always capable of fully articulating an answer to this question,[27] and (2) that if the object one disinterestedly likes is shown not to merit disinterested pleasure, one is under rational pressure to reexperience the object and to be open to revise one's pleasure.[28]

---

27 Similarly, believing for a reason, for example, that the Eiffel Tower is in Paris, need not be the explicit conclusion *actually* drawn from the premises one has for this conclusion.

28 In the aesthetic case, responding to the rational pressure to revise is not independent of reexperiencing the object for oneself (e.g., CPJ, 5:284–285).

To see how aesthetic pleasure is shaped by responsiveness to what
is to be felt for its object, it is useful, first, to notice that avowing or
rejecting aesthetic pleasure, just like avowing or rejecting a belief or intentional action, is not a matter of introspection, but of reconsidering
the beauty of the object in its relation to the subject's judgmental
activity, and second, to contrast aesthetic pleasures with agreeable
pleasures. I discuss these two points in the rest of the section.

First, being subject to the question "what is to be felt disinterestedly?" means that aesthetic pleasure involves a consultation with the
world that explains what one feels by reference to what is to be felt:

> For the judgment of taste consists precisely in the fact that it calls a
> thing beautiful only in accordance with that quality [*Beschaffenheit*]
> in it by means of which it corresponds with our way of receiving it.
> (CPJ, 5:282)[29]

> That object the form of which . . . in mere reflection on it . . . is
> judged as the ground of a pleasure in the representation of such an
> object—with its representation this pleasure is also judged to be
> necessarily combined. (CPJ, 5:190)

According to Kant, aesthetic pleasure is conscious of the "form of
purposiveness in the representation through which an object is given
to us" (CPJ, 5:221). Accordingly, when I am asked "Do you really like
The Tree of Life?" I don't look inside myself in quest of the relevant
feeling, but reflect upon the film, possibly watch it again, and attend
to its cinematography, the way this cinematography brings out aspects
of the story, connects to the soundtrack, and constitutes the distinctive point of view of a child that is essential for a proper engagement
with the questions that the film raises about the beginning of life,
childhood, parental love, and grace. To answer a question about my

---

29 Judgments of natural beauty, according to Kant, also have their ground "in the object and its shape
[*Gestalt*]" (CPJ, 5:279).

pleasure in this film, I have to attend to the film in its relation to the form of my reflecting upon it in this and similar ways; I cannot simply "connect" to my emotions, or reimagine my feelings, as I would likely do if I were asked "Do you really like oatmeal?" Introducing this last question is meant to bring in agreeable pleasures, which I will now contrast with aesthetic pleasures because this contrast sheds light on the responsive character of the latter.

The way I just introduced pleasures in the agreeable may raise a worry: do I mean to imply that questions about agreeable pleasures are fully answered by introspection?

Well, of course, I may be able to explain why I like oatmeal, and explain it in part by reviewing the properties that oatmeal has. I do not deny *that*.[30] But such explanations are *necessarily* grounded also in my *idiosyncratic* likings, inclinations, and desires. (I may say that I like oatmeal because its texture and warmth soothes *me* in the morning, given my specific constitution.) "Between that which pleases merely in the judging and that which gratifies [*vergnünt*] (pleases in the sensation) there is . . . an essential difference. The latter is something that one cannot, like the former, require of everyone" (CPJ, 5:330–331). Explanations of agreeable pleasures are not intersubjectively sharable as explanations of beliefs, intentional actions, and aesthetic pleasures are. The former do not unfold the reasons why *everyone* in the same position should be in the same state, and so they are not responsive to the question "what is to be felt?," which is a *universal* or *intersubjective* question (a question for everyone in the same situation—not a question about what the object may happen to elicit in any specific

---

30 At the same time, I do *not* claim that aesthetic pleasure is grounded in the qualities that an object has independently of the mind, but only that it *is* independent of any private aspect of the mind. For Kant, the relevant ground is the *relation* between the form of the object and the form of the subject's judgmental activity as expressing the form of the human capacity to judge *in general*—the form of human subjectivity, not the form of any particular human subject. Yet, the internality of pleasure to each particular judgment of taste indicates that the self is built in to them, the same self that must autonomously feel pleasure in the object, rather than merely repeat another person's judgment without feeling any pleasure.

person). Insofar as they are not responsive to this question, pleasures in the agreeable are not exercises of rational agency.

Another way of putting the difference between aesthetic pleasures and agreeable pleasures (and thus, another way of explaining the rationality of the former) is in terms of desert or merit: "hence one says of the agreeable not merely that it **pleases** but that it **gratifies**. It is not mere approval that I give it, rather inclination is thereby aroused" (CPJ, 5:207). But: "the beautiful is closer than the agreeable to the good because of the freedom that occurs with it . . . we give the beautiful, like the good, our approval."[31] Questions about what the object *merits*, not what it elicits from us, are internal to aesthetic judgment and pleasure, but alien to judgments of the agreeable and their grounding pleasures. And these questions are equivalent to the question about what to judge with a disinterested pleasure. The relevance of this "merit question" is one of the marks of the rationality of aesthetic pleasure.

One might worry that Kant ignores the way in which we regularly revise our agreeable pleasures in light of certain demands, pressures, and norms and take even guilty pleasures to be criticizable and revisable in terms of what is good to do or to feel. But I don't think he does. All that Kant claims is that agreeable pleasures are positioned differently vis-à-vis the world because of their different relation to sharable reasons and to questions of desert and merit. Agreeable pleasures are not responsive to a question about what to feel in the same way that aesthetic pleasures are because (1) they are never independent of the person's subjective desires, needs, and inclinations; (2) their actuality does not depend on endorsement (more on that below); and (3) if and when agreeable pleasures are responsive to sharable reasons, standards, or norms, these are external both to the pleasure and to its objects— they usually come in the shape of practical or moral pressures (e.g., CPJ, 5:331).[32]

---

31 Quoted from students' notes of Kant's lectures, edited as *Metaphysik Dohna,* in LM, 28:676.

32 One might still worry that Kant's way of drawing the distinction obliterates the very idea of food criticism. On one level, this objection seems justified: Kant himself did not fully recognize the

Up to here, my explanation of aesthetic pleasure as responsive to the question "what is to be felt disinterestedly?" has been part of arguing that it is an exercise of rationality insofar as it is constituted and maintained by consciousness of what makes it called for and of its own propriety. But the responsiveness to this question brings out yet another mark of the rationality of aesthetic pleasure, or, at least, another way of capturing its rationality: aesthetic pleasure is an exercise of rational agency insofar as it is grounded in this kind of consciousness and thus insofar as the basis for *actually* feeling it is *endorsement*, not what the object happens to produce in me. While the actuality of agreeable pleasures depends on how subjects are affected by an object, the actuality of aesthetic pleasures presupposes the affective self-consciousness of its propriety to the object. This relation between endorsement and actuality—the dependence of an attitude on being endorsed as the proper attitude to have—is a central mark of rational agency.[33]

While both intentional action and belief have already been explained along similar lines, I argue that Kant encourages us to recognize that aesthetic pleasure should be understood as an analogous exercise of rational agency.

_____

possibility of food criticism as an exercise of taste. Nevertheless, I believe that his distinction between agreeable and aesthetic pleasures leaves room for such kind of criticism, for I take his view on the matter to imply the following. If, for example, your delight in dark chocolate (as the delight of the food critic) is grounded in an exploration of different kinds of chocolates, tastings, and in a careful reading of expert reviews of different chocolates, so that if others do not appreciate and enjoy the dark chocolates that you do, you would regard it as a failing on their part, then this delight is *not* agreeable but may well be an aesthetic pleasure. If a pleasure's constitution and maintenance is grounded in endorsing it as a pleasure that ought to be felt by everyone in the same situation, it is not a pleasure in the agreeable, but in the beautiful. Moreover, as value-laden as this contrast may sound, it is meant neither to degrade pleasures in the agreeable nor to undermine their role in human life. Pleasures in the agreeable *do* play a significant role in our capacity to live a balanced, full life. But no matter how humanly important pleasures in the agreeable are, and how related they indeed are to the capacity for practical reason, they are categorically different from aesthetic pleasures. Only the latter are rational agential states.

33 In making this claim, I follow Matthew Boyle, "Active Belief," *Canadian Journal of Philosophy*, supp. vol. 35 (2010): 141. Notice that I do not explain rationality in terms of *conceptual* shape or conceptual capacities (for that view, see John McDowell, *Mind and World* [Cambridge, MA: Harvard University Press, 1996]). The picture of rationality portrayed here is more capacious (and perhaps closer to the kind of rationality that McDowell takes to be operative in our "second nature").

2. RESPONSE TO THE OBJECTION
OF OVERINTELLECTUALISM

One might object to this argument by raising the worry that I emphasize the reflective and responsive nature of aesthetic pleasures *at the price of* their receptive nature. Even if Kant explains aesthetic pleasures (and displeasures) in terms of their relation to the power of judgment (which he regards as a "high," "intellectual" and "cognitive" power of spontaneity), rather than to sensibility, are they not affective states that belong to our receptive nature?

This objection—fundamentally, the objection of overintellectualization—suggests that my proposal conflicts not only with the receptive and affective nature of pleasures but also with Kant's own view, for, allegedly, it goes against Kant's famous demand of the aesthetic judge to "listen to no reasons and arguments [*keine Gründe und kein Vernüfteln*], [but] rather believe that those rules of the critics are false or at least that this is not the case for their application than allow that [his] judgment [i.e., the judgment of taste] should be determined by means of *a priori* grounds of proof, since it is supposed to be a judgment of taste and not of the understanding or of reason" (CPJ, 5:284–285). Treating aesthetic pleasure as a rationally responsive mental attitude may seem to contradict both the letter and the spirit of Kant's *Critique*.

I respond to this objection along two lines, which I will first list, and then elaborate on. First, although the responsiveness to reasons that I take to be internal to aesthetic pleasure means that it is an active state, the kind of activity that characterizes this pleasure does not imply that it is produced at will, and so it does not contradict the receptive and affective character of pleasure. Second, the reasons to which aesthetic pleasure is responsive are neither evidential, like theoretical reasons for belief, nor practical. They are aesthetic reasons for feeling disinterested pleasure in an object. The rest of this essay is devoted to explaining these points.

First, the reflectively active nature of aesthetic pleasure is compatible with its receptive character since it does not entail that it is produced "at will." In contrast to beliefs, judgments, and actions, pleasures are undoubtedly receptive, though Kant suggests that the pleasure in the good and the pleasure in the beautiful are not merely receptive states: they are exercises of our *human* nature; expressions of ourselves as *spontaneous-receptive beings*. Receptive as they are, these pleasures are modes of consciousness, responsive either to the demands of reason or to the call of beauty. But this responsiveness is shaped and made possible by a form of activity that is fully compatible with the receptive nature of pleasures, that is, with their not being produced "at will." To see that, we need to distinguish between two different kinds of causality, two notions of responsibility, and two distinct senses of activity.

There are at least two different ways in which we may be the causes of our attitudes, and two corresponding ways of having responsibility over them. Intuitively, we seem to be passive with regard to most of our sensations (say, headaches and other pains), and agreeable pleasures (enjoying white but not dark chocolate, flourishing in hot weather but loathing the cold). These mental attitudes seem to force themselves on us—to be generated by causes to which we do not necessarily contribute. Such attitudes are, of course, ours, but ours in being episodes in our psychological histories and mental lives.

The responsibility we have over these attitudes can be called "external" or "third-person" responsibility. Richard Moran, who first made the distinction I am introducing here, points out that the attitudes over which I have only external responsibility "are not an expression of *my* will, but nonetheless I can exert some influence over them."[34] Surely, sensations and agreeable pleasures may guide our actions, and if we endorse any of them as good to feel and pursue, they might even become,

---

34 Richard Moran, "Frankfurt on Identification," in *Contours of Agency*, ed. Sarah Buss and Lee Overton (Cambridge, MA: MIT Press, 2002), 200.

through this reflective endorsement, expressive of our wills.[35] But, in contrast to beliefs, intentional actions, rationally responsive desires, and (I argue) aesthetic pleasures, sensations and agreeable pleasures are not modes of rational responsiveness to questions about what to do or what to feel. Hence, their *actuality* does not depend on consciousness of their fitness to their ground (or reflective endorsement). Hence, external responsibility is the responsibility we have over attitudes that are not marked by rational agency.

Notice that external responsibility is not tied to attitudes that are *not* caused "at will," and that "causing at will" is neither necessary nor sufficient for what I am going to call "internal" or "agential" responsibility. This is the kind of responsibility we have over attitudes that are exercises of rational agency insofar as they are constituted by being conscious of their fitness to their ground. I can cause myself "at will" to have a sensation of pain, say by pinching myself, and yet have no internal responsibility over this sensation. No matter how caused, this sensation is not an expression of who I am or what I am committed to, but only an episode I undergo—part of my psychological history, but not part of my identity as a reflective self. If so, causing my attitudes "at will" is not a sufficient condition for internal responsibility. But nor is it a necessary condition. We need not assume that beliefs, and "responsive desires" (desires that are not merely the result of, say, hunger or fatigue, but are shaped by a sense of what is good) have to be formed "at will." The kind of activity relevant for these attitudes—free rational endorsement—is sufficiently different from willing, choosing, or deciding, but is proper for explaining the subject's taking the state to be an attitude she is committed to. We are agentially responsible for an attitude, which is an expression of who we are—paradigmatically, a belief, an action, a "rationally responsive" desire, less paradigmatically an emotion, a concern, and, I add, aesthetic pleasure—*not* insofar as

---

35 That will turn agreeable pleasures into practical, *non*pathological pleasures—pleasures in the good. On this transformation, see Engstrom, *Form of Practical Reason*, 69.

it is caused "at will," but insofar as the attitude is subject to a "why" question, or, as Kant puts it, insofar as it is a matter of "approval."[36]

If this is right, then agential responsibility is neither a matter of having control over an attitude, nor is it a matter of producing it. Rational and responsible agency over a state is compatible with us not having *external* control over the state—with us not causing it "at will." And so, the receptive nature of aesthetic pleasure does not prevent it from being an exercise of rational agency. Aesthetic pleasure can, without contradiction, be both a receptive and rational attitude. The requirement on the agential nature of an attitude is that its actuality depend on its endorsement as an attitude *to have*. And, as I suggested earlier, the actuality of aesthetic pleasure *does* depend on its affective, self-conscious endorsement. Feeling such a pleasure *is* being responsive to beauty as that which "has a claim on everyone's satisfaction." And so, although aesthetic pleasure is not produced "at will," it is characterized by the kind of activity that is necessary and sufficient for any attitude to be a rationally free attitude.

It is time to turn to the second line of response to the objection I am treating on these pages: the line of response that distinguishes aesthetic rationality from theoretical rationality and from practical rationality.

I do not suggest that one can offer the reasons one is responsive to when properly making an aesthetic judgment as evidence for one's judgment, or as a universally accessible and objective proof of the propriety of one's pleasure. This is not Kant's view, and, I think, not the right view to hold. Reasons for aesthetic pleasure are neither evidential nor practical, but aesthetic through and through. And yet, like belief and action, this pleasure is also subject to the question "why." The main

---

36 Notice that I need not be able to give the exact reason for acting that way, having this desire, or feeling this pleasure in order to be thusly responsible for it. As G. E. M. Anscombe argues, answers like "for no particular reason" or "now, why did I do this/feel this/desire this?" are compatible with the relevance of the rational "why" question, and so they need not exclude the attitude from the domain of agential responsibility. This *relevance*, but not recognition of actual reasons, is required for the kind of rationality, responsibility, and agency I am discussing here. See Elizabeth Anscombe, *Intention* (Cambridge, MA: Harvard University Press, 1957).

point behind my insistence that aesthetic pleasure is responsive to this question is that it is not a product of brute receptivity, but an exercise of rationality insofar as it is constituted and maintained through self-consciousness of propriety and aptness; insofar as its actuality depends on endorsement.[37]

But being rational in that way does not render aesthetic pleasure a "cognitive" act in the Kantian sense of the term "cognitive," only an act of rational agency. "Pleasure is . . . a basic property . . . which cannot be reduced to anything, thus not also to the faculty of cognition" (LM, 28:674–675). For Kant, this means that aesthetic pleasure is not supported by conceptual representations, general principles, reasons for believing, or reasons for acting. Yet, it is part of the space of reasons. For aesthetic pleasures are nonetheless explained and justified by *aesthetic* reasons.[38] What are these?

One might think that the difference between aesthetic reasons on the one hand and theoretical and practical reasons on the other is that aesthetic reasons can only provide likelihood but no guarantee. Those reasons, the line goes, do not entail the aesthetic goodness of the object in question.[39] It may be maintained, for example, that Cate Blanchett's fine acting explains and justifies, but does not guarantee, the excellence of Woody Allen's film *Blue Jasmine*, and so, allegedly, is no reason for aesthetically liking it.

But this way of differentiating the three kinds of reasons is mistaken. For one thing, talk about guarantee and entailment is as misplaced in the practical domain of reasons as it is in the aesthetic domain. The end

---

37 I agree with Moran, "Frankfurt," 211–212, that *no* pleasure, not even pleasures in the agreeable, are a matter of *brute* receptivity in the same way that sensations are. But given his admission that an agreeable pleasure may well survive the realization that it is not worthy, and that it is "not being based on reasons," I suspect that Moran would agree with me that agreeable pleasures are not exercises of rational agency in the way that aesthetic pleasure are.

38 I take it that this is partly why Kant has come to believe that the faculty of pleasure and displeasure has a high, intellectual part—the power of judgment—that endows this faculty with a priori principles.

39 E.g., Frank Sibley, *Approach to Aesthetics: Collected Papers on Philosophical Aesthetics* (Oxford: Oxford University Press, 2001), 40.

of being benevolent, for example, does not entail my taking care of my neighbor's child during her mourning over her husband even if it is a reason for doing so, and the aim of completing my essay is a reason for my sitting at the computer right now, even though the former does not guarantee the latter.

Talk about likelihood, guarantee, and certainty is misplaced in the aesthetic and the practical domains on normative and logical grounds because such talk is about *proofs* or *evidence*. And proofs and evidence support *beliefs*, neither actions *nor* aesthetic judgments and pleasures. An expression of your *belief* that an object is beautiful, Kant insists, is *not* an aesthetic judgment, but a theoretical, or as he often refers to it, a "logical judgment" (e.g., CPJ, 5:284). If you judge "*The Tree of Life* is an excellent film," and explain your judgment and the pleasure it expresses by claiming "I haven't seen the film, but A. O. Scott wrote a raving review of it," your judgment is not an aesthetic judgment, but a theoretical judgment: an expression of your belief that the film is good, backed up by the evidence of experts. If Kant is right, aesthetic judgment is not such an expression of belief but an expression of a disinterested pleasure that everyone is to feel for the object; it is an expression of the responsive liking that I described above. And since it is not an expression of belief, aesthetic judgment is not backed up by proofs or by any reasons for *believing* that the object is beautiful.

Nor is it supported by reasons for taking some action with regard to the object. If you tell me that *The Tree of Life* is good because it can improve one's relationship with one's parents, you have neither explained nor justified your aesthetic appreciation of the film, but expressed a practical judgment supported by reasons for acting a certain way: reasons to go and watch the film, not reasons to aesthetically like or appreciate it.

So what supports aesthetic judgment? In brief, rather than reasons for believing or acting, aesthetic reasons are reasons for (disinterestedly) feeling, or more precisely, for appreciating, where appreciating stands for the affective, imaginative, and intellectual activity that Kant calls "aesthetic judgment": the activity of feeling disinterestedly in accordance with the free harmony of the imagination and the understanding in responsiveness to the relevant object. If we merely believe that the film is great, but don't feel the appropriate kind of pleasure, we may be responsive to theoretical reasons, but not to any aesthetic reasons, and so we *fail* to appreciate the object, that is, to aesthetically judge it. Making an aesthetic judgment is being responsive to the object's *claim to a universal pleasure* (CPJ, 5:280–281) through this very pleasure, and, thus, it is a mode of responsiveness to the reasons in which this claim figures, namely, reasons for feeling a specific kind of pleasure.

Notice that this affective rational responsiveness to (or appreciation of) a beautiful object is also an affective responsiveness to a certain parts-wholes relationship. To judge beauty *aesthetically*, we must *appreciate* (rather than believe)—through our own affective engagement with the object—the necessity of the unity of the "beauty-making features" of the object for the beauty of *this* object as a whole (even if it is not necessary for the beauty of *every* object of its kind). And we appreciate *that* when we appreciate the reciprocal relation between the object as a *whole* and its "beauty-making-parts" *by* liking the whole and the parts disinterestedly.[40] Aesthetic reasons, then, have a holistic shape, which is *to be felt* or appreciated. Appreciating the fitness or discord between the parts of an object and the object as a whole *is* a matter of feeling. And so being responsive to aesthetic reasons is *not* feeling pleasure on the basis of *believing* that pleasure is called for, but *feeling* that the pleasure that one actually feels is called for. As I explained above, when proper, aesthetic pleasure is the affective mode through which we are responsive to what is to be felt disinterestingly. And since it is also conscious of its own propriety, aesthetic pleasure is both object-oriented and self-oriented.

---

40 On this reciprocal part-whole relation, see K. Gorodeisky, "A Tale of Two Faculties," *British Journal of Aesthetics* 51.4 (2011): 415–436.

Accepting the distinctive reasons for appreciating as *reasons* is challenging, but the challenge is worthy. For the assumption that rationality has the form of *theoretical* rationality—that it is disjunctively either deductive or inductive and includes only reasons for believing— is a false assumption. A more fruitful way of thinking about rationality is in the terms I introduced in section 1. Even if reasons for aesthetic appreciation are often hard to articulate, aesthetic pleasure *is* responsive to reasons because of the dependence of its actuality on endorsement, and because of its being affectively conscious of its propriety to its ground. In contrast to answers about agreeable pleasures, the answer to the question "why do you (aesthetically) like it?" is "because it is beautiful," which means, for Kant, "because it merits a disinterested pleasure (from everyone).[41]

Accordingly, aesthetic pleasures and judgments *are* responsive to reasons, but to specifically *aesthetic reasons*. The main distinguishing mark of aesthetic reasons is that they are neither reasons for believing nor reasons for acting but for *feeling* a distinctive kind of disinterested pleasure that purports to reveal its object and its own propriety.

One of the virtues of this proposal is that it seems to do justice to the character of aesthetic discourse. It explains why we often ask for and give reasons for our aesthetic likings. And it suggests a way of thinking about the dependence of aesthetic judgments and the rational explanations of our likings on individual appreciations. It explains, in other words, why it is not enough to say "the performance was brilliant because it was so precise" independently of liking the individual performance as brilliant in the way that it is. For another person, consulting her experience, may say that it is exactly this precision that

---

41 Again, based on what Joseph Raz called the "explanatory-normative nexus," we can also say that an exercise of rational agency is one grounded in normative reasons, where normative reasons explain by being normative: they explain an attitude (e.g., belief, intentional action, emotion) insofar as they not only prompt but also guide it through the agent's rational awareness of them as reasons for this attitude. Aesthetic pleasure is responsive to reasons on this account too. See Raz, *From Normativity to Responsibility*.

made the performance sound mechanical and lacking in passion—her dislike of the performance *is* her finding the precision a demerit *here*. If I am right, then the fact that aesthetic judgments and their rational explanations do not compel anyone else to agree with me *independently of the person's coming to appreciate what I do through her own affective experience* may look less puzzling. On this Kantian-inspired account, finding the piece's precision to be either a merit or demerit *is* (i.e., can be achieved only in and through) one's own experience of pleasure or displeasure.[42]

And so, I insist that, while aesthetic pleasure *is* rational, it is an exercise of a form of rationality that is categorically different from the more familiar theoretical and practical forms of rationality. Aesthetic pleasure is an exercise of aesthetic rationality.

---

42 This means also that my proposal explains why aesthetic explanations are not proofs or whatever we call the support of an action, but *rational* guides of appreciation. See James Shelley, "Critical Compatibilism," in *Knowing Art*, ed. Matthew Kieran and Dominic McIver Lopes (Dordrecht: Springer, 2007), 125–136. Following Sibley, though, Shelley regards them as "guides to *perception*," while I regard them as rational guides to *appreciation*, which is an expression of *liking*.

Reflection

MUSICAL PLEASURE, DIFFICULT MUSIC

Roger Mathew Grant

Can a melody provide us with pleasure? Plato certainly thought so, as do many today. However, it is difficult to discern just how this comes to pass.[1] Early modern music theorists took as their point of departure the notion that the tones of a musical melody could work together with a text in order to imitate and so further represent natural sentiments and the features of the natural world captured in the text. This mimetic ideal, which was a major component of eighteenth-century aesthetics in particular, held that experiencing representations of the various passions was itself pleasurable. "Just as the painter imitates the features and colors of nature," the Abbé Bateux explained, "so the musician imitates the tones, accents, sighs, inflections of the voice, and indeed all of those sounds with which nature exudes the sentiments and passions."[2] Musical tones

---

1 See in particular Plato, *Laws* 2.655c–656b; see also Francesco Pelosi, *Plato on Music, Soul, and Body* (Cambridge: Cambridge University Press, 2010), especially 53–55.

2 "Ainsi que le Peintre imite les traits & les couleurs de la nature, de même le Musicien imite les tons, les accens, les soûpirs, les inflexions de voix, enfin tous ces sons à l'aide desquels la nature même exprime ses sentiments & ses passions. Tous ces sons, commme nous l'avons déjà exposé, ont une force merveilleuse pour nous émouvoir, parce qu'ils sont les signes des passions instituez par la nature dont ils ont reçû leur énergie." Jean-Baptiste Dubos, *Reflexions critiques sur la poesie et sur la peinture* (Paris: Jean Mariette, 1719), vol. 1, 634–635.

FIGURE 1 J. S. Bach, melody from the Fugue in C Major, in *The Well-Tempered Clavier,* book 1, mm. 1–2

had a marvelous power to augment the meaning of poetry in song by conveying the sentiments the poetry expressed.

But what of melodies without texts—tunes that are not songs? Consider for instance the melody reproduced here, the opening line of the Fugue in C Major from J. S. Bach's *Well-Tempered Clavier,* book 1 (1722; fig. 1). It is difficult to say which, if any, natural sentiments this melody depicts. At the crest of the melody, its melodic intervals—the distances between the pitches—grow larger, a quality some eighteenth-century theorists associated with joy.[3] The tail end, however, returns to smaller intervals and shorter durations, which could suggest a more frivolous character. It might be difficult, then, to say that this melody expresses one unified sentiment.

For some eighteenth-century thinkers, the difficulty of pinpointing the exact nature and content of musical representation was a virtue. Pleasure, on this view, came from the indefiniteness and open-endedness of musical expression. "Painting shows the object itself," Diderot explained; "poetry describes it, but music only excites an idea of it. . . . How is it then that of the three arts that imitate nature, the one whose expression is the most arbitrary and least precise speaks most forcefully to the soul? Is it that in showing less of its objects it leaves more to the imagination?"[4] Diderot's suggestion was shared in Thomas Twinning's interpretation of this problem in

3 See for example Johann Mattheson, *Der vollkommene Capellmeister* (Hamburg: Christian Herold, 1739), 16.

4 "La Peinture montre l'objet même, la Poësie le décrit, la Musique en excite à peine une idée. Elle n'a de ressource que dans les intervalles & la durée des sons; & quelle analogie y a-t'il entre cette espéce de crayons, & le printems, les ténébres, la solitude, &c. & la plûpart des objets? Comment se fait-il donc

musical representation. Twinning, commenting on Aristotle's *Poetics*, went so far as to jettison music's responsibility to mimesis altogether.

> Music . . . is not *imitative*, but if I may hazard the expression, merely *suggestive*. But, whatever we may call it, this I will venture to say,— that in instrumental Music, expressively *performed*, the very indecision itself of the expression, leaving the hearer to the free operation of his *emotion* upon his *fancy*, and as it were, to the free *choice* of such ideas are, *to him*, most adapted to react upon and heighten the emotion which occasioned them, produces a pleasure, which nobody, I believe, who is able to feel it, will deny to be one of the most delicious that Music is capable of affording.[5]

Bach's melody in this view gives rise to a huge host of ideas and therefore generates pleasure for the listener in the free choice thereof. This thesis is exactly opposed to that of the mimetic theorists, for whom music evokes pleasure in the specificity of its depicted sentiments.

Bach's melody in figure 1 is only the short opening fragment of a longer composition written in the form of a fugue. Fugues open with a single melody—the subject—that is transformed and replayed throughout the composition in a systematic fashion. Imitation in fugues is not of nature, but instead of the fugue subject itself. Fugues are written in a polyphonic texture, meaning that each individual musical line is an independent entity worthy of being called a melody in its own right, though all of these lines are coordinated with each other in counterpoint so that they can overlap and interweave. The result is a complex composition that

---

que des trois arts imitateurs de la nature, celui dont l'expression est la plus arbitraire & la moins précise, parle le plus fortement à l'ame? Seroit-ce que montrant moins les objets, il laisse plus de carriere à notre imagination . . . ?" Denis Diderot, *Lettre sur les sourds et muets* (Paris, 1751), 302–304.

5 *Aristotle's Treatise on Poetry, Translated: with Notes on the translation and on the original; and Two Dissertations, on Poetical, and Musical, Imitation*, trans. Thomas Twining (London, 1789), 60.

maintains several simultaneously active registers of narrative; it can be difficult even for a professional musician to hear all the elements of a fugue spinning out at once. These pieces are not just difficult to hear in their entirety, they are also difficult to compose. Eighteenth-century theorists referred to them as "worked-out" (*ausgearbeiteten*), or carefully preplanned.

Bach's Fugue in C Major is a model of the fugue form. The first eight measures are given in figure 2. After the entrance of the subject we hear the entrance of the answer: the same melody, but played at a different pitch level. The answer must then harmonize correctly with the ongoing line of music that the subject began. Following on the answer, we hear the entrance of the subject in a lower register, adding a third strand of material to the composition. As this version of the subject unfolds, the other two lines borrow elements, or motives, from the subject to create lines that are closely related to the ideas initially set out in the opening. Finally we hear the fourth contrapuntal strand enter, again with the same subject's melody, though at the lowest pitch level yet. Now four independent strands of music respond to one another with similar gestures, and

FIGURE 2   J. S. Bach, Fugue in C Major, in *The Well-Tempered Clavier*, book 1, mm. 1–8

it becomes increasingly difficult—if not impossible—to hear every allusion and modification of the subject that Bach has written into this complex contrapuntal web.

Elaborate counterpoint, like the writing featured in this fugue, was a concern for eighteenth-century writers on music. Some wondered whether and how this difficult music could be pleasurable, and others worried about its capacity to raise any specific sentiment in its listeners. The Berlin theorist and musician Christian Gottfried Krause worried that the composers of this sort of music had "even forgot the affections altogether."[6] But he also described another experience associated with this difficult music: "it was noticed that when all the voices were worked-out, as the composers say, this expresses a grandeur, an admiration, a great zeal, and a general pleasure, and the heart is filled by it with certain elevated and strong feelings."[7] Here Krause does not describe an experience of affective mimesis but instead comes close to a description of the sublime, which sometimes characterized critical reactions to complex counterpoint. The inability to hear every nuanced reference to the subject and to track the unfurling of all of the intricate and interlacing lines of a Bach fugue has the capacity to generate the melancholy awe and subsequent pleasure associated with the Kantian mathematical sublime.[8] Krause, like Diderot, found in the indefiniteness of musical representation a potential for the experience of limitlessness.

In certain respects, then, the most difficult music might also be some of the most pleasurable. Like spicy food and roller-coaster

---

6 Christian Gottfried Krause, *Von der musikalischen Poesie* (Berlin: Johann Friedrich Voß, 1752), 32.

7 "Man merkte, wenn alle Stimmen arbeiten, wie die Tonkünstler reden daß solches eine Pracht, eine Bewunderung, eine allgemeine Freude, einen grossen Eyfer ausdrückt, und daß das Herz davon mit gewissen hohen und starken Empfindungen erfüllet wird." Krause, *Von der musikalischen Poesie*, 32.

8 On this point in particular see Elaine Sisman, *Mozart: Jupiter Symphony* (Cambridge: Cambridge University Press, 1993), 68–79; for a rather different view of the sublime in music—one that emphasizes liminality rather than transcendence—see Kiene Brillenburg Wurth, *Musically Sublime: Indeterminacy, Infinity, Irresolvability* (New York: Fordham University Press, 2009).

rides, difficult music pushes us past where we are comfortable in order to produce an aesthetic experience—disorientation, shock, immersive innumerability, or even the sublime—that can ultimately offer up intense feelings of pleasure. So when we intuit that melodies are good at providing us with pleasure—be it through their capacity for mimesis or because of their indefiniteness—we ought also to remember that four at once can sometimes do even better than one.

CHAPTER NINE

John Stuart Mill

"PLEASURE" IN THE LAWS OF PSYCHOLOGY AND

THE PRINCIPLE OF MORALS

Dominique Kuenzle

John Stuart Mill's concept of pleasure is a candidate for the top ten list of most-discussed concepts, relative to the work of specific philosophers, within the entire history of philosophy. The concept is all too obviously all too central to Mill's work, especially within his development of Bentham's theory in *Utilitarianism*. Many of the issues that ensure Mill's continued presence in philosophy seminars hinge on the concept of pleasure: the questions of Mill's alleged psychological hedonism and egoism, the principle of utility, the qualitative distinction between different kinds of pleasure, and the related evaluation of "higher" and "lower" pleasures that set Mill apart from Bentham, as well as his "proof" of the principle of utility.

This contribution will not join any of these discussions; there are countless introductory texts on Mill covering these issues, some of them easily accessible online.[1] Instead, I shall take a step away from these controversies to identify the questions that ought to be answered, according to Mill's own presuppositions within the philosophy of science and language, in order to determine the conceptual content of "pleasure" in the first place. This will be done in three sections: first, I will examine those parts of Mill's own philosophy of language, as extensively discussed in his *System of Logic*, that are required to determine what he sees as the semantics of the words "pleasure" and "pain."

Because Mill states conditions under which terms can be redefined for scientific purposes, and because Mill's own work allows for identifying a plausible scientific home language game for "pleasure" and "pain," I will next examine their role and content within the associationist psychology ("associationism") of Mill's time. The focus will be on his father James Mill's *Analysis of the Phenomena of the Human Mind*, the first volume of which was written by his father when Mill was just sixteen years old (1822) and the second a few years later (1829). Much later, in 1869, a quarter century after publishing the *System of Logic* (1843) and eight years after the original publication of *Utilitarianism* (in installments in *Fraser's Magazine*), Mill reedited both volumes and added a preface and many instructive comments.

Mill's work in the philosophy of language, jointly with his epistemology, result in the claim that the conceptual content expressed by general concepts can be determined by epistemic criteria of appropriateness. Accordingly, we need to determine the epistemic criteria that govern the use of "pleasure" within associationist psychology in order to understand what Mill takes pleasure to be. I attempt to show that for Mill, as for his father, pleasures just are pleasurable sensations; they are only subjectively and phenomenally identifiable. It could, but need

---

1 David Brink, "Mill's Moral and Political Philosophy," in *The Stanford Encyclopedia of Philosophy* (Winter 2016 Edition), edited by Edward N. Zalta, accessed March 3, 2018, http://plato.stanford. edu/archives/fall2008/entries/mill-moral-political/. Fred Wilson, "John Stuart Mill," in Zalta, *Stanford Encyclopedia of Philosophy* (Fall 2014 Edition), accessed June 16, 2015, http://plato.stanford. edu/archives/spr2014/entries/mill/. Christopher Macleod, "John Stuart Mill," in Zalta, *Stanford Encyclopedia of Philosophy* (Spring 2018 Edition), accessed March 3, 2018, http://plato.stanford.edu/ archives/spr2018/entries/mill/.

not, turn out that pleasures are not just aspects of such sensations, but detachable parts; this question would be settled empirically, not by psychology alone (introspection and [self-] observation as sources of evidence), but by what the neurosciences find out about how pleasurable sensations are caused. If we consider action explanations as a source of additional criteria for the scientific appropriateness of "pleasure," we get the full, complex picture of how, according to Mill, the concept is individuated.

1. The Connotations of "Pleasure": Mill's Philosophy of Language

"Pleasure" is a linguistic expression. In order to specify the concept that Mill sees as expressed by the use of this word, we need to make explicit a range of presuppositions and decisions within his own epistemology and the philosophy of language, as presented in the *System of Logic* (1841).

Propositions and Names

Mill sees propositions, rather than concepts, as the core unit of semantic content; after all, we use sentences, not words, to make epistemic progress, mainly by asking questions and seeking answers. Propositions count as answers to questions, propositions stand in the inductive and deductive inferential relations that are at the core of Mill's epistemological work. We get to the semantic content of *sub*sentential expressions by first explaining the content of propositions, then breaking it up by means of the notion of predication. By stating a proposition, we attribute a predicate to a subject. The proposition is true if and only if the predicate applies to the subject.

Linguistic entities that are appropriately used as subjects or predicates are called "names." Because any linguistic expression that can be used as a subject or predicate within a proposition thereby counts as a name, Mill's is a nonstandard use of the term "name." Not only "Carlyle" counts as a name, but so do "the present secretary-general of the United Nations," "she," and "dog" (but not "not" or "by"; not every English expression can be used as subject or predicate). Names are singular ("Carlyle") or general ("dog").

The semantics of all Millian names is modeled on the meaning of proper names. First and foremost, names denote existing or imaginary entities (SL, 27). Accordingly, all three of "Barack Obama," "John Stuart Mill," and "Sherlock Holmes" denote. General names denote what we would today call their extension: "dog" denotes all existing, past, future, and imaginary dogs; every entity of which it can be truly affirmed.

While the semantic content of proper names is exhausted by their denotation, this does not hold of other types of names. All names except for proper names denote entities via their *connotation*, which is roughly what we have in mind when we speak of the meaning or sense of a linguistic expression (SL, 34). Take, for example, the Millian name "dog": the denotation of "dog" consists of all real and imaginary dogs, but this isn't what we tend to think of as the meaning of the expression. The meaning of the expression "dog" is its connotation. Connotative names can be defined, their connotation is the definiendum. The definition is "the proposition which declares its connotation" (SL, 133).

Connotations as semantic entities correspond to *attributes* on the ontological level. Many attributes that are connoted by singular and general names can be denoted themselves. Mill calls the names that denote attributes "abstract" and gives "whiteness," "humanity," and "old age" as examples (SL, 29). There are singular abstract names denoting just one attribute such as "visibleness" or "equality," as well as general ones denoting "classes of attributes" such as "color," "whiteness," "magnitude," or indeed "attribute" itself. These abstract names have no connotation; their meaning is exhausted by their denotation (SL, 105).

If a speaker commits herself to the truth of a proposition, she first claims that the entity or entities denoted by the proposition's subject are a subset of the entities of which the predicate is true. Second, the predicate's connotation is related to the entity or entities denoted by and/or to the attribute connoted by the subject. If the subject is a proper name ("Mill is clever"), then the proposition's meaning is constituted by the individual thing being denoted by the subject having the attributes connoted by the predicate (SL, 97). If the subject connotes, too ("Dogs are mammals"), then the meaning of the proposition depends on its logical structure. For epistemological and logical reasons, Mill is particularly interested in affirmative universal propositions of the form "All Xs are Ys." Although such statements still affirm that the entities denoted by the subject possess the attributes connoted by the predicate, they do so not by "individually designating" what is denoted by the subject, but by expressing a relation between the connoted attributes. Mill calls this relation, which enables the subject to denote an indefinite number of entities, "constant accompaniment" of attributes (SL, 97–98).

The Semantics and Metaphysics of General Connotative Names

General connotative names may connote just one attribute, as "white" does, or a plurality, as "bachelor" does. In the latter case, the name counts as semantically complex and its definition can be called an "analysis" of the name (SL, 134). While simple attributes such as whiteness are undoubtedly subject to further epistemological and metaphysical inquiry, it is not clear whether Mill is willing to count this further inquiry as part of the *semantic analysis* of the name "white." Committing himself to a version of a semantic empiricism, he is explicit, though, about the metaphysical and epistemological *point* of this further analysis: "no assertion can be made, at least with a meaning, concerning [substances or attributes,] these unknown and unknowable entities, except in virtue of the Phenomena by which alone they manifest themselves to our faculties" (SL, 100). Accordingly, some names denote and/or connote "noumena," that is, substances or attributes that are (unknowable) causes of "phenomena." This is not only true of what "Socrates" denotes or "mortal" connotes (SL, 98), but even of semantically simple names that may appear phenomenal to us: "whiteness may be defined, the power or property of exciting the sensation of white" (SL, 136). Accordingly, whiteness counts as an (unknown or unknowable) attribute, given to us (and thus rendering propositions involving the general name "white" meaningful) by causing the sensation of white, thereby constituting a phenomenon. "Matter," Mill famously writes, "is nothing but the permanent possibility of perception" (SL, 58).

Accordingly, "whiteness" is a general abstract name denoting the class of "unknown or unknowable" attributes that causes our sensations of shades of white (SL, 29–30; see above). "White" is a general connotative name denoting all past, present, future, and fictional things having these attributes and connoting these attributes. "Sensation of white," to finish the discussion of the semantics of words with sensory content, denotes all past, present, future, and fictional sensations of white, while it connotes a subjectively experienced sameness class of sensations:

> The only names which are unsusceptible of definition, because their meaning is unsusceptible of analysis, are the names of the single feelings themselves. These are in the same condition as proper names. They are not, indeed, like proper names, unmeaning; for the words *sensation of white* signify, that the sensation which I so denominate, resembles other sensations which I remember to have had before, and to have called by that name. But as we have no words by which to recall those former sensations, except the very word which we seek to define, or some other which, being exactly synonymous with it, requires definition as much, words cannot unfold the signification of this class of names, and we are obliged to make a direct appeal to the personal experience of the individual whom we address. (SL, 136)

The Epistemology of General Connotative Names:
Mill's "Real Kinds"

We are free to introduce and define any general connotative names we would like by abstracting from a range of entities or events an idea or "conception" of some sameness relating those entities or events. "White animals," for example, is a perfectly valid general connotative name, because the underlying concept tracks the attribute of whiteness among animals (SL, 650–656).

However, not all general connotative names, that is, not all general conceptions or ideas, are useful, that is, epistemically fruitful, which is addressed by Mill by means of the two criteria of *clarity* and *appropriateness*. "Clear" general conceptions are based on knowledge of the criteria of sameness (SL, 658), which results in their corresponding general names having "precise connotations" (SL, 659). It follows from what Mill says about the names of sensations that the knowledge of the connoted attributes can remain implicit, because the connotations of terms denoting sensations (including "pleasure" and "pain") cannot be stated (see above). What is required for clear connotation are rather epistemic skills or virtues: "habits of attentive observation, extensive experience, and a memory which receives and retains an exact image of what is observed" (SL, 659).

For a general conception to count as *appropriate*, it must be based on "real" resemblances (SL, 656). Real resemblances in turn are epistemically constituted. Real resemblance is a sameness or similarity relation between individuals that allows for induction, that is, the formulation of causal laws, and thereby for explaining and understanding relevant phenomena (SL, 656, 660). While the clarity of our use of general names depends on virtues of observation such as carefulness and accuracy, the appropriateness of our general names increases with our epistemic *activity*: The more research we conduct, the more we are willing to group and regroup phenomena according to potentially fruitful similarities, the better our chance to increase the appropriateness of our conceptions. Ideally, then, we find out that at least some of the resemblances picked out by our general names constitute "real kinds," which are roughly equivalent with what we would today call "natural kinds."

What it is for a kind to be "real," to be "in nature" is explained via the semantics of natural kind terms. Mill's examples of such names are "animal," "plant," "sulphur," and "phosphorus." These names, just as are appropriately connotative names in general, are characterized by their inductive potential. What distinguishes a real kind name "X" from other general connotative names is that it makes sense to ask what Xs are, that the inquiry into "common properties" of Xs is epistemically fruitful. Animals and plants, according to Mill, share numerous properties that are not caused by the criterial properties that allow language users to correctly apply the name; "white things," by contrast, share only their whiteness and those properties that are causally connected with whiteness (SL, 122).

Accordingly, neither white animals nor mobile phones constitute real kinds, while animals and sulphur do. "Animal" and "sulphur" connote (are semantically contentful) in an epistemically fruitful and nontransparent way in that the connotations required for language users to competently use these names do not provide them with the criteria that determine whether something is, in fact, an animal or a piece of sulphur.

Nonscientific and Scientific Language Use

Since general connotative names in everyday use often lack precise connotations (Mill's clarity criterion), they are unsuitable for scientific induction (SL, 668). The "philosophical language" needed for scientific purposes either replaces everyday general names with stipulatively defined names (making explicit the attributes connoted by the terms) or adjusts the meaning of existing names. This is done partly by a process of historical and/or psychological analysis: the logician examines first what Mill calls "the natural history of the variations in the meaning of terms" (SL, chapter 5). She thereby identifies common social, linguistic, and historical causes for shifts or extensions of the connotation of general names. In addition, the logician seeks causal psychological explanations of "what points of resemblance among the different things commonly called by the name, have produced in the common mind this vague feeling of likeness; have given to the things the similarity of aspect, which has made them a class, and has caused the same name to be bestowed upon them" (SL, 669). "The meaning of a term actually in use is not an arbitrary quantity to be fixed, but an unknown quantity to be sought" (SL, 671).

Once the vague existing connotation of a name is established, similarity to it serves as one, but not the main, let alone the only, criterion for the new definition's success (SL, 671). The established usage of the term should be preserved, but not at all costs. As established earlier, the main criteria for scientifically adjusted names are clarity and appropriateness, where "appropriateness" requires that the name connotes attributes (common to all individuals denoted by the name) that allow for induction. Suitable attributes for such scientifically (or "logically") regimented connotation are those on which "many others depend, or at least which are sure marks of them, and from whence, therefore, many others will follow by inference" (SL, 672). Such attributes can be connoted themselves, or they can be partly constitutive of real kinds, whose specimens share innumerable properties not connoted by their names.

Accordingly, inductive progress can involve replacing inappropriate general names with appropriate ones, and ideally with names of real kinds. Mill himself describes this process in terms of us *discovering* whether a general name picks out a real kind or not. He discusses categories of human beings: "old people," "teenagers," "white people," and "men" are general names. Once Mill's criterion of clarity is met, it could *turn out*, Mill says, that they pick out real kinds, because it is possible that our progress in physiology establishes that the differences between these classes cannot be causally explained by a small number of "primary differences" between human beings (SL, 124). If it turns out that women differ from men in "innumerable" ways that are independent of the criterial ones that allow for competent use of the names, then "women" and "men" pick out real kinds.

Scientific definitions of general names, therefore, are always works in progress; "every enlargement of our knowledge of the objects to which the name is applied, is liable to suggest an improvement in the definition," Mill writes; "It is impossible to frame a perfect set of definitions on any subject, until the theory of the subject is perfect: and as science makes progress, its definitions are also progressive" (SL, 672).

The Connotation and Denotation of "Pleasure" as a General Name

"Pleasure," according to what has been said, is undoubtedly a name, because it is useable both as a subject and a predicate in propositions. It is a *general concrete* name, because it can be truly affirmed of an indefinite number of entities. Depending on whether it will turn out to connote one or several attributes (a "combination of attributes"; SL, 105), it is a simple (such as "white") or complex (such as "bachelor") name. "Pleasurableness," in turn, is an abstract name; depending on whether pleasures are "variable in degree or in kind," it will turn out to be a singular or general abstract name (SL, 30).

As I have shown in this chapter, this connotation is determined by the name's regimented scientific language use, which to some extent takes the word's established everyday use into account (via a "natural history" of this use), but then determines its denotation and connotation by ensuring its clarity and appropriateness within scientific contexts. As a next step in this inquiry, therefore, I need to make explicit what Mill sees as the relevant inductions providing the criteria for the appropriateness of the scientifically regimented conception of pleasure and pain. With Mill describing psychology as the basis of all scientific endeavors to explain, predict, and govern the behavior of human beings, and with "pleasure" being a core concept within the cutting-edge psychological theory of Mill's time, it is obvious that his father's and others' associationist psychology is the primary source of the epistemic pressures on the constitution of "pleasure" as an appropriate (general connotative and/or abstract) name.

2. PLEASURE IN ASSOCIATIONIST PSYCHOLOGY

Book 6 of the *Science of Logic*, "On the Logic of the Moral Sciences," situates the goals, methods, and conceptual basis of psychology, sociology, economy, and ethics within Mill's epistemology and philosophy of science. These "Moral Sciences," as Mill calls them, have two kinds of ambitions: (1) they descriptively aim to improve our explanations and predictions of human behavior by articulating the general laws and special conditions that determine such behavior, and (2) they normatively issue and justify rules or precepts to govern and improve such behavior. If the moral sciences follow their descriptive ambitions, Mill calls them "Science"; in their normative or "imperative" moods, he labels them "Art" (SL 8, 943).

When aiming at descriptive goals, the key idea behind the moral sciences is that the "uniformity of causation" extends to human behavior and thinking, which are thereby subject to scientific explanation. As in other branches of science, the moral sciences, too, aim at resolving special and/or complex phenomena into general and/or simple ones.[2] Psychology provides the foundations for all other moral sciences. Here, Mill embraces the *associationist psychology* explored by his father, which is the relevant immediate home language game of Mill's concept of pleasure. Associationist psychology attempts to explain mental phenomena by subsuming them to the "laws of the mind" (SL, chapter 4). Once the laws of the mind are established, they can be

---

2 Mill's "Preface," in APHM 1, v–vi.

assembled to investigate the laws that govern how human beings form
their characters. This is the subject of the moral science of *ethology* (SL,
chapter 5). Generalizations of social human behavior allow for the formulation of empirical laws of human nature and society, which should
eventually enable us to explain and predict individual human beings'
behavior in concrete circumstances.[3]

James Mill on the Nature and Constitution of Pleasure and Pain (1822/1829)

When discussing methodological issues of psychology as the science
of mental phenomena in his *System of Logic*, Mill originally references
only his father's *Analysis of the Phenomena of the Human Mind* from
1822, which he later published in a new edition, with a preface and additional notes by himself and Alexander Bain (1869). In later editions
of the *System*, Mill added a reference to Alexander Bain's *Treatise of the
Human Mind* (1855/1859). Because Mill explicitly says that conceptual
content is determined by criteria of clarity and appropriateness within
scientific contexts, his own concept of pleasure must be traced within
James Mill's associationist psychology as adopted by John Stuart Mill
and Alexander Bain.

James Mill takes *sensations* to be the simple building blocks of all
mental phenomena. He treats them as a species of "feelings" (APHM
I, 3). "Feeling," for the Mills, was just a synonym for "state of consciousness": "everything is a feeling of which the mind is conscious" (SL, 51).
Accordingly, sensations are necessarily conscious. Sensations are provided by the five senses, as well as by muscular activity and by means
of the digestive tract (APHM I, 3); they are provided by an organ and
caused by an object (APHM I, 8–9).

Interestingly, pleasure and pain are not discussed in James Mill's
section on sensations, although they are mentioned in passing as

---

3 John Skorupski, *The Arguments of the Philosophers: John Stuart Mill* (London: Routledge,
1989), 260.

something that other mental, conscious states ("feelings") "partake of" (e.g., APHM 1, 31) and as examples (pleasure of scratching an itch [APHM 1, 39], pleasure of "violent exercise" [APHM 1, 43], pleasure of stretching one's muscles [APHM 1, 43], pleasures of alcohol and opium [APHM 1, 46]). Only later, when the second volume of his *Analysis* (originally published in 1829) turns to the motivating role of ideas, their "active powers" (APHM 2, chapter 16), are pleasure and pain extensively discussed:

> Some sensations, probably the greater number, are what we call indifferent. They are not considered as either painful, or pleasurable. There are sensations, however, and of frequent recurrence, some of which are painful, some pleasurable. The difference is, that which is felt. A man knows it, by feeling it; and this is the whole account of the phenomenon. I have one sensation, and then another, and then another. The first is of such a kind, that I care not whether it is long or short; the second is of such a kind, that I would put an end to it instantly if I could; the third is of such a kind, that I like it prolonged. To distinguish those feelings, I give them names. I call the first Indifferent; the second, Painful; the third, Pleasurable; very often, for shortness, I call the second, Pain, the third, Pleasure. (APHM 2, 184)

> The state of consciousness under the [pleasurable] sensation, that is, the sensation itself, differed from other sensations, in that it was agreeable. A name was wanted to denote this peculiarity; to mark, as a class, the sensations which possess it. The term, Pleasure, was adopted. (APHM 2, 191)

According to this view, pleasures and pains are not *caused* by sensations; jointly with "indifferent," they provide an exhaustive classification of all sensations, which can then be combined with a classification according to the senses (APHM 2, 185). Hence we get pleasurable sensations of the eye or the digestive tract, indifferent sensations of touch, painful sensations of the taste or of muscular activity, etc. Nothing about this account of pleasure suggests that all pleasures are in any way similar to each other, or that pleasurable sensations are the result of a mental ("associationist") addition of pleasure (as a simple, detachable sensation) to other simple sensations. Pleasures are simply pleasurable sensations; pleasurable sensations are those we subjectively phenomenally recognize because we would like them to last longer.[4] All these sensations can yield *ideas*, which are the "states of consciousness" that result when the objects causing the sensation are removed (APHM 2, 189). "Trains of ideas" themselves can be "agreeable" or "disagreeable" to have, but because ideas are not sensations, James Mill is careful not to call these mental phenomena "pleasurable" (APHM 2, 190).

The idea of a future pleasurable sensation, Mill continues, in a move not entirely agreed with by his son, is a *desire* for this sensation if it is "associated with the future" (APHM 2, 191; John Stuart Mill's note 37 in APHM 2, 194–195; see "Pleasure in Action Explanations" below). The combination of the idea of a pleasurable sensation with the idea of an action that is thought to result in this sensation is a *motive* (APHM 2, 258). With material approvingly quoted by John Stuart Mill from his father's *Fragment on Mackintosh* (1830), it emerges that actions are by definition directed at ends, that these ends can be classified, and that the idea of pleasure (pleasurable sensation) is the genus of these ends: "motive, then, taken generically is pleasure." Sensuality, ambition, avarice, glory, sociality are named as examples of "species" of this

---

4 Richard Brandt, *A Theory of the Good and the Right* (Oxford: Clarendon Press, 1979), 40–41, offers a definition of "pleasurable experience" very much in line with James Mill's account. Jeremy Bentham on the other hand appears to differ from his friend's view, treating pleasure and pain as separable sensations ("interesting perceptions," 5.1) that can themselves be simple or complex, depending on whether they consist of just one or several (simple) pleasures and pains. See Jeremy Bentham, *An Introduction to the Principles of Morals and Legislation*, reedited by J. H. Burns, H. L. A Hart, and F. Rosen (Oxford: Clarendon Press, 1996, originally published 1789). Bentham's, but not James Mill's, view is arguably subject to the heterogeneity worries about pleasures raised by Gilbert Ryle, "Pleasure," *Proceedings of the Aristotelian Society*, supp., 28 (1954): 135–146, and Anthony Kenny, *Action, Emotion and Will* (London: Routledge and Kegan Paul, 1963), chapter 6.

"genus" (APHM 2, 263; John Stuart Mill's quotes from *Fragment on Mackintosh* in note 69). The *will* is then defined as a specific form of associating an immediate action with the idea of a pleasurable sensation as the action's end (APHM 2, 364). It differs from a mere motive mainly by including an idea of how it feels to call the muscles into action. James Mill intends this disambiguation of "the idea of the action" to solve the problem of how we can sometimes merely entertain a motive (merely desiring something) without acting on it.

John Stuart Mill: Pleasure as Related by the Laws of the Mind

Mill agrees with his father that pleasure and pain are sensations (APHM 1, 7n2, 66n22). Sensations are one of four main kinds of mental phenomena, along with thoughts, emotions, and volitions (SL, 849):

> It is usual indeed to speak of sensations as states of body, not of mind. But this is the common confusion, of giving one and the same name to a phenomenon and to the proximate cause or conditions of the phenomenon. The immediate antecedent of a sensation is a state of body, but the sensation itself is a state of mind. If the word mind means anything, it means that which feels. Whatever opinion we hold respecting the fundamental identity or diversity of matter and mind, in any case the distinction between mental and physical facts, between the internal and the external worlds, will always remain, as a matter of classification: and in that classification, sensations, like all other feelings, must be ranked as mental phenomena. (SL, 849)

At least all sensations, and perhaps the other main categories of mental phenomena, too, have *physical causes*; their explanations are part of "physiology" (SL, 850). Although it could eventually turn out that all laws of the mind are derivative from "laws of animal life," and that "their truth may therefore depend on physical conditions" (SL, 851), we can relate mental phenomena to other mental phenomena via general (or "elementary") and special laws of the mind, independently of the question of the physiological causes.

Following his father, as well as the first part of Alexander Bain's *Treatise of the Human Mind* (*The Senses and the Intellect* [1855], part 2, *The Emotions and the Will* [1859]), Mill accepts the laws of association as the most general and elementary laws of psychology. These laws ought to be established by proper induction, and they ought to provide criteria of adequacy for the scientifically regimented use of "pleasure" and "pain."

Mill takes no exception to his father's view that "pleasure" and "pain" are abbreviations of "pleasurable" and "painful" sensations, respectively. He agrees with his father, too, that there are many different kinds of pleasure and pain, which can be categorized according to the organs or senses. According to his own accounts of abstract names, this variability in kind means that "pleasurability" and "painfulness" are *general* abstract names (see "The Semantics and Metaphysics of General Connotative Names" above). The main methods for examining pleasures and pains are the subject's "practised self-consciousness and self-observation, assisted by observation of others" (U, chapter 4, 237). The social sciences and history, too, can contribute to the task of "eliminative induction,"[5] which is needed to establish the causation of mental phenomena.

Accordingly, both eating chocolate and reading Wordsworth are pleasurable sensations. To classify both as pleasures is just one way of identifying shared attributes (as connoted by "pleasure" and denoted by "pleasurableness"). Before we turn to the neuronal basis of these sensations, the question of the attribute or attributes connoted by "pleasure" must be answered in terms of the laws of association linking these sensations to other mental phenomena such as ideas and ultimately motives, desires, and actions.

Pleasurable and painful sensations result in *ideas* of pleasurable and painful sensations (SL, 695). At least at one point, Mill identifies these ideas with conscious states ("feelings") of varying intensity (SL, 857).

---

5 Skorupski, *Arguments of the Philosophers: John Stuart Mill*, 178.

Abstraction, in turn, yields the ideas of pleasurableness or painfulness. These can be associated with different ideas (SL, 695), resulting in desires and thus playing important roles in action explanations. However, the fact that such associationist laws relate desires to pleasurable experiences does not imply that pleasure is a product of introspective analysis of desires. Complex ideas, Mill says, can be "chemically" constituted.

The idea of an orange is an example of a *mechanically* constituted complex idea, because it consists of our simple ideas of a certain color, form, taste, and smell (SL, 854). *Chemically* generated complex ideas on the other hand appear simple themselves and can be of a different kind than their constituent simple ideas. Our visual perception of the shape of an object, for example, involves ideas of form and extension that have been generated by tactile perception. These simple ideas cannot be identified by introspective analysis of our visual perception of the form of the object; they have chemically "generated," and not mechanically "composed," the (seemingly simple) complex idea (SL, 854). Pleasure and pain can, but need not, result in emotions and desires that are more than their aggregates "or in any respect homogenous with them" (SL, 442).

Chemically generated complex ideas, as well as mental phenomena such as thoughts, emotions, and volitions, cannot be introspectively analyzed; they need to be causally explained by means of experiments and observation. On the one hand we proceed by what Mill calls the "Method of Agreement," comparing instances of mental phenomena types looking for shared conditions (simple ideas). The method of agreement needs to be combined with the "Method of Difference," whereby we observe or experimentally induce mental effects under varying circumstances (SL, 855). As Mill states in a note from 1865 with reference to the fifth chapter of *Utilitarianism*, there are mental phenomena such as the moral sentiments that cannot be explained by means of observation and experimentation alone, but need to be illuminated by the methods of history and the social sciences (SL, 855n).

According to the emerging picture, it is not quite correct that, as a common narrative within the history of philosophy has it, there is a shared tendency between Locke and the associationists (Bentham and James Mill) to treat pleasure as a simple, measurable sensation represented by a simple idea. Bentham and James Mill, according to this account, explain complex ideas as analyzable, whereas John Stuart Mill's notion of the chemical constitution of complex ideas allows him to conceive of pleasures and pains as inseparable aspects of complex mental phenomena.

By contrast, it is James Mill, rather than John Stuart Mill, who unequivocally states that pleasure and pain are mere aspects or qualities of sensations. The difference between mechanical and chemical production of complex ideas does not straightforwardly apply to the relation between pleasures and other sensations per se. It is true that on the level of *ideas* (constituting thoughts and volitions), John Stuart Mill develops his father's model by introducing chemically generated complex ideas. It is true, too, that this then implies that introspective analysis of these complex ideas does not allow for the identification of simple ideas of pleasure and pain; empirical observation and experimentation is needed, as may be, in the case of the moral sentiments, historiography, and the social sciences (SL, 855).

However, this complication on the level of ideas is consistent with his and his father's view that the simple ideas of something being pleasurable or painful are mere abstractions, merely one way of classifying sensations, ultimately to be judged in the context of the inductive success of the associationist model as a whole. "Pleasure" and "pain" connote the attribute or attributes that make us want to prolong or shorten our respective sensations. It is true, as I will show in the next subsection, that John Stuart Mill considers the possibility that pleasures and pains are separable parts of complex *sensations*, but this is not a result of any considerations on the level of ideas. Instead, he suggests methodologically moving on from a narrow conception of associationist psychology to further inductive research into the *physiological causes* of sensations. This, according to Mill, could show pleasure and pain to be isolable parts of more complex sensations.

Pleasure as "Detachable Part" and the Question of Physiology

In a 1869 comment on his father's discussion of the nature of pleasure and pain, Mill raises the possibility that pleasure and pain, and "especially the pleasure," is a *detachable part* of the sensation, rather than just its "aspect or quality" (APHM 2, 185n36). Mill thereby takes up a question going back to John Locke, who appears to waver over the question of whether ideas resulting from pleasurable and painful sensations are combinations of separable simple ideas or whether they are at least sometimes not "wholly separated," but instead "blended" together.[6]

Mill takes this to be an empirical question, with independent variation, in this case of subjective psychological phenomena such as the gradual loss of pleasure resulting from mere repetition of a pleasurable sensation, to count as evidence. And with the connotation, that is, the conceptual content, of the terms "pleasure" and "pain" depending on their role within induction in general (and not just associationist psychology narrowly conceived), he even links the question of whether pleasure is an aspect or part of a pleasurable sensation to the question of its physiological cause:

> in the case of many pleasurable or painful sensations, it is open to question whether the pleasure or pain, especially the pleasure, is not something added to the sensation, and capable of being detached from it, rather than merely a particular aspect or quality of the sensation. It is often observable that a sensation is much less pleasurable at one time than at another, though to our consciousness it appears exactly the same sensation in all except the pleasure.

---

6 John Locke, *Essay Concerning Human Understanding*, ed. P. H. Nidditch (Oxford: Oxford University Press, [1689] 1975), 2.7.3–5.

This is emphatically the fact in cases of satiety, or of loss of taste for a sensation by loss of novelty. It is probable that in such cases the pleasure may depend on different nerves, or on a different action of the same nerves, from the remaining part of the sensation. (APHM 2, 185n36)

Pleasure in Action Explanations and the Laws of Morals

Given that the conceptual content of the concepts of pleasure and pain are subject to scientific regimentation, and given that Mill situates psychology at the basis of all attempts to explain human behavior by means of subsuming such behavior under (if not causal, certainly "empirical") laws, action explanations depend on a suitable concept of pleasure and provide potential evidence for general laws linking pleasure and pain with other mental states, especially volitions: if we know in what precise way the idea of pleasure contributes to an agent acting the way she does, we can link up the action with the agent's subjective and objective circumstances. We can then potentially vary these circumstances, or observe variations of these circumstances, and check the agent's behavior.

However, unfortunately Mill's account of the role of pleasure and pain in human behavior is not quite clear enough. Quite apart from many of the notorious difficulties with Mill's "proof" of the principle of utility in the fourth chapter of *Utilitarianism*, there is a tension between two passages in which he discusses the relation between pleasure and desire. In *Utilitarianism* (1861), Mill famously makes the following claim: "desiring a thing and finding it pleasant, aversion to it and thinking of it as painful, are phenomena entirely inseparable, or rather two parts of the same phenomenon; in strictness of language, two different modes of naming the same psychological fact: that to think of an object as desirable (unless for the sake of its consequences), and to think of it as pleasant, are one and the same thing; and that to desire anything, except in proportion as the idea of it is pleasant, is a physical and metaphysical impossibility" (U, 237–238). Here, Mill unequivocally seems to say that statements of the form "S desires O" constitute the same proposition as "S thinks of O as pleasant" and "S finds O pleasant," as long as we are talking about the same agent (S) and object (O). Because Mill does not mention, as his father does, that "desire," as opposed to "idea of a pleasurable sensation," connotes futurity, this is a slight simplification even of his father's view, who, after all, insists on "desirableness, and the idea of something pleasurable, being convertible terms" (APHM 2, 193). It is certainly a simplification of John Stuart Mill's own views, as expressed in the context of associationist psychology, because eight years after *Utilitarianism*, in his notes on the very passages in which his father expresses this view, he explicitly states that desire is *not* to be identified with the idea of a future pleasurable sensation (APHM 2, 194–195n37). The idea of a future pleasurable sensation may be an *expectation*, but not a desire; we can expect something without desiring it (and vice versa). Desire, instead, is "the initiatory stage of the Will," in that in what we call "desire" there is "always included a positive stimulation to action," a "tendency to action" (APHM 2, 194n37).

Mill seems to think that what it means for pleasure to turn into, or to partly constitute, a desire is accounted for by his father's theory of volition, with which he largely agrees. Either account—the oversimplified one in *Utilitarianism*, as well as his father's theory of volition—ensures that the idea of pleasure, via the notion of volition, can in principle be inductively inferred on the basis of observable human behavior. The concept of pleasure, via the idea of pleasure, plays an important role in action explanations. This is, as it were, a second inductive machine in which the concept of pleasure needs to be plugged in.

However, the crucial role afforded to character and the science of ethology ensures that Mill's account of human behavior (into which the concept of pleasure ought to fit) is more sophisticated than Bentham's or his father's. Ever since "Remarks on Bentham's Philosophy" (1833), and prominently in "Bentham" (1838), "Coleridge" (1840), the *System of Logic* (1843), and *Utilitarianism* (1861), Mill seeks to expand the associationist model of action. He agrees with both Bentham and his father that ideas of pleasure and pain are essential for all action explanations, and that many actions are indeed best explained in terms of motives, that is, associations of ideas of pleasurable or painful sensations with objects and/or behavior that causes them. The general names denoting these actions, as well as other causes of pleasure and pain, may then connote agreeableness or painfulness; our desires are directed either at the pleasurable sensations or at the object or action that causes them (SL, 842).

The interdependence of psychology and ethology ensures a more general model of action explanation than the one provided by his father's and Bentham's hedonistic calculus by incorporating habits, character traits (virtues, vices), and (moral and other) emotions. Indeed, in his criticism of Bentham's application of the principle of utility, Mill explicitly states that we need "much deeper insight into the formation of character, and knowledge of the internal workings of human nature, than Mr. Bentham possessed" ("Remarks on Bentham's Philosophy" in *Collected Works*, vol. 10, 8).

The desires of human beings differ according to their constitutions and biographies; they are malleable. In *Utilitarianism*, Mill gives the example of a miser who associates an idea of pleasure with spending money, until he ends up associating pleasure with the state of being rich (U, 236). In "Bentham" ((1838), *Collected Works*, vol. 10, 95–96), Mill mentions motives such as spiritual perfection, developing one's character according to one's own standards of excellence, self-respect, "the love of beauty, the passion of the artist; the love of order." The consciousness of virtue, according to this account, is a pleasure (U, 235), and Mill's way of putting this point indicates that altruistic acts, too, can and should be (or be made by means of self-education) pleasurable.

Associationist psychology and action explanations serve as the descriptive basis for the normative "arts" within the social sciences, which determine actions and policies by means of the "Principle of Utility" or "Greatest Happiness Principle," which states that "actions are right in proportion as they tend to promote happiness" (U, chapter 2). Mill famously equates "happiness" with "pleasure, and the absence of pain," before he goes out of his way to ensure that his concept of pleasure applies not only to eating, sleeping, and sex, but contains "higher," qualitatively better pleasures such as watching an opera or conducting a discussion, too.

3. ACCOUNTING FOR MILL'S USE OF "PLEASURE"

I have identified three epistemic criteria determining inductively motivated conceptual change: (1) similarity to common established nonscientific uses of the term, as identified via its "natural history"; (2) clarity, and (3) appropriateness of the term's connotation as responding to inductive progress. In order to determine the meaning of Mill's use of "pleasure" and "pain," I will now examine whether, and how, these criteria are met within associationist psychology, in additional inductive contexts discussed by Mill, and when the descriptive ambitions of the moral sciences are supplemented by normative and evaluative goals, turning the moral sciences into "Arts."

John Stuart Mill on "Pleasure" within Associationist Psychology

Mill is not hugely concerned with anything like a "natural history" of nonscientific uses of the term "pleasure." We seem to more or less call enjoyable events, external objects, or experiences "pleasures," which is roughly the use James Mill seems to track with his subjective and phenomenal characterization of the term. Attributive uses as part of folk psychological action explanations ("She did it because she expected it to be pleasurable") and everyday moral judgments ("One ought to help others when they're in pain") are not discussed.

The scientific home language game of the concept of pleasure is the associationist psychology of Mill's time, as exemplified by his father's

Analysis of the Phenomena of the Human Mind and the works of David
Hartley and Alexander Bain. Within associationist psychology narrowly conceived, "pleasures" and "pains" as general names that denote all real and imaginary pleasurable or painful sensations via their
connotations. At first sight, pleasure's role as a phenomenal given
seems to keep things simple. To have pleasure and to know that one
has pleasure, states James Mill, are the same thing. His son agrees with
this perceived epistemic simplicity of the phenomena and supplies a
methodological justification for construing "pleasure" and "pain" as
denoting sensations, rather than unknown or unknowable causes or
external events or objects: associationist psychology establishes mental
laws. If we connect this agreement with Mill's views of the semantics of
general names, it emerges that within this context, "pleasure" denotes
pleasurable sensations themselves, even though an attitude toward
these sensations serves as the criterion of applicability. Just like "sensation of white," "pleasure" cannot be defined (its connotation cannot be
explicitly stated), but unlike proper names it does not lack meaning: its
connotation is constituted by the use of the term's implicitly claiming
similarity of the denoted sensation with a range of previous sensation
(SL, 136).

Irrespective of the concept's role in everyday English, it is up to associationist psychology to ensure that the term's connotation is clear and
appropriate. Because clarity does not require explicit definitions, but
instead epistemic virtues such as "habits of attentive observation" and
memory (SL, 659), James Mill's insistence that we all subjectively know
that some sensation is pleasurable when we have it ensures that the
clarity criterion is met, even in the absence of a definition. And in case
the rule of "you'll know one when you'll have one" should fail to work,
the elder Mill supplies an additional rule for identifying pleasures: it's
just those sensations that we all wish would go on for longer (APHM
2, 184).

Whether James Mill's conception of pleasure is epistemically *appropriate* depends on the inductive success of associationist psychology,

on the "laws of the mind" linking up various kinds of sensations that can be empirically discovered. The scientifically regimented semantics of "pleasure" and "pain," as proposed by the Mills, is at least provisionally correct if and only if the class of sensations these names denote are similar in ways that allow for an explanatorily and predictive "science of the mind" to be successful (SL, 851). Despite pleasure, as a mental phenomenon, being subjective, we can establish associative law-like relations between pleasurable and other sensations by means of self-observation within experimental and/or observational settings.

The one major complication of this view of pleasure within associationist psychology concerns the role of pleasure in volition. This, after all, is how the subjectively observable mental phenomena that are the primary subject of the inductions of the "Science of the Mind" are tied up with observable behavior. In the context of James Mill's *Analysis*, father and son agree that actions are to be explained by means of complex ideas consisting of ideas of actions and pleasurable sensations, which are then fed into a theory of volition. This, of course, raises additional questions with regard to the concept's appropriateness, because it is by no means guaranteed that the very same "laws of the mind" allow for predictions and explanations of agents (1) confirming in laboratory settings that they are having a sensation that they would call "pleasurable" and/or like to continue and (2) acting in certain ways.

"Pleasure" outside Associationist Psychology: The Prospect of Unified Neuroscience

As I have shown, words, answering to inductive progress, can change their meanings. And although the associative "laws of the mind" can be examined independently of their causal base, the relations of associationist psychology "to the science of physiology must never be overlooked or undervalued" (SL, 851). All sensations, including pleasures, have physiological causes, and according to Mill it is possible,

or even "extremely probable," that all mental laws will prove to be reducible to physiological laws (SL, 850–851).

If psychology were to be turned into a "mere branch" of "the science
of physiology," then this would affect the semantics of the names
denoting mental phenomena, because their appropriateness would
have to be reevaluated. In the note to his father's *Analysis* discussed
above (APHM 2, 185n36), Mill hints at such a reevaluation of the
semantics of "pleasure" by pointing at independent variation of the
pleasure-aspect of sensations as potential reason for counting pleasures
as detachable parts, not as mere aspects, of pleasurable sensations.

Mill does not spell out the full implications of this possibility, but
the following two consequences are explicit: first, to identify pleasures
as "detachable parts" must mean more than the possibility of mentally
abstracting from other aspects of the sensation and our ability to consciously attend to the pleasurable aspect itself. Because these capacities
are granted by James Mill, too, his son must have in mind something
like an isolable feeling internal to the pleasurable sensation, perhaps a
component common to all pleasurable sensations, when he suggests
that pleasure might be "something added to the sensation, and capable
of being detached from it, rather than merely a particular aspect or
quality of the sensation" (APHM 2, 185n36).

Second, one way it could turn out that pleasures are parts rather than
aspects of sensations lies in our identification of specific kinds of physiological causes. It could turn out that the pleasure-aspect of our pleasurable sensations is caused by "different nerves" from those causing
other aspects of the sensation (or it could be caused "in different ways"
by the same nerve).

Accounting for independent variation and physiological causation of pleasure and pain would not imply, of course, that pleasures
and pains are *caused* by sensations. "Pleasure" and "pain" can still be
construed as general names denoting past, present, future, and fictional sensations themselves. However, because Mill sees conceptual
content as answerable to epistemic criteria, such a discovery ought to

have implications for the conceptual content, the connotation of the terms, which must be reevaluated in the light of their new inductive potential within a unified science of physiology (see section 1). If it turns out that pleasure and pain are caused by certain kinds of neuronal process, then this allows for suitable changes to their connotation (conceptual content, meaning). It is conceivable, for example, that "pleasurableness," analogously to "whiteness," could turn out to be best construed as an abstract general name denoting the attribute that causes sensations to be pleasurable—that is, in this case, their physiological causes.

One way (if not the only way) pleasures could turn out to be a part, instead of a mere aspect, of sensations, could be that we find out that pleasures constitute a *real kind*. As I have shown (section 1), Mill's real kinds are *epistemically* constituted; a kind is real if and only if its specimens share "numerous or innumerable" properties that are causally independent of those that count as criteria for competent use of the name. If "X" is a real kind name, then it makes sense to ask what Xs are; the inquiry into shared properties of Xs is epistemically fruitful.

Now, if "pleasure" were just an abbreviation of "pleasurable sensation," and if the semantic content of "pleasurable sensation" is constituted by a similarity class of sensations, then it would not make sense to ask what pleasures are. By discussing independent variation of the pleasure aspect and its potential physiological base, and by allowing for real kinds to emerge as a product of inductive progress, Mill allows for pleasures to turn out to be real kinds, which means that the properties that allow for competent use of the term "pleasure" are not the attributes constitutive of the kind.

Just as it wasn't clear for Mill whether "men" and "women" denote real kinds of human beings (SL, 124), we might not yet know, at any given time of inductive research, whether "pleasure" and "pain" denote real kinds of detachable parts of sensations. If this were the case, their semantics could change radically. We could still use the subjective sensation or even the attitudes of wanting these sensations prolonged or shortened as the criteria for identifying pleasures and pains in competent language use, but the terms' connotations would now be of a neurophysiological nature. We could consistently agree that sensations previously considered to be pleasant or painful by competent language users "have turned out to be not really pleasant or painful." "But it is often necessary to define the class by some property not familiarly known, provided that property be the best mark of those which are known" (SL, 675). The criteria for accepting such a conclusion would be entirely epistemic (scientific; psychological-physiological); the counterintuitive nature of this consequence could feasibly be softened by divorcing the scientifically regimented concept of pleasure from the one in everyday use. If this is right, then the content of the concepts of pleasure and pain depends not only on their inductive potential for explanatory and predictive laws of the mind, but potentially and probably on their function in a unified neuroscience of mental phenomena and their physiological base.

"Pleasure" outside Associationist Psychology: The Principle of Utility

I have now shown that the criteria of clarity and appropriateness establish three kinds of pull on the appropriateness of the connotation of "pleasure" and "pain" within the context of the moral sciences: (1) explanatory and predictive success with regard to subjectively and phenomenally experienced pleasurable and painful sensations, (2) explanatory and predictive success with regard to actions (via the role of pleasure in volitions), and (3) neurophysiological causation of sensations in the context of a unified science of man.

Moving from the purely descriptive moral sciences to the genuinely normative and evaluative moral "arts," we see that Mill's wide concept of pleasurable sensation is well suited to reject any claims that the principle of utility commits us to the promotion of "bodily" pleasures. Enjoying an opera and the experience of helping others can be pleasurable sensations, after all. It is only when Mill extends the notion of pleasure to states other than sensations, such as "pleasures of the intellect, of the feelings and imagination, and of the moral sentiments" (U, 211) that the concept begins to be strained. James Mill, as I have shown, discussed enjoyable thoughts, but made sure to call them "agreeable." Mill exacerbates this problem for his official view that pleasures are pleasurable sensations when he categorizes these "intellectual" pleasures as qualitatively different and of higher value than those "of mere sensation" (U, 211).

What are we to make of Mill's points in *Utilitarianism*—that there are "intellectual pleasures" that aren't "mere sensations"—in the context of our general reconstruction of his concept of pleasure? First, we could stay close to his text and take into account that "mere sensations" is immediately followed by talk of "mental" and "bodily pleasures," suggesting that "mere sensation" here is merely a loose way of differentiating "bodily" pleasures from the "higher" pleasures accompanying intellectual activities, virtuous acts, and the production and consumption of art.

More substantially, it seems likely that Mill, when sketching his moral theory in *Utilitarianism*, oversimplifies his own position within the moral sciences, especially by failing to explicitly mention the provisional, work-in-progress state of contemporary psychology and ethology. The methodological basis for the move from the purely descriptive ambitions of the moral sciences to the genuinely normative attempt to set up values, principles, laws, policies, etc. is laid out in chapter 12 of the sixth book of the *System of Logic* (SL, 943–952). Mill describes the relation between descriptive and normative work as a temporal process: first, art identifies and formulates an end, "and hands it over to the science": "the science receives it, considers it as a phenomenon or effect to be studied, and having investigated its causes and conditions, sends it back to art with a theorem of the combinations of circumstances by which it could be produced" (SL, 944). Art takes this scientific study back and decides whether these combinations and circumstances are in the human power; then it pronounces the end attainable or not. As a consequence of this procedure, an end cannot properly be said to be attainable and turned into practical rules, laws, or policies until "the whole, and not a part merely, of the operation which belongs to science, has been performed" (SL, 945). For practical reasons, we often do set up rules based on "less than this ideally perfect theory," but these rules cannot be fully relied on without constantly referring back to the scientific laws on which they are founded; without our constant readiness to reopen scientific investigations.

The concepts of pleasure and pain are, as I have shown, plainly under development; Alexander Bain's associationist theory of action has not yet fully proven to "make good on its footing," and even more radically, pleasures and pains could turn out to be real kinds, connoting neurophysiological bases of our subjective sensations. Depending on the progress of the moral sciences, we might have reason to redraw the conceptual boundaries of "pleasure" and "pain." This might, Mill happily could have conceded, affect the precise formulation of the principle of utility, but the question of whether we are properly said "to desire everything, and only, that which we find pleasurable," or "to desire pleasurable sensations and agreeable thoughts" doesn't change the fact that we ought to help others to do what they enjoy and to avoid things that hurt them.

4. Conclusion

If in general we cannot spell out the conceptual content of specific linguistic expressions without being explicit about the underlying theory of what kind of a concept we are dealing with, and what it means, in general, to spell out, or clarify, or analyze conceptual content, then much less can we do so in the case of a philosopher who offers all of these background views himself. In this contribution, I have attempted to take a step back from the much-discussed issues of Mill's psychological hedonism and egoism, of his "proof" for the principle of utility and his distinction between "higher" and "lower" pleasures.

Instead I have shown that the concept of pleasure, in its scientifically regimented use, faces appropriateness criteria (criteria that ensure that it's a good, suitable, well-chosen concept) from three sources: (1) within associationist psychology, pleasures are inductively linked, via laws of the mind, to other subjectively experienced mental phenomena; (2) simultaneously, pleasures are reduced to their physiological causes, determining whether they are detachable parts or mere aspects of the pleasurable sensations the general connotative name "pleasures" denotes; and (3) they feature prominently in action explanations (via the idea of pleasure in volition).

The resulting account sees "pleasure" in Mill as a technical term, expressing a concept-under-construction, answering to appropriateness criteria, and thus owing its conceptual content (its connotation) to the above three sources. "Pleasures" are pleasurable sensations; "pleasurable sensation" cannot be defined (semantically analyzed). Instead, "pleasurable sensation" connotes an attribute shared by sensations, thus categorizing sensations into subjectively and phenomenally recognizable classes. Depending on the progress of psychology and potentially the causal explanations by the neurosciences ("physiology"), this attribute could turn out to be either constitutive of pleasures, or merely criterial for identifying a natural kind (Mill: "real" kind). The famous account provided in *Utilitarianism* offers an oversimplification of the moral theory's scientific base (psychology, ethology, action theory) and thus a distortion of the concept of pleasure. However, normative theorizing always ought to take into account the provisional, work-in-progress status of the underlying science, and the connotations of key terms. The moral precepts set up by the principle of utility are thus bound to be changed in the light of inductive progress in associative psychology, ethology, and the neurosciences.

Reflection

PLEASURE EXPERIENCE IN SCHIZOPHRENIA

Ann M. Kring and Amy H. Sanchez

In this Reflection, we consider the role of pleasure in one of
the most severe mental disorders: schizophrenia. We will first
review the symptoms of schizophrenia that impact pleasure
experience and then discuss the contributions of affective
science research that have informed our understanding of
pleasure in schizophrenia. Along the way, we will discuss the
ways in which pleasure is defined and measured in psychology
and neuroscience, and we will discuss the conceptualization
of pleasure in schizophrenia as it relates to motivation and
cognition.

Schizophrenia includes a wide range of symptoms that impact
everything about us that makes us human: the way we think, the
way we feel, and the way we behave. Of relevance to this book
is the symptom anhedonia. Simply defined, "anhedonia" refers
to a lack of pleasure. From a clinical perspective, anhedonia
is typically assessed via an interview with a mental health
professional in which a person with schizophrenia is asked
about pleasure and enjoyment in various life activities such
as socializing, eating, working, and participating in hobbies.
Anhedonia is one of the most common schizophrenia symptoms;

as many as three-quarters of people with schizophrenia experience it.[1]

In our own work, we have adopted the methods, theories, and measures of affective science to better understand anhedonia in schizophrenia. Affective science theory and research is grounded in the notion that emotions, such as pleasure, are more fully captured through comprehensive, multimethod assessment. In our research, we assess emotional responses broadly (i.e., we measure facial expression, reports of experience, brain activity, body responses) when people with and without schizophrenia are engaging with emotionally salient stimuli in our laboratory (e.g., films, pictures, foods, narratives about their own lives) as well as in their daily lives. Some have questioned whether people with schizophrenia can accurately and reliably report on their feelings given that they often have cognitive and language disturbances. However, we (and others) have shown that people with schizophrenia provide reliable and valid reports of their emotional experience, as evidenced by high internal consistency and test-retest reliability of emotion experience reports, even when assessments occur across changes in symptoms and medication status.[2] Furthermore, people with schizophrenia represent their emotion knowledge in the same two-dimensional structure (valence and arousal) as do people without schizophrenia.[3]

One of the most well-replicated affective science findings in schizophrenia is that people with schizophrenia report experiencing similar (or slightly less) amounts of positive emotion

---

1 William P. Horan, Ann M. Kring, and Jack J. Blanchard, "Anhedonia in Schizophrenia: A Review of Assessment Strategies," *Schizophrenia Bulletin* 32.2 (April 2006): 259–273.

2 Ann M. Kring and Kelly S. Earnst, "Stability of Emotional Responding in Schizophrenia," *Behavior Therapy* 30 (1999): 373–388.

3 Ann M. Kring, Lisa Feldman Barrett, and David E. Gard, "On the Broad Applicability of the Affective Circumplex: Representations of Affective Knowledge among Schizophrenia Patients," *Psychological Science* 14.3 (May 2003): 207–214.

compared to those without schizophrenia in the presence of
emotionally evocative stimuli and in daily life,[4] regardless of
changes in medication status.[5]

If as many as three-quarters of people with schizophrenia have
the clinical symptom anhedonia (i.e., lack of pleasure), how can
they report experiencing as much pleasure as people without
schizophrenia when they are presented with pleasant things?
When people with schizophrenia are presented with pleasurable
stimuli either in a research setting or in daily life, they can and
do derive pleasure from these experiences. However, we and
others have shown that people with schizophrenia are less likely
to *anticipate* that future events will be pleasurable, are less likely
to experience pleasure in anticipation of things to come (i.e.,
anticipatory pleasure), and thus may be less likely to seek out
pleasurable experiences.[6] We have argued for the importance
of characterizing the time course of emotion to distinguish
anticipatory from in-the-moment (i.e., *consummatory*) emotion

4 Alex S. Cohen and Kyle S. Minor, "Emotional Experience in Patients with Schizophrenia
Revisited: Meta-analysis of Laboratory Studies," *Schizophrenia Bulletin* 36.1 (January 2008): 143;
Ann M. Kring and Erin K. Moran, "Emotional Response Deficits in Schizophrenia: Insights
from Affective Science," *Schizophrenia Bulletin* 34.5 (September 2008): 819–834; Katiah Llerena,
Gregory P. Strauss, and Alex S. Cohen, "Looking at the Other Side of the Coin: A Meta-analysis
of Self-Reported Emotional Arousal in People with Schizophrenia," *Schizophrenia Research* 142.1–3
(December 2012): 65–70.

David E. Gard, Ann M. Kring, Marja Germans Gard, William P. Horan, and Michael F. Green,
"Anhedonia in Schizophrenia: Distinctions between Anticipatory and Consummatory Pleasure,"
Schizophrenia Research 93.1–3 (July 2007): 253–260; Inez Myin-Germeys, Philippe A. E. G.
Delespaul, and Marten W. DeVries, "Schizophrenia Patients Are More Emotionally Active Than
Is Assumed Based on Their Behaviour," *Schizophrenia Bulletin* 26.4 (2000): 847–854; Margreet
Oorschot, Thomas Kwapil, Philippe Delespaul, and Inez Myin-Germeys, "Momentary Assessment
Research in Psychosis," in "Special Section: Psychopathology in Daily Life: Using Ecological
Momentary Assessment Methods," *Psychological Assessment* 21.4 (December 2009): 498–505;
Margreet Oorschot, Tineke Lataster, Viviane Thewissen, Mariëlle Lardinois, Marieke Wichers, Jim
van Os, Philippe Delespaul, and Inez Myin-Germeys, "Emotional Experience in Negative Symptoms
of Schizophrenia—No Evidence for a Generalized Hedonic Deficit," *Schizophrenia Bulletin* 39.1
(January 2013): 215–220; Amy H. Sanchez, Lindsey M. Lavaysse, Jessica N. Starr, and David E. Gard,
"Daily Life Evidence of Environment-Incongruent Emotion in Schizophrenia," *Psychiatry Research*
220.1–2 (July 28, 2014): 89–95.

5 Kring and Earnst, "Stability of Emotional Responding in Schizophrenia."

6 Gard et al., "Anhedonia in Schizophrenia."

experience.[7] Several behavioral, psychophysiological, and fMRI studies find difficulties among people with schizophrenia in anticipatory pleasure.[8]

Anticipating whether something in the future will be pleasurable requires myriad cognitive skills, including imagination, reflection, drawing upon past experiences, and maintaining an image or emotional state. To illustrate, consider the problem of where to go on vacation. You consider a beach vacation, which may then lead you to call forth a past vacation you took in Hawaii. This prompts you to predict that your vacation will be relaxing and enjoyable, and indeed you experience pleasure now, knowing you will soon be sitting on the beach (anticipatory pleasure). These processes will support your motivational system such that you will make your travel reservations (approach motivation and behavior), and once you take your vacation, you will experience in-the-moment, or consummatory, pleasure. You will savor (maintain) the pleasure from the vacation, and this experience will be encoded into memory. Thus, the next time you need to make a vacation choice, this memory may be called upon to restart the temporal process again.

One way that we have assessed the phenomenological experience of pleasure in anticipation is using a self-report measure of physical/sensory anticipation experience called the

7 Ann M. Kring and Janelle M. Caponigro, "Emotion in Schizophrenia: Where Feeling Meets Thinking," *Current Directions in Psychological Science* 19.4 (August 2010): 255–259; Ann M. Kring and Ori Elis, "Emotion Deficits in People with Schizophrenia," *Annual Review of Clinical Psychology* 9 (2013): 409–433.

8 For instance, G. F. Juckel, M. Schlagenhauf, T. Koslowski, A. Wustenberg, B. Villringer, J. Knutson, J. Wrase, and A. Heinz, "Dysfunction of Ventral Striatal Reward Prediction in Schizophrenia," *Neuroimage* 29.2 (2006): 409–416; Fabien Trémeau, Daniel Antonius, John T. Cacioppo, Rachel Ziwich, Pamela Butler, Dolores Malaspina, and Daniel C. Javitt, "Anticipated, On-line and Remembered Positive Experience in Schizophrenia," *Schizophrenia Research* 122 (2010): 199–205; Jonathan K. Wynn, William P. Horan, Ann M. Kring, Robert F. Simons, and Michael F. Green, "Impaired Anticipatory Event-Related Potentials in Schizophrenia," *International Journal of Psychophysiology* 77.2 (August 2010): 141–149.

Temporal Experience of Pleasure Scale.[9] This measure includes items assessing both anticipatory pleasure experience and in-the-moment (consummatory) pleasure for different physical sensations (e.g., "When I think about eating my favorite food, I can almost taste how good it is"). People with schizophrenia score lower on the anticipatory pleasure scale compared to people without schizophrenia, but they report comparable consummatory pleasure. This pattern has been found among people who are at risk for developing schizophrenia, people who are early in the course of the illness, people who have had the illness for many years, and people with schizophrenia from different countries and cultures. Newer research is examining anticipatory pleasure in social life specifically.

Our work on anticipatory pleasure has brought anhedonia research in schizophrenia squarely into the cognitive realm. Other contemporary approaches to studying anhedonia in schizophrenia draw heavily from neuroscience research,[10] in part because the quest for pharmacological treatments is informed by what we know about the human brain. In particular, the neuroscience of motivation, which includes several processes that are associated with overlapping brain regions and networks, has been used to understand anhedonia in schizophrenia. Motivation processes include a calculation of how much effort is needed to achieve a desired outcome (e.g., a reward), a plan of how to obtain that reward, and a behavioral response to get the reward. In many ways, this approach has shoved the study of anhedonia into a motivational corner, leaving less room for other approaches. Nevertheless, the neuroscience approach has illuminated a number

---

9 David E. Gard, Marja Germans Gard, Anne M. Kring, and O. P. John, "Anticipatory and Consummatory Components of the Experience of Pleasure: A Scale Development Study," *Journal of Research in Personality* 40 (2006): 1086–1102.

10 Ann M. Kring and Deanna M. Barch, "The Motivation and Pleasure Dimension of Negative Symptoms: Neural Substrates and Behavioral Outputs," *European Neuropsychopharmacology* 24.5 (2014): 725–736.

of key findings about anhedonia in schizophrenia. Psychological and neuroscience research shows that people with schizophrenia have difficulties both in computing the value and effort needed to obtain rewarding outcomes and in exerting effort to achieve rewards.[11]

This research has identified brain regions and networks that are not working as efficiently for people with schizophrenia compared to people without schizophrenia,[12] and the hope is that these discoveries will inform the development of next-generation treatments for motivation difficulties in schizophrenia. However, this approach does not fully capture *pleasure experience* in schizophrenia. Indeed, this type of research does not typically assess the phenomenological experience of people with schizophrenia.

Our work on anticipation brings the study of anhedonia into a more traditionally cognitive realm that is nevertheless fully integrated with neuroscience approaches to anhedonia in schizophrenia. Current human neuroscience research on brain networks that support cognition, emotion, and perceiving other people has demonstrated that many of the brain's networks participate in the support of these psychologically diverse processes

---

11 See James M. Gold, Gregory P. Strauss, James A. Waltz, Benjamin M. Robinson, Jamie K. Brown, and Michael J. Frank, "Negative Symptoms of Schizophrenia Are Associated with Abnormal Effort-Cost Computations," *Biological Psychiatry* 74.2 (2013): 130–136; James M. Gold, James A. Waltz, Tatyana M. Matveeva, Zuzana Kasanova, Gregory P. Strauss, Ellen S. Herbener, Anne G. E. Collins, and Michael J. Frank, "Negative Symptoms and the Failure to Represent the Expected Reward Value of Actions: Behavioral and Computational Modeling Evidence," *Archives of General Psychiatry* 69.2 (2012): 129–138; E. A. Heerey, K. R. Bell-Warren, and J. M. Gold, "Decision-Making Impairments in the Context of Intact Reward Sensitivity in Schizophrenia," *Biological Psychiatry* 64.1 (July 2008): 62–69.

Deanna M. Barch, Michael T. Treadway, and Nathan Schoen, "Effort, Anhedonia, and Function in Schizophrenia: Reduced Effort Allocation Predicts Amotivation and Functional Impairment," *Journal of Abnormal Psychology* 123.2 (2014): 387–397; Michael T. Treadway, Joel S. Peterman, David H. Zald, and Sohee Park, "Impaired Effort Allocation in Patients with Schizophrenia," *Schizophrenia Research* 161.2–3 (2015): 382–385.

12 Kring and Barch, "Motivation and Pleasure Dimension of Negative Symptoms."

and functions, rendering the search for psychological process-specific networks nearly obsolete.[13]

In summary, diminished pleasure in schizophrenia is most apparent when it comes to anticipating future events. That is, people with schizophrenia report *expecting* less pleasure from enjoyable activities, and experience less pleasure *when anticipating* future events, than people without schizophrenia. However, when actually doing pleasant activities, people with and without schizophrenia report experiencing the same amount of pleasure. The example of anhedonia in schizophrenia illustrates that pleasure is not a single process. Instead, pleasure emerges from a host of interacting cognitive, affective, and motivational systems, dysfunction in any one of which may lead to problems with pleasure.

---

13 Lisa Feldman Barrett and Ajay Satpute, "Large-Scale Brain Networks in Affective and Social Neuroscience: Toward an Integrative Functional Architecture of the Brain," *Current Opinion in Neurobiology* 23.3 (2013): 361–372.

CHAPTER TEN

A Contemporary Account
of Sensory Pleasure

Murat Aydede

What sort of a difference is the difference between having a taste sensation that I enjoy and having a taste sensation to which I am indifferent or having one that I dislike? Here I use the word "enjoy" in the sense of finding the sensation *pleasant*. Is the difference a phenomenological one—a difference in the way the sensations *feel* to me? Is it therefore a difference that I can normally be introspectively aware of? Or does the difference necessarily involve a difference in (some combination of) my desires, preferences, attitudes, inclinations, dispositions, motivations, or drive states, without necessarily making a phenomenological difference? Or is it a difference consisting of both—phenomenological and attitudinal?

Many thanks to Matt Fulkerson, Dom Lopes, and Lisa Shapiro for their useful comments. Special thanks to Lisa Shapiro for inviting me to participate in this project and the fantastic conference that preceded this book.

The ordinary notion of sensory pleasure takes the difference to be phenomenological: pleasant sensations necessarily *feel* good, unpleasant sensations *feel* bad, others feel neither bad nor good. And this *feeling* good (or, bad) is a conscious difference that is normally open to introspection. Thus, the ordinary conception takes sensory pleasure as a feeling episode. Call any view that takes sensory pleasure to be a feeling a *felt-quality view.*[1]

It is less clear where the ordinary conception stands about the modality of the relationship between sensory pleasure and various conative attitudes. Sure, I normally (perhaps always) want or desire the sensation that I find pleasant, or am inclined to pursue it in some sense. But prima facie it is not clear whether the sensation's pleasantness itself consists in my desiring or wanting the sensation or my being inclined toward it in some way. In fact, common sense seems to take the converse view: I want or desire or am inclined toward the sensation for the reason that it feels pleasant. Why would anybody be tempted to think otherwise, that is, think that what *makes* a sensation a pleasant one is one's conative or evaluative attitudes (desiring, wanting, liking, etc.) toward the sensation? Call any view of this kind an *attitudinal view* of sensory pleasure. Attitudinal views became increasingly more popular in twentieth-century philosophy and continue to gain momentum to this day. Despite commonsense opposition, to understand why, we need to attend to various puzzles that arise when sensory pleasure is thought of as a felt-quality of our sensory experiences.

In what follows, I will present some of these puzzles, clarify the explanatory target, and develop a positive account of sensory pleasure (sensory affect, in general, positive or negative) that will combine elements from felt-quality and attitudinal views but will be markedly different from them. It will also solve the puzzles in a way that will

---

1 I will follow F. Feldman, "Hedonism," in *The Encyclopedia of Ethics*, ed. L. C. Becker and C. B. Becker (New York: Routledge, 2001), 662–669, as well as others for the terminology in what follows.

remain faithful to the phenomenology and the ordinary and intuitive understanding of sensory pleasure. It is in fact three proposals—each proposal pitching the account of sensory pleasure at a different level. Thus, the account to be proposed may be called, depending on the level, an adverbialist, a functionalist, or an experiential-desire account. The adverbialist proposal offers a model or framework for a proper conceptualization of the complexity and structure of the qualitative phenomenology of affective or sensory experiences. The functionalist proposal then offers an account about the metaphysical realization of this phenomenology. When these two levels are considered simultaneously, another descriptive level between the two becomes intuitively compelling: this is the view according to which a pleasant sensation is an *experiential* desire and belief directed at the same worldly stimulus.

I. PUZZLES
Heterogeneity

Suppose that the ordinary understanding of sensory pleasure as a feeling episode is correct: sensory pleasure is a kind of feeling in the broad sense in which any phenomenal element in one's experience is a feeling—it is a phenomenological occurrence generally accessible to one's introspection. So the ordinary framework is realist about the phenomenology of sensory pleasure. This entails that there is some common phenomenology to all sensory pleasures. But right herein seems to lie one of the puzzles about sensory pleasure. The moment we start asking what this common element is—common to all pleasant sensations in all their rich variations and differences—we seem to draw a blank. If there is a common phenomenological element to all pleasant sensations, it seems elusive. All we can say seems something like: all pleasant sensations *feel* good.

Think of some examples: the sensations I have when I taste or smell a fresh ripe strawberry, a Castelvetrano olive, a freshly cut Meyer lemon, a piece of Lindt blackcurrant dark chocolate, or when I feel a chilled

peach or a golf ball on my fingers, the gentle kiss of my lover on my
lips, or when I hear the laughter of my son or the opening of Albinoni's
Adagio, or when I see the turquoise waters of Bodrum Bay, and many
others as diverse as these—I like them all. I find them pleasant. Yes,
they all feel good, but I am at a loss when I reflect on what phenomenological element is supposed to be common to them all. What felt-
quality unites them as pleasant? If there is one I can't seem to locate it
in introspection.

In the literature, this difficulty is known as the "heterogeneity
problem." This is not only a puzzle for the ordinary understanding of
sensory pleasure but also a philosophical problem in its own right for
all *felt-quality views* of sensory pleasure. These are views that endorse
the ordinary understanding and claim that sensory pleasure is a kind
of felt phenomenal quality common to all pleasant sensations. There
are basically two discernable variants of felt-quality views in the literature:[2] those who take sensory pleasure to be (1) a *distinctive feeling*,[3]
or (2) a *hedonic tone*.[4] The former variant is not very popular; the latter
has quite a few adherents. The felt-quality views, building on the ordinary understanding, insist that the pleasantness of sensations has

2 See Feldman, "Hedonism," for the terminology and very helpful discussion of the relevant
categorizations.

3 Early G. E. Moore, *Principia Ethica*, ed. T. Baldwin (Cambridge: Cambridge University Press,
[1903] 1993), 12, is probably the most explicit statement of the view. But also see David Brink, *Moral
Realism and the Foundations of Ethics* (Cambridge: Cambridge University Press, 1989), 221: "the one
and only intrinsic good is pleasure, which is understood as a simple, qualitative mental state." A more
recent defense is B. Bramble, "The Distinctive Feeling Theory of Pleasure," *Philosophical Studies* 162
(2011): 201–217: "for an experience to be pleasant (or unpleasant) is just for it to involve or contain
a distinctive kind of feeling, one we might call 'the feeling of pleasure itself,' or simply 'the pleasant
feeling' (or, in the case of unpleasant experiences, 'the unpleasant feeling')." See also T. L. S. Sprigge,
"Is the Esse of Intrinsic Value Percipi? Pleasure, Pain and Value." *Royal Institute of Philosophy*, supp.
vol. 47 (2000): 119–140.

4 See, among others, C. D. Broad, *Five Types of Ethical Theory* (London: Routledge and Kegan Paul,
1930); K. Duncker, "On Pleasure, Emotion, and Striving," *Philosophy and Phenomenological Research* 1
(1941): 391–430; S. Kagan, "The Limits of Well-Being," *Social Philosophy and Policy* 9 (1992): 169–189;
R. Crisp, *Reasons and the Good* (Oxford: Oxford University Press, 2006); A. Smuts, "The Feels Good
Theory of Pleasure," *Philosophical Studies* 155 (2011): 241–265; and I. Labukt, "Hedonic Tone and the
Heterogeneity of Pleasure," *Utilitas* 24 (2012): 172–199.

a phenomenological reality that has a detectable occurrence in our sensory experiences. Very roughly, the distinctive feeling views take this reality to be a phenomenologically uniform occurrence across all pleasant experiences, whereas the hedonic tone views allow for variations in the phenomenological character of this occurrence without losing its type-identity. Although the hedonic tone views are meant to be more nuanced and subtle in this regard, they are somewhat more difficult to grasp, since it is not clear how to understand this variable but somewhat identifiable phenomenal character (hedonic tone). I will get back to this below and offer a framework in which we can make better sense of the notion of hedonic tone.

Motivation and Intrinsic Value

It is also part of the intuitive ordinary understanding that pleasant sensations are inherently motivating and in some sense noninstrumentally (≈ intrinsically) good—and surely these two features are intimately related. Puzzles arise, however, when we try to understand how all this could be so. If pleasantness is a kind of feeling somehow modifying a sensation, it is somewhat mysterious that it can be the kind of thing that can inherently motivate or be intrinsically good. We know *that* pleasantness is motivating and good, but we don't know *how* it could be so if it is just a kind of feeling that somehow "attaches" to sensations.

There are several related but distinct puzzles here that we need to expose. First, start with motivation. Pleasant sensations are inherently motivating. *Inherently*, because it seems that, in order for them to motivate, the experiencer need not have any further motivating beliefs and desires. It appears that a pleasant sensation all by itself can motivate. It seems mysterious how a mere feeling can have such a power.

Second, *what* is it that pleasant sensations are said to inherently motivate? It is notoriously difficult to answer this question in an abstract and completely general way. Intuitively, we would like to say something like: they (defeasibly)[5] motivate behavior *intended* to do whatever it is that would sustain undergoing the sensation as long as it remains pleasant.[6] This would make the pleasant *sensation* (a mental state) the target of intention—thus, the target of the end state that the behavior is aimed to bring about. But this is problematic. Motivated behavior is not merely caused behavior. Motivation is intentional, and so is motivated behavior—it is behavior performed with an end *in mind* (however simple or complex, frivolous or serious, misguided or smart this may be). That is why understanding the motivations of an agent behaving in a certain way can make the agent's behavior *intelligible* by identifying the *reasons* for which the agent behaves the way she does. These reasons may be good or bad, justified or unjustified, based on correct or incorrect information or reasoning. But they will make us understand *why* the agent does what she does. On one way of looking at the target of motivation, this seems to require that the agent be capable of perceiving or thinking of (in general, being in an intentional state *about*) the object or state of affairs that she aims for. The end state for which the agent is motivated needs to be thought of by the agent in some way or other. So, even if we put aside our own conception of our motivations, there are animals and young children who obviously can experience pleasant sensations and be motivated by them without having the capability of even thinking of their own sensations—let alone forming *intentions about them*. So, sensation-directed intentional behavior cannot always be what pleasant sensations motivate for *all* who are capable of experiencing pleasant sensations.

Perhaps it is more plausible to say that the behavior is intended to "consume" whatever object or physical feature of the object that

---

5 The kind of motivation under discussion is always *defeasible* motivation, in the sense that it can always be *overridden* with other stronger motivating factors. So I will leave this aside.

6 A parallel claim can be made for unpleasant sensations such as pain: they (defeasibly) motivate behavior intended to do whatever it is that would stop undergoing the sensation as long as it is unpleasant. As said, although the focus is on sensory pleasure, the discussion and analysis can be extended to all sensory affect, positive and negative.

happens to be the causal source of one's pleasant sensation. This would make the "consummatory" behavior itself (e.g., the act of eating, smelling, feeling, hearing, etc., or their proper objects) the target of intention and the end state aimed at. Unlike that in the former proposal, this is behavior that is extra-mentally directed—roughly, world-directed. It doesn't require the capability of forming intentions about one's sensations, or one's mental states in general.

But is it really more plausible to say that what gets motivated by pleasant sensations is *always* and *exclusively* the consummatory behavior—world-directed behavior? This may be true for animals and most young children (and perhaps even for most of us most of the time) but doesn't seem to generalize easily to all cases. When I take a bite from this piece of watermelon, my primary reason may be that I feel hungry (and thus may be aware that a bodily need is to be satisfied). But if you ask me why I took a bite from the watermelon rather than this piece of pineapple, all else being equal, the answer would have to change to something like "because I like watermelon better than pineapple." This may just be another way of saying "the taste of watermelon is more pleasant to me than the taste of pineapple" where "taste" refers to the taste sensation. And this may be the end of the matter in the sense that there may be no further end to which my having this pleasant sensation (as opposed to that one) is a means. This brings us to sensory pleasure itself being an intrinsic good in the sense that it may be *an* end in itself, something that is not only desired but *desirable* noninstrumentally. Furthermore, the sensation by being pleasant seems generally manifest to me as intrinsically desirable—even if it may *also* be desirable instrumentally.[7] As such, it will motivate me to sustain the sensation qua pleasant. This is sensation-directed behavior, not merely world-directed behavior.

---

7 Again, all else being equal. Most of the time all else may not be equal. Remember, we are operating under the assumption that all such desires are defeasible. I. Goldstein, "Why People Prefer Pleasure to Pain," *Philosophy* 55 (1980): 349–362, argues that desiring pleasure over pain is a matter of rationally grasping what is evident. I agree with him on this point.

Thus, sensory pleasure is Janus-faced: it has a motivational face looking both outward and inward. A pleasant sensation of an object motivates both object-directed behavior and sensation-directed behavior. It does the former because sensations themselves are outward looking—they are sensations *of* worldly (extra-mental) objects or events, and are normally diaphanous to their owners, and are generally caused or sustained by the owners' worldly behavior. It does the latter because on reflection we can grasp the intrinsic goodness of sensory pleasure—that is, we can *aim* or *intend* to have pleasant sensations as ends in themselves and act accordingly. This requires that we be able to have thoughts and desires about our own sensations and their pleasantness. It turns out that it is practically impossible to act to bring about sensory pleasure without bringing about the sensation, and impossible to bring about the sensation without engaging in the relevant consummatory behavior. If you think about it, this arrangement is a brilliant design feature of our affective/perceptual systems.

But it is puzzling how pleasantness as a kind of feeling that "attaches" to sensations can do all of this. Take the sensation produced upon feeling a peach with your fingers. To most, this is a sensation that is neither pleasant nor unpleasant—it is affectively neutral. But to a few, it is an intensely unpleasant feeling—and reliably so. To some, it is a pleasant feeling—I, for one, like feeling the velvety texture of peaches. So we have a tactile feeling indicating a certain kind of texture of a surface that seems, at the core, affectively neutral. What do we need to add to this feeling (sensation) to turn it into a pleasant or unpleasant one understood as inherently motivating and intrinsically good/bad? Another kind of feeling? Saying yes is puzzling, saying no is puzzling. We draw a blank but we want to understand.

Opposite Valences

A third puzzle is about how feelings can have opposites. A sensation can be pleasant or unpleasant. The ordinary understanding of sensory pleasure conceives of pleasantness and unpleasantness as kinds of feeling modifying otherwise affectively neutral sensations to different degrees. This seems to imply that feelings can be opposites in whatever sense the pleasantness and unpleasantness are opposites. But how mere feelings could have opposites seems mysterious.

2. CONTEMPORARY ACCOUNTS

There are other puzzles about sensory pleasure, but the above should do for the moment to motivate a search for an account better equipped to deal with these puzzles, which seem to spring from understanding sensory pleasure as a felt-quality of sensory experiences. This is why the main competitor to the felt-quality views has been the increasingly more popular attitudinal views, which treat sensory affect as a kind of proattitude toward a given sensation said to be pleasant. The nature of this attitude varies from philosopher to philosopher, but the main theme has been that this is a *conative* or *evaluative* proattitude, such as wanting, desiring, liking, etc.[8] Here is a recent statement of one of the best worked-out accounts of this kind of view given by Heathwood:

---

8 Here the list is long. H. Sidgwick, *The Methods of Ethics*, 7th ed. (New York: Macmillan, [1907] 1981), may have started things going, but things are complicated—he used "desirable" rather than "desired." See, among others, W. Alston, "Pleasure," in *The Encyclopedia of Philosophy*, ed. P. Edwards (New York: Collier-Macmillan, 1968): 244–250; W. A. Davis, "Pleasure and Happiness," *Philosophical Studies* 39 (1981): 305–317, and "A Causal Theory of Enjoyment," *Mind* 91 (1982): 240–256; R. Brandt, *A Theory of the Good and the Right* (Oxford: Clarendon Press, 1979); F. Feldman, "On the Intrinsic Value of Pleasures," *Ethics* 107 (1997): 448–466, and *Pleasure and the Good Life* (New York: Oxford University Press, 2004); C. Heathwood, "The Reduction of Sensory Pleasure to Desire," *Philosophical Studies* 133 (2007): 23–44, among others, for defenses of attitudinal theories. D. Parfit, *On What Matters*, vol. 1 (Oxford: Oxford University Press, 2011), and M. Brady, "Pain and the Euthyphro Dilemma," paper presented at the Pain Conference, University of Glasgow, June 18–20, 2013, develop the attitudinal theory in terms of liking (or disliking) a sensation, where this hedonic attitude is taken to be different from desiring in that it is not meant to be responsive to reasons (see M. Aydede, "How to Unify Theories of Sensory Pleasure: An Adverbialist Proposal," *Review of Philosophy and Psychology* 5 [2014]: 119–133, for a critical evaluation). W. S. Robinson, "What Is It Like to Like?," *Philosophical Psychology* 19 (2006): 743–765, gives an account of sensory pleasure that is hard to classify but seems closer to the attitudinal theories, as he takes the pleasantness to essentially involve intentional and evaluative directedness toward sensations. See also D. M. Armstrong, *Bodily Sensations* (London: Routledge and Kegan Paul, 1962); G. Pitcher, "Pain Perception," *Philosophical Review* 79 (1970): 368–393; M. Tye, *Ten Problems of Consciousness: A Representational Theory of the Phenomenal*

(DESIRE-THEORY)

a sensation S, occurring at time t, is a sensory pleasure at t if, and only if, the subject of S desires, intrinsically and *de re*, at t, of S, that it be occurring at t.[9]

Attitudinal theories are developed, more or less, as reactions to the difficulties and puzzles inherent in the ordinary understanding of sensory pleasure and the felt-quality views that attempt to turn this framework into a more systematic account of sensory pleasure. Indeed, the heterogeneity worry is explicit in most attitudinal theorists. For instance, Heathwood writes: "the phenomenology just doesn't bear it out—there doesn't seem to be any one feeling (or even 'hedonic tone') common to all occasions on which we experience pleasure or enjoyment."[10]

If anything like the desire-theory is true, we can see how the puzzles raised above can be resolved. The heterogeneity problem presumably is no longer a problem since what unites all the qualitatively different pleasant sensations is not the presence of a unique kind of mental quality or feeling, which has proved to be elusive, but is rather a conative attitude toward those sensations: they are all desired in the way specified.

The second puzzle about motivation and intrinsic value can be resolved too. It is generally the accepted view among philosophers that an explanation of motivation in terms of desires (or similar conative states) is not problematic. In fact, this view is so prevalent that it may be the factor responsible for the generation of the puzzle in the first place: how to make sense of the motivational power of a mental state in the absence of any sort of desire, or a desire-like conative state, somewhere in the vicinity? A mere feeling seems powerless to move.

Mind (Cambridge: MIT Press, 1995); R. Hall, "Are Pains Necessarily Unpleasant?," *Philosophy and Phenomenological Research* 49 (1989): 643–659; and G. Kahane, "Pain, Dislike and Experience," *Utilitas* 21 (2009): 327–336, for proposals that can be categorized as attitudinal.

9 Heathwood, "Reduction of Sensory Pleasure," 32.

10 Heathwood, "Reduction of Sensory Pleasure," 26.

According to the desire-theory, pleasant sensations are *inherently* motivating because they are made up of desires: at bottom, a pleasant sensation is a desired sensation. So a pleasant sensation doesn't need any further beliefs and desires to motivate—it is motivating all by itself.

Moreover, pleasant sensations motivate *sensation-directed* behavior— behavior gauged to sustain the sensation as its ultimate aim. But, as I have shown, practically this requires outward "consummatory" behavior directed to sustain the physical stimulus causing the sensation. So, according to the desire-theory, pleasant sensations are both sensation-directed and world-directed in their motivational structure.

As to why pleasant sensations are intrinsically good and desirable: that is because they are satisfied desires—desiring of a sensation that is simultaneously satisfied by the presence of the very same sensation.[11] This relies on the strong intuition that, all else being equal, satisfaction of a desire is noninstrumentally good for the agent. Properly understood, very few people would reject this intuition.

The third puzzle is also easily solved. A sensation can be pleasant or unpleasant. The oppositeness is simply a reflection of different attitudes. This can be handled in either of two ways by saying that an unpleasant sensation is one that is *not* desired (unwanted, disliked, etc.) or by saying that its *cessation* is desired (wanted, liked, etc.). Either way, there doesn't seem to be a deep mystery here.

But the attitudinal theories have their own problems. Here I don't have space to discuss them in any detail except to briefly touch upon a few intuitively graspable difficulties.[12] Attitudinal theory is irrealist about the phenomenology of sensory pleasure. It denies the existence of any phenomenological element common to all pleasant sensations.

---

11 See, for instance, C. Heathwood, "Desire Satisfactionism and Hedonism," *Philosophical Studies* 128 (2006): 539–563, and "Desire-Based Theories of Reasons, Pleasure, and Welfare," *Oxford Studies in Metaethics* 6 (2011): 79–106.

12 See Aydede, "How to Unify," for a more extensive criticism.

Instead it proposes that what is common is a mental attitude: they are all desired in a certain manner. For this to be a successful response to the heterogeneity problem, the desiring (or, whatever attitude is proposed) needs to contribute no phenomenology to sensations that are said to be pleasant, so that there is no phenomenological difference among an affectively neutral sensation, an unpleasant sensation, and a pleasant sensation, even when the phenomenology of the sensation is kept the same. For instance, the difference between a smell sensation that you find very pleasant on a given occasion and the same sensation you find unpleasant on another occasion is not a difference you can discern by relying on how the two *feel*. The attitudinal theorist can certainly grant that we are unreflectively prepared to say that the former feels good and the latter bad. But the theorist needs to insist that this is shorthand for some way of differentiating between the two that is not based on how the two experiences *feel*. This is counterintuitive and implausible, especially in the absence of a credible answer, on the part of the attitudinal theorist, to the question "how else is one to tell them apart?"

There is also the much discussed "Euthyphro problem" for attitudinal theories. Focusing on the desire-theory, we can pose the problem by asking a question: If a sensation is pleasant for a subject and the subject desires it (intrinsically, contemporaneously, de re, etc.), is the sensation pleasant because the subject desires it, or does the subject desire the sensation because it is pleasant? The desire-theorist is committed to an affirmative answer to the former question.[13] The "because" here need not be interpreted as *merely* asking a causal question (asking for causal explanation), but rather as inquiring into the *reasons* why the experiencer desires the sensation that she does. The difficulty here is that we would like to say intuitively that one desires a sensation for the reason that the sensation is pleasant. But the desire-theorist, by taking the converse route, is precluded from saying that one desires a

---

13   As readily acknowledged by Heathwood himself in "Reduction of Sensory Pleasure," 38–40.

sensation for that reason. In fact, the desire-theorist seems stuck with the fact that she cannot say that the sensation is desired for any reason at all. For suppose it is said that a sensation is desired for a reason other than just having the sensation itself. This would make the desire instrumental. Hence, the attitudinal theories cannot explain why one desires a sensation on the occasion that the sensation is pleasant. This doesn't of course preclude the desire-theorist from saying that pleasant sensations provide good reasons for desiring them. This just means that desired sensations provide good reasons for us to desire them—that is, to desire the desired sensations. This makes sense only if we are using the term "desire" differently in its two occurrences.

Attitudinal theories of sensory pleasure have other problems. They were meant to advance our understanding of what sensory pleasures are and go beyond what felt-quality views can offer. In my opinion, they don't do that. In fact, they make things even worse by first denying that sensory pleasure is a matter of phenomenology and then offering an account that requires sensations to be the intentional target of a proattitude for no reason at all just to turn them into pleasant ones.

Attitudinal and felt-quality views have been the most popular and dominant attempts to give philosophical accounts of sensory pleasure in the last one hundred years or so. Various core elements of these views appeared earlier in the history of philosophy, of course.[14] But surprisingly there hasn't been any other sustained attempt in recent years. In particular, philosophy of mind doesn't have much to offer about sensory pleasure. Recent years have seen a lively debate and a plethora of theories on pain and in particular on the affective aspect of pains.[15] But apart from some brief remarks here and there, no systematic attempt

---

14 See Dominique Kuenzle, chapter 9 here, for the intellectual background of these views. Lisa Shapiro, chapter 6 here, and Melissa Frankel, chapter 7 here, demonstrate the seeds of adverbial accounts of sensory (and so pleasure) perception, as part of more complex accounts, in the early modern period.

15 See, for instance, B. Cutter and M. Tye, "Tracking Representationalism and the Painfulness of Pain," *Philosophical Issues* 21 (2011): 90–109; M. Martínez, "Imperative Content and the Painfulness of Pain," *Phenomenology and the Cognitive Sciences* 10 (2011): 67–90; B. O'Sullivan

has been made to address the nature of sensory pleasure and the puzzles it gives rise to.[16]

What follows is, as advertised, a three-level proposal that will combine elements from felt-quality and attitudinal views, and will solve the puzzles in a way that will remain faithful to the phenomenology and the intuitive understanding of sensory pleasure.

3. A Three-Level Account of Sensory Pleasure

One of the interesting things about the debate between the defenders of felt-quality and attitudinal views is that both camps claim that introspective evidence favors their side. It is notoriously difficult to settle a debate of this sort. On the one hand, following common sense, we would like to say that sensory pleasure is a kind of *feeling*. But feelings are paradigmatic phenomenal episodes: they are conscious phenomenological occurrences. On the other hand, when we try to introspectively spot a phenomenological commonality to all the different

---

and R. Schroer, "Painful Reasons: Representationalism as a Theory of Pain," *Philosophical Quarterly* 62 (2012): 737–758; D. Bain, "What Makes Pains Unpleasant?," *Philosophical Studies* 166 (2013): 60–89; C. Klein, "What Pain Asymbolia Really Shows," *Mind* 124 (2015): 493–516; and M. Aydede and M. Fulkerson, "Reasons and Theories of Sensory Affect," in *The Philosophy of Pain: Unpleasantness, Emotion, and Deviance*, ed. David Bain, Michael Brady, and Jennifer Corns (forthcoming).

16 Subsequent to Ryle's attack on mental episodes as inner causes of behavior and his attack on pleasure as an inner feeling episode, the 1950's through mid-1970s experienced a lively debate about whether pleasure was more dispositional than episodic as Ryle claimed. This debate in some ways parallels the worries that split the felt-quality and attitudinal theorists. See M. Aydede, "An Analysis of Pleasure vis-à-vis Pain," *Philosophy and Phenomenological Research* 61 (2000): 537–570, for a critical survey of this debate. See also D. Wolfsdorf, *Pleasure in Ancient Greek Philosophy* (Cambridge: Cambridge University Press, 2013), chapter 9, which contains a very helpful critical survey of this debate and related others. The work of Tim Schroeder, "Pleasure, Displeasure, and Representation," *Canadian Journal of Philosophy* 31 (2001): 507–530, and *Three Faces of Desire* (Oxford: Oxford University Press, 2004), is an exception to the claim I make in the main text above: although his work tends to focus on desire, he has developed a scientifically informed account of pleasure that is generally friendly to the view I present below. See also Leonard D. Katz, "Hedonism as Metaphysics and Value" (Ph.D. diss., Princeton University, 1986), and "Pleasure," in *The Stanford Encyclopedia of Philosophy* (Spring 2014 edition), ed. Edward N. Zalta, last modified 2006, http://plato.stanford.edu/archives/spr2014/entries/pleasure/, whose views, to the extent I can pin them down, are congenial.

kinds of pleasant sensations, we seem to come up empty-handed. What to do?

Adverbialism

Most hedonic tone versions of the felt-quality views have been developed with this problem in mind—the heterogeneity of pleasant sensations that still *feel* good. Although there seems to be serious confusion about how exactly to interpret these theories, the intention has always been that the affective tone of an experience isn't like the phenomenology of sensory qualities (qualia, sensations) but is to be understood rather like sensory qualities "affectively toned"—the intuition being that this affective tone is a higher-order property (or a dimension) of first-order sensory qualities of experiences (or, a property of their instantiation). Thus affect has been thought by the hedonic tone theorists to have a peculiar phenomenology somehow piggybacking on the ground-level phenomenology of the sensory qualities. But hedonic tone is a phenomenological occurrence, and in this sense, a feeling. How to make sense of this sort of intuition? How should we conceptualize the phenomenological structure of pleasant sensations? My first proposal is: *adverbially*.

We need to distinguish the phenomenology of sensations from the phenomenology of pleasantness that modifies or qualifies these sensations. Sensations are, in the narrow sense in which I have been using the word, the fundamental qualities of our perceptual experiences that register a range of complex physical features or magnitudes of objects that we encounter when we sense our environment. Psychophysics has been in the business of cataloging what these features/magnitudes are and what the corresponding sensory qualities are that register them. It turns out that the sensations proper to each sensory modality have a rich and complex systematicity to them that we can represent as multidimensional *quality spaces*. The best known example of this is the three-dimensional color solid consisting of brightness, hue, and saturation.

Every shade of any humanly visible color quality is a point in this space. The quality space or spaces of other sensory modalities are not as well known or understood—partly because the number of dimensions involved is controversial and they are very difficult to study empirically.[17] But progress is being made, and there is not much controversy about the existence of these quality spaces for most sensory modalities.

Can affect be added as a separate dimension to any given quality space that characterizes a given sensory modality? The answer is yes and no. No, because pleasantness of a given sensation as a phenomenological occurrence doesn't register an objective feature or magnitude of the stimulus in the way the sensation itself does (in our narrow sense)—a given sensation can be pleasant or unpleasant or affectively neutral without this variation necessarily corresponding to any physical variation in the stimulus. But also, yes, in a way, because affect is a *way* a stimulus is presented to us in sensing it: whatever sensations we may be undergoing registering physical features of a stimulus, these sensations occur modified with affect, thus presenting the stimulus of the sensation under an "affective light." Thus the instantiation of sensory qualities is modified in an affective dimension registering the reaction of the subject to the perceived object (to the stimulus or the physical features of this stimulus). I want to model this structure by saying that affect (pleasantness) is an *adverbial* modification of the instantiation of sensations. An analogy may be helpful here: think of dancing (≈ perceptual experience) different dances (tango, waltz, swing, etc. ≈ different sensory qualities, sensations) fast, moderately, or slowly (≈ affective modification of sensory qualities as pleasant, neutral, unpleasant, etc.). Similarly, when I find the taste of the watermelon pleasant, I am undergoing a taste sensation registering certain

---

17 See A. Clark, *Sensory Qualities* (Oxford: Oxford University Press, 1996) for an overview of psychophysical studies of quality spaces of various sensory modalities and the practical difficulties involved in conducting the experiments (multidimensional scaling experiments) required to map out these spaces. I should add, however, that I don't need the assumption of quality spaces for the main account I develop in this chapter.

physical features of the piece in my mouth, but at the same time the sensation is being affectively or hedonically "toned," making the object of the sensation (this piece of watermelon in my mouth) affectively, thus motivationally, salient to me. This toning is the affective adverbial modification of the relevant sensory qualities.

Ryle was onto something when he said, in a similar context discussing pleasure, "the enjoyment of a walk is not a concomitant, e.g., an introspectable effect of the walking, such that there might be two histories, one the history of the walk, the other the history of its agreeableness to the walker."[18] My proposal is, in a certain sense, to internalize Ryle's behavioral adverbialism, making it a matter of *how* the sensory qualities with their different and heterogeneous phenomenology are instantiated in conscious experience. This is the affective dimension of experiences with a continuum ranging from positive, passing through neutral, to negative hedonic tone.[19] Likewise, in my story, there are no two separate histories because there are no two separate phenomenological existences. The realization of one is the adverbial realization of the other.

This model explains why, when we try to "isolate" a quality or a feeling peculiar to sensory pleasure, we always seem to end up with the sensory qualities themselves directing our attention to the external objects whose sensible properties they present. In fact, that's why we *also* attribute affective qualities (like pleasantness or unpleasantness) to the (physical) *objects* of experiences.[20] Try to isolate the fastness of a fast waltz or a fast tango; you can't do it without paying close

---

18 Ryle, "Pleasure," *Proceedings of the Aristotelian Society*, supp., 28 (1954): 138.

19 So there are no affectless sensory experiences. But some sensory experiences are affectively neutral—they have a neutral affect, so to speak. Think of affective dimension as always present and as having a continuous scale with a neutral value somewhere in between the positive and negative ends. The implementation of this hedonic bivalent scale may use different neural structures.

20 In M. Aydede and M. Fulkerson, "Affective Qualities," presentation at the annual meeting of the Pacific Division of the American Philosophical Association, San Francisco, April 2013, Matt Fulkerson and I argue for a largely Lockean dispositional account of affective qualities as qualifying the worldly objects of our affective experiences.

attention to the waltz or the tango itself. Nevertheless, the "fastness" or "slowness" common to the different token dances can be discerned. In fact, some dance types can themselves be classified as fast or slow— these might perhaps correspond to relatively hard-wired affective responses to certain kinds of sensations (e.g., sweet tastes). Just as the fastness or slowness of dances can be recognized across different types of dances, the pleasantness or unpleasantness common to various otherwise quite different sensations is detectable, indeed introspectively available.[21]

The alleged difficulty of spotting a phenomenological quality common to all pleasant sensations is due to a faulty model of what it is to introspect phenomenological elements of experiences and what it is to be such a phenomenological element. The critics of hedonic tone theories have in mind the phenomenology of sensations (in my narrow sense) and they don't pay much attention to how the hedonic tone theorists want to explain the peculiarities of affective phenomenology. The adverbialist model offers a better framework for understanding affective phenomenology in line with hedonic tone views. Just as the tempo of various dances can be discerned as, say, fast, the pleasantness of various quite different sensations can be introspectively discerned as a higher-order affective dimension ("hedonic tone") of the sensation, but at the same time, what is being discerned is clearly a phenomenal element of our sensory experiences: it is a modification of *sensations*—it is a *way* sensations are instantiated in experiential consciousness. Thus, the adverbialist model of how to understand the phenomenological structure of sensory pleasure respects both intuitions mentioned at the beginning of this section. It thus resolves the puzzle of how sensory pleasure can be a kind of common feeling for which the heterogeneity of sensory phenomenology is not a problem.

---

21 The analogy with dancing is only just that, of course—an analogy, intended to help understand how we can conceive of hedonic tone as adverbial/affective modification of sensory qualities. But it shows that there is nothing mysterious about the peculiar phenomenology of sensory affect—or at least, there needn't be any.

But what does the adverbial modification of a sensation consist of, metaphysically speaking? What are the naturalistic underpinnings of this adverbialist model?

Psychofunctionalism

There is a prima facie plausibility to attitudinal views of sensory pleasure: in undergoing a pleasant sensation we are in a state that seems to have a certain kind of motivational tug or pull. We experience this pull as a kind of motivational bias, or even a premotoric oomph—some kind of felt urge. In short, some kind of desire-like state is involved somewhere in feeling a pleasant sensation. I have argued elsewhere that the ordinary intuitive notion of desire, or indeed, of any proattitude like wanting or liking, isn't up to capturing this, especially when directed toward the sensation involved.[22] The notion the attitudinal theorists seek is, intuitively, a *functional role* notion,[23] only partially and superficially capturable in terms of ordinary conative or evaluative notions. Let's introduce the term "p-desire" to denote the state type with the psychofunctional role of processing the incoming sensory information in whatever ways that realize the pleasantness of sensations.[24] What would this involve? Answering this question isn't an armchair affair, but a quick look at affective neuroscience suggests

22 See Aydede, "How to Unify Theories of Sensory Pleasure: An Adverbialist Proposal." *Review of Philosophy and Psychology* 5 (2014): 119–133.

23 Actually, a *psychofunctional* role notion—see below. See N. Block, "Troubles with Functionalism," in *Readings in Philosophy of Psychology*, vol. 1, ed. Ned Block (Cambridge, MA: Harvard University Press, 1980), 268–305, for the distinction between functionalism and psychofunctionalism.

24 See Aydede, "Pleasure vis-à-vis Pain," where p-desiring was called "desiring*." For a similar treatment of pain affect, see A. Clark, "Painfulness Is Not a Quale," in *Pain: New Essays on Its Nature and the Methodology of Its Study*, ed. M. Aydede (Cambridge, MA: MIT Press, 2005), 177–198. The framework to be presented below was, in outline form, part of an essay cowritten with Matt Fulkerson that was presented at the annual meetings of the Pacific Division of the American Philosophical Association in San Francisco, 2013, and in San Diego, 2014. We plan to continue collaborating on this topic. For a critical survey of theories of affect (pain affect, in particular) developed in contemporary philosophy of mind, see our forthcoming joint work, and for a sustained criticism of strong representationalism about sensory affect (about pain), see M. Aydede and M. Fulkerson, "Affect: Representationalists' Headache," *Philosophical Studies* 170 (2014): 175–198.

that this role consists of a complex processing of incoming sensory information that, among other things,[25]

- Sets interruptible motivational parameters (motivational biasing—"more-of-this" or "less-of-this" or "stop-this" incoming stimulus)
- Prepares the effector or psychomotor systems of the organism, providing action-preparedness (motor biasing)
- Provides appraisals of the incoming sensory information for its significance for the organism and for its potential for enhancing its behavioral repertoire (epistemic biasing)
- Influences action preferences on the basis of the sensory stimuli's informational content for present and future behavior through associative or cognitive learning, habituation, incentive sensitization, etc.
- Provides steady earmarked input to more centralized concept-wielding cognitive, conative, and decision-theoretic systems.

We can think of p-desiring as a complex modification (filtering, enhancing, biasing, amplifying, consolidating, etc.) of the incoming sensory information that will causally influence, in the above ways, the subject's motivational, cognitive, and behavioral priorities in such a way that makes some of this available to the subject's conscious thoughts and conative attitudes. This may result, when appropriate or needed, in the subject's *judging* that she likes the taste or that she finds the taste pleasant, where judging is a conceptual affair epistemically based on her pleasant sensation, that is, on her affectively modified perceptual experience.

---

25 See, among others, K. Berridge, "Motivation Concepts in Behavioral Neuroscience," *Physiology and Behavior* 81 (2004): 179–209; E. T. Rolls, *Emotion and Decision-Making Explained* (Oxford: Oxford University Press, 2014); J. Panksepp and L. Biven, *The Archeology of Mind* (New York: Norton, 2012). For a bit more discussion of the relevance of scientific work to philosophical theorizing about sensory affect, see Aydede, "Pain and Pleasure" in *Routledge Handbook of Emotion Theory*, ed. A. Scarantino (New York: Routledge, forthcoming).

P-desiring is for now largely a placeholder for whatever the scientific research will eventually reveal about the nature of this psychofunctional role. The claim here is that the metaphysics of sensory affect consists in a certain kind of causal processing or modification of incoming sensory information. P-desiring incoming sensory information is mostly a subpersonal process revealed in consciousness as a pleasant or unpleasant sensation. But its functional nature is not altogether hidden at the personal level. As I have said, this is what makes attitudinal theories prima facie plausible. The pleasantness of the taste of a piece of watermelon consists literally in my being motivationally (motorically, epistemically, etc.) *biased* toward that very taste, and toward the watermelon for that matter, in the very experiencing of that taste. This is *how* that taste (and the watermelon) is being *presented* to my consciousness. The pleasantness, in this sense, is the "felt evaluation" of that taste.[26]

So, sensory pleasure—as the adverbial modification of the way a sensation is instantiated in experiential consciousness—metaphysically consists of p-desiring incoming sensory information at the subpersonal level, where p-desiring is to be cashed out at the level of engineering design of learning-capable autonomous agents that consume sensory information, that is, psychofunctionally. Adverbialism offers a personal-level framework within which we can properly conceptualize *affective* phenomenology as adverbial/affective modification of *sensory* phenomenology. Psychofunctionalism then offers the naturalistic underpinnings of how this modification is realized as a certain kind of functional role (p-desiring) at the (largely) subpersonal level.[27] Figure 10.1 summarizes the emerging picture.

---

26 Terminology is borrowed from B. Helm, "Felt Evaluations: A Theory of Pleasure and Pain," *American Philosophical Quarterly* 39 (2002): 13–30—although his position differs from mine in significant ways. Here in this paragraph, it is actually helpful to leave "taste" ambiguous between the taste sensation and its worldly object (say, molecules on your tongue). As discussed above, either will do in this context.

27 I should note, however, that a property dualist about mental properties can easily accept the framework I am offering: just interpret the realization relations (indicated by double arrows in

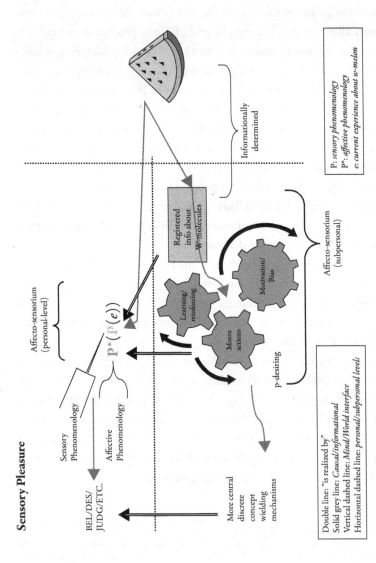

Sensory Pleasure

Affecto-sensorium (personal-level)

Sensory Phenomenology

BEL/DES/JUDG/ETC.

Affective Phenomenology

$\mathbf{P^*(P}(e))$

More central discrete concept wielding mechanisms

Registered info about *w*-molecules

Learning/reinforcing

Motor actions

Motivation/Bias

Affecto-sensorium (subpersonal)

p-desiring

Informationally determined

P : *sensory phenomenology*
P* : *affective phenomenology*
e : *current experience about w-melon*

Double line: "is realized by"
Solid grey line: *Causal/informational*
Vertical dashed line: *Mind/World interface*
Horizontal dashed line: *personal/subpersonal levels*

FIGURE 10.1 Diagram of the metaphysical and phenomenological structure of sensory pleasure

World-Directed Experiential (Phenomenal) Desire Interpretation of Sensory Pleasure

There is a long and venerable tradition in philosophy of mind that treats the phenomenology of perceptual experience as *representational*. There are different versions of this story with varying degrees of metaphysical or reductionist ambitions. Consider the (weak) representationalist claim that sensory phenomenology consists of nonconceptual (analog) representation of the complex physical sensible properties of objects we perceptually encounter in our environment. Indeed, very few would dispute the claim that sensory experiences carry information about certain ranges of physical properties or magnitudes of perceptible objects or events. If we add that this is in fact their proper function, it would be quite natural to treat sensory experiences as essentially representational. The character of sensory representation would then be differentiated by its peculiar representational content, format, and functional role as an interface between the world and the more central concept wielding mechanisms. On this view, sensory representation would have accuracy conditions: they can be veridical or not, true or false. In the picture above, the mental predicate P would nonconceptually (in analog form) represent certain physical features of the watermelon (call these features W). We may, for convenience, call this form of representation *phenomenal believing* or, for short, *p-believing* (p-believing that x is W).[28] *Ordinary* perceptual beliefs with conceptual structure, such as the belief that the watermelon is crisp and juicy, would then be causally generated and, when appropriate,

---

fig. 10.1) as causal (or noncausal, for that matter) *correlations* between the instantiations of physical and mental properties.

28 Compare Byrne's *exing that P*, roughly experiential *"believing" that P* that feeds normally into the mechanisms of ordinary perceptual belief formation. See A. Byrne, "Experience and Content," *Philosophical Quarterly* 59 (2009): 429–451. Here the referential position indicated by "x" would be transparent and de re. The choice of the term "phenomenal believing" isn't entirely happy, but the emphasis is on the perceptual experiences' *assertoric force* in reporting what one's immediate physical environment is like in modality-specific ways.

epistemically justified by the relevant perceptual experience (p-belief) or, more precisely, by the relevant sensory phenomenological aspects of the experience—these aspects having an analog indicative function.

As I have pointed out, pleasant sensations generally give rise to *ordinary* desires with conceptual structure that we can express, for instance, linguistically. If I find the taste of watermelon pleasant on the basis of how it tastes affectively, ceteris paribus, I may form an ordinary desire to taste or continue tasting the watermelon as long as it tastes pleasant. What rationalizes and justifies this desire of mine is how the watermelon tastes to me affectively—how the taste sensation, and thus the watermelon, strikes me affectively in experiencing it. This is the pleasantness of the sensation. We have, then, a parallel relationship between the affective phenomenology of the taste experience, p-desiring (or P^*), and the conceptually structured conative or evaluative states formed on the basis of, and justified by, this affective phenomenology.[29]

On this way of looking at the picture, the pleasantness of a sensation is, crudely put, an experiential (phenomenal) desire that is world-directed, just as the sensation involved is itself world-directed. If my taste sensation of the watermelon is pleasant, I am both p-believing and p-desiring (certain physical features of) the watermelon (W), which together constitute my taste experience of it.[30] The affective phenomenology is ontologically dependent on the sensory phenomenology involved in this experience—p-desiring being the adverbial/functional modification of p-believing.

---

29 See Aydede, "Pleasure vis-à-vis Pain," 559–560, for an earlier version of this, at bottom functionalist, story where I called p-desiring the incoming sensory information, desiring*, and equated it with the sensory pleasure associated with sensing the world through our sensory modalities. This was an attempt to agree with Ryle's naturalism (as against the excessive mentalism of his opponents) while still insisting that sensory pleasure is not merely a dispositional affair, but a phenomenological occurrence in one's consciousness.

30 Those who are familiar with the results of recent affective neuroscience might think that this claim is in tension with the increasing recognition of a distinction between "liking" and "wanting" that Kent Berridge and his colleagues have been urging for (see Berridge, "Motivation Concepts"). The tension can be resolved. Unfortunately, I cannot take up this issue in this chapter, but see Aydede, "Pain and Pleasure."

An advantage of this way of looking at sensory pleasure is that we seem to have a good explanation of why or how it could be intrinsically good for the agent. For the pleasantness (P^*) of a sensation (P) of a sensible property W, roughly, amounts to p-desiring the instantiation of W while p-believing it—that is, it amounts to having one's p-desires being *satisfied* as registered by the relevant p-beliefs. It seems intuitively obvious that if any psychological fact is intrinsically good, experiential registration of the satisfaction of one's desires is intrinsically good.

So suppose I taste this piece of watermelon. I find the taste pleasant: I am having a pleasant sensation. On the present proposal, I am p-believing that a certain complex sensible property (W) is being instantiated on my tongue, where the whole that-clause is to be read transparently but in the format of the relevant sensory code (P): whatever it is that is causally responsible for the distinctive watermelon taste I am having, *that* is W (W being instantiated on my tongue). I am also simultaneously p-desiring (P^*) that *this* W be "occurring." This is the affective-sensory experience and its phenomenology. To summarize, then, the pleasant taste sensation caused by W on my tongue is nothing but the *experiential/phenomenal* believing and desiring that W is/be instantiated.

But, being reflective, I may *also* form the ordinary *perceptual* belief that *that* is W, and the ordinary desire that *this* W continue, which I can express by saying, for instance (depending on the context), that *this* is good watermelon, or that this watermelon tastes pleasant, or that I want this watermelon, etc. But also, being *really* reflective, I may additionally form the *introspective* belief that this watermelon tastes like *that*, where the latter demonstrative refers to the characteristic way the watermelon tastes to me—its distinctive phenomenal character. As well, I may form the introspective desire that I continue having this sensation. Thus, my pleasant taste sensation may generate and justify two ordinary desires: one is world-directed and the other experience-directed. The ordinary world-directed desire is epistemically justified by the fact that I p-desire the watermelon, and the ordinary experience-directed desire is normatively justified by the fact that the pleasant sensation I am having is intrinsically good ($\approx$ I am having a p-desire I am p-believing to be satisfied), and I can grasp it as such.

If sensory pleasure is a form of world-directed desire (an experiential or phenomenal desire of, say, sensible property W in the very act of sensing W), then we have a fairly straightforward account of the motivating and justifying power of sensory pleasure as a kind of feeling realized psychofunctionally (roughly, as p-desiring W while sensing W). Moreover, the puzzle about opposite valences finds a good solution if we note that we can have *experiential aversions*—p-aversions, as it were, psychofunctionally understood in ways analogous to p-desires. The unpleasantness or painfulness of pains, or indeed, of many sensations, can then be understood, at the personal level, as adverbial modifications of incoming sensory information realized, at the subpersonal level, as certain psychofunctional roles.

4. CONCLUSION

I have described my account as having three levels: an adverbialist and a psychofunctionalist level, and a level in between at which we can describe sensory pleasure as world-directed experiential desire. Adverbialism is meant to provide a model for understanding the elusive and puzzling phenomenology of sensory pleasure (and sensory affect in general). This is fully at the personal level. I invite you to pay close attention to your own sensory affective phenomenology, based on lived experiences, and see whether my proposal makes better sense than my rivals'. Accurate phenomenological observations are hard to make, and disagreements about how the phenomenology of certain kinds of experiences is structured are particularly difficult to settle. But my primary argument for adverbialism is its intuitive explanatory and unifying power: it makes sensory pleasure a phenomenal episode (a kind of feeling) without falling prey to the heterogeneity problem that plagues all felt-quality views. I believe it makes better sense of what hedonic tone theorists have had in mind all along when they have claimed that the pleasantness of a sensation is an affective "toning" of the relevant sensation. It also captures the truth in the attitudinal theories by taking sensory affect to modify (or, apply to) sensations. The metaphysical essence of this modification is functional: sensations carry information for autonomous intentional organisms who *use* it for their various aims (consciously or unconsciously). The affect of a sensation is a way of marking the teleological significance of that sensation, and thus, of what that sensation represents, for the organism. There is something essentially desire-like in a pleasant sensation.

The psychofunctionalist proposal is meant to cash out the naturalistic underpinnings of this adverbial modification of sensations. I have introduced the term "p-desire" to stand for whatever complex psychofunctional role realizes the affective modification of incoming sensory information. The essence of this role is to get the organism to "move" or prepare for moving, as well as to make it learn what to desire for future contingencies—the role is inherently motivational and learning-theoretic. The choice of "desire" in this quasi-technical term "p-desire" is not accidental: when you look at the various aspects of this role in detail (as crudely illustrated above), it becomes conceptually compelling to treat the role as conative and motivational. But this is the role of affect that makes sense only in the context of processing the incoming sensory *information about the world*, in other words, only in the context of cognition (broadly speaking, including evaluative cognition) of the world with which we are perceptually in contact.

However, as the attentive reader might have noticed, I have also occasionally used the term "p-desire" above deliberately to describe something that makes phenomenological sense in the light of what is said at these two levels: to describe sensory pleasure as a world-directed experiential desire in phenomenal form. When I am tasting the watermelon in my mouth, the sensory pleasure I experience draws me to the watermelon. Although it is my taste sensation that is primarily pleasant, this pleasantness as a phenomenal episode *is* an experiential desiring of the watermelon in the very act of tasting/sensing it—this is what p-desiring reduces pleasantness to. Thus, we can see how the pleasantness of a sensation is inherently motivational and can play a justificatory role in the formation of ordinary beliefs and desires. The attitudinal theorists were right in insisting that there is a conative attitude involved in sensory pleasure, but they got the intentional object of this conative attitude wrong. Clearly, when I have a pleasant sensation S of a sensible (physical) property W, I generally desire, want, or like S. But this is not what constitutes the pleasantness of the sensation. What is constitutive is the fact that my p-desiring W is being satisfied as registered by my sensing W—revealed phenomenologically as S being affectively/adverbially "toned" (modified). Thus the present view is a form of desire-satisfaction account of what constitutes the intrinsic goodness of sensory pleasure.

I wish I had a catchier and descriptively more revealing name for my three-level account of pleasure. But good and comprehensive theories are hard to nail down by single descriptive names: thus, my adverbialist, functionalist, and experiential-desire view of sensory pleasure (indeed, sensory affect in general) is one view describing the same phenomenon at three different levels.

Bibliography

PRIMARY SOURCES

Alberti, Leon Battista. *On Painting and On Sculpture*. Edited and translated by
 Cecil Grayson. New York: Phaidon, 1972.

Anonymous. *Shahvat-afzā*. MS British Library Or. 11841.

Aquinas, Thomas. *Opera omnia*. Editio Leonina. Rome: Commissio
 Leonina, 1888–.

Aquinas, Thomas. *Scriptum super Sententiis*. Edited by Pierre Mandonnet and
 Maria Fabianus Moos. 4 vols. Paris: Lethielleux, 1929–1947.

Aristotle. *The Arabic Version of the Nicomachean Ethics*. Edited by Anna Akasoy and
 Alexander Fidora. Translated by D. M. Dunlop. Leiden: Brill, 2005.

Aristotle. *Aristotle's Treatise on Poetry, Translated: with Notes on the translation
 and on the original; and Two Dissertations, on Poetical, and Musical, Imitation.*
 Translated by Thomas Twining. London, 1789.

Aristotle. *Metaphysics Lambda*, in *Arisṭū 'ind al-'Arab*. Edited by 'Abd al-Raḥmān
 al-Badawī. Kuwait: Wikālat al-maṭbū'āt, 1978.

Aristotle. *Nicomachean Ethics*. Edited by I. Bywater. Oxford: Clarendon, 1894.

Aristotle. *Nicomachean Ethics*. Translated with commentary by T. H. Irwin. Indianapolis: Hackett, 1999.

al-Ashʿarī, Abū-l-Ḥasan. *Maqālāt al-islāmīyīn wa-ʾkhtilāf al-muṣallīn*. Edited by H. Ritter. Istanbul: Maṭbaʿat al-dawla, 1930.

Augustine. *On the Trinity*. Edited by W. J. Mountain and F. Glorie. 2 vols. Turnhout: Corpus Christianorum, 1968.

Auriol, Peter. *In Quatuor Libros Sententiarum*. 2 vols. Rome, 1596/1605.

Auriol, Peter. *Scriptum Super Primum Sententiarum. Prologue. Distinctions I–VIII*. Edited by Eligius M. Buytaert. 2 vols. St. Bonaventure, NY: Franciscan Institute, 1952/1956.

Avicenna. *Avicenna's De Anima, Being the Psychological Part of Kitāb al-Shifāʾ*. Edited by F. Rahman. London: Oxford University Press, 1959.

Avicenna. *al-Taʿlīqāt*. Edited by ʿAbd al-Raḥmān al-Badawī. Cairo: al-Hayʾa al-miṣrīya al-ʿāmma li-l-kitāb, 1973.

Ayāz, Maḥmūd. *Laṭāʾif-i Shāhī*. MS British Library India Office Islamic 1330, fols. 104–223.

Ayāz, Maḥmūd. *Miftāḥ al-surūr-i ʿĀdilshāhī*. MS British Library India Office Islamic 2473, dated 1738.

Bentham, Jeremy. *An Introduction to the Principles of Morals and Legislation*. Reedited by J. H. Burns and H. L. A Hart, with a new introduction by F. Rosen. Oxford: Clarendon Press, 1996. Originally published 1789.

Berkeley, George. *The Works of George Berkeley, Bishop of Cloyne*. 9 vols. Edited by A. A. Luce and T. E. Jessop. London: Thomas Nelson, 1948–1957.

Bilgrāmī, Āzād. *Ghizlān al-hind*. Edited by Siryūs Shamīsa. Tehran: Ṣadā-yi muʿāṣir, 2003.

Boethius. *The Consolation of Philosophy*. Translated by S. J. Tester. Loeb. Cambridge, MA: Harvard University Press, 1973.

Boethius. *De consolatione philosophiae, libri V*. Leiden: Franciscus Raphelengius, 1590.

Cicero. *Tusculan Disputations*. Edited by J. E. King. Cambridge, MA: Harvard University Press, 1927.

Descartes, René. *Oeuvres Complètes*. 11 vols. Edited by Charles Adam and Paul Tannery. Paris: Vrin, 1996.

Descartes, René. *The Philosophical Writings of Descartes*. 2 vols. Edited and translated by John Cottingham, Robert Stoothoff, and Dugald Murdoch. Cambridge: Cambridge University Press, 1984.

Descartes, René. *The Philosophical Writings of Descartes*. Vol. 3. Edited and translated by John Cottingham, Robert Stoothoff, Dugald Murdoch, and Anthony Kenny. Cambridge: Cambridge University Press, 1991.

Diderot, Denis. *Lettre sur les sourds et muets*. Paris, 1751.

Dubos, Jean-Baptiste. *Reflexions critiques sur la poesie et sur la peinture*. Vol. 1. Paris: Jean Mariette, 1719.

Duns Scotus, John. *Opera omnia*. Vatican City: Typis Polyglottis Vaticanis, 1950–.

Fārābī, Ābū Naṣr. *Al-Farabi on the Perfect State: Abū Naṣr al-Fārābī's Mabādī ārā' ahl al-madīna al-fāḍila*. Edited and translated by R. Walzer. Oxford: Clarendon Press, 1985.

Ghazālī, Abū Ḥāmid. *Kīmīyā-yi sa'ādat*. Edited by Ḥusayn Khadīvjām. Tehran: Intishārāt-i 'ilmī va farhangī, 1975.

Ghazālī, Abū Ḥāmid. *On Disciplining the Soul and on Breaking the Two Desires: Books XXII and XXIII of the Revival of the Religious Sciences*. Translated by Tim Winter. Cambridge: Islamic Texts Society, 1995.

Homer. *Odysseae libri XXIIII*. Cologne: Eucharius Cervicorn, 1534.

Ibn 'Arabī. *al-Futūḥāt al-Makkīya*. Cairo: Būlāq, 1911.

Jāmī, Muḥammad Qulī. *Kūk shāstra yā ladhdhat al-nisā'*. MS British Museum Add 17489.

Kant, Immanuel. *Akademie Ausgabe: Kants gesammelte Schriften*. Hrsg. von der Königlich Preußischen Akademie der Wissenschaften. Berlin: de Gruyter, 1902.

Kant, Immanuel. *Critique of the Power of Judgment*. Edited and translated by Paul Guyer and Eric Matthews. Cambridge: Cambridge University Press, [1790] 2000.

Kant, Immanuel. *Critique of Practical Reason*. Edited and translated by Mary Gregor. In *Practical Philosophy*. Cambridge: Cambridge University Press, [1788] 1996.

Kant, Immanuel. *Kant's Lectures on Metaphysics*. Edited as *Metaphysik Dohna, Metaphysik Vigilantius (K3)*, and *Metaphysik L2*, in *Lectures on Metaphysics*. Edited and translated by Karl Ameriks and Steve Naragon. Cambridge: Cambridge University Press, [1792–93 and 1794–95] 1997.

Kant, Immanuel. *The Metaphysics of Morals*. Edited and translated by Mary Gregor. In *Practical Philosophy*. Cambridge: Cambridge University Press, [1797] 1996.

Kindī. *The Philosophical Works of al-Kindī*. Translated by Peter Pormann and Peter Adamson. Karachi: Oxford University Press, 2012.

Kokkoka. *The Koka Shastra Being the Ratirahasya of Kokkoka*. Translated by W. G. Archer. London: Allen and Unwin, 1964.

Krause, Christian Gottfried. *Von der musikalischen Poesie*. Berlin: Johann Friedrich Voß, 1752.

Locke, John. *An Essay Concerning Human Understanding*. Edited by Peter H. Nidditch. Oxford: Oxford University Press, [1689] 1975.

Majlisī, Muḥammad Bāqir. *Biḥār al-anwār al-jāmi'a li-durar akhbār al-a'immat al-aṭhār*. Beirut: Mu'assasat al-A'lamī, 2008.

Majlisī, Muḥammad Bāqir. *Ḥilyat al-muttaqīn*. Qum: Dhawī-l-qurba, 2003.

Malebranche, Nicolas. *Dialogues on Metaphysics and on Religion*. Edited and
    translated by Nicholas Jolley and David Scott. Cambridge: Cambridge
    University Press, 1997.

Malebranche, Nicolas. *Oeuvres Complètes*. 4th ed. Edited by André Robinet.
    Paris: Vrin, 1991.

Malebranche, Nicolas. *The Search after Truth*. Edited and translated by Thomas M.
    Lennon and Paul J. Olscamp. With *Elucidations of the Search after Truth*. Edited
    and translated by Thomas M. Lennon. Cambridge: Cambridge University
    Press, 1997.

Mattheson, Johann. *Der vollkommene Capellmeister*. Hamburg: Christian
    Herold, 1739.

Molière. *Le Malade imaginaire*. Vol. 4. Edited by L. Aimé-Martin.
    Paris: Lefèvre, 1837.

Mill, James. *Analysis of the Phenomena of the Human Mind*. Vol. 1.
    London: Longman, Green, Reader and Dyer, 1822.

Mill, James. *Analysis of the Phenomena of the Human Mind*. Vol. 2.
    London: Longman, Green, Reader and Dyer, 1829.

Mill, James. *Analysis of the Phenomena of the Human Mind*. Edited with notes by
    John Stuart Mill and Alexander Bain. 2 vols. 2nd ed. London: Longman, Green,
    Reader and Dyer, 1869.

Mill, John Stuart. "Bentham" (1838). In *Collected Works of John Stuart Mill*, edited
    by J. M. Robson, vol. 10, 75–115. Toronto: University of Toronto Press, 1963.

Mill, John Stuart. "Coleridge" (1840). In *Collected Works of John Stuart Mill*, edited
    by J. M. Robson, vol. 10, 117–163. Toronto: University of Toronto Press, 1963.

Mill, John Stuart. *Collected Works of John Stuart Mill*. Edited by J. M. Robson.
    Toronto: University of Toronto Press, 1963–1991.

Mill, John Stuart. *An Examination of Sir William Hamilton's Philosophy*
    (1865). In *Collected Works of John Stuart Mill*, edited by J. M. Robson, vol. 9.
    Toronto: University of Toronto Press, 1979.

Mill, John Stuart. *The Subjection of Women* (1869). In *Collected Works of John Stuart
    Mill*, edited by J. M. Robson, vol. 21, 259–340. Toronto: University of Toronto
    Press, 1984.

Mill, John Stuart. *System of Logic, Ratiocinative and Inductive* (1843). In *Collected
    Works of John Stuart Mill*, edited by J. M. Robson, vols. 7–8. Toronto: University
    of Toronto Press, 1974.

Mill, John Stuart. *Utilitarianism* (1861). In *Collected Works of John Stuart Mill*,
    edited by J. M. Robson, vol. 10, 203–259. Toronto: University of Toronto
    Press, 1985.

Miskawayh. *Tahdhīb al-akhlāq* [The refinement of character]. Translated by C. Zurayk. Beirut: Maktabat al-Lubnān, 1968.

Mullā Ṣadrā. *al-Ḥikma al-mutaʿāliya fī l-asfār al-ʿaqlīya al-arbaʿa*. Edited by G. Aʿvānī et al. Tehran: Sadra Islamic Philosophy Research Institute, 2004.

Nakhshābī, Żiyāʾ al-Dīn. *Juzʾīyāt va kullīyāt*. MS British Library India Office Islamic 905, dated 1595.

Nakhshābī, Żiyāʾ al-Dīn. *Ladhdhat al-nisāʾ*. MS British Library India Office Islamic 908.

Nakhshābī, Żiyāʾ al-Dīn. *Ladhdhat al-nisāʾ*. MS Ganjbakhsh Library Islamabad (Pakistan) 3949.

Nakhshābī, Żiyāʾ al-Dīn. *Ladhdhat al-nisāʾ*. MS Ganjbakhsh Library Islamabad (Pakistan) 791.

Nakhshābī, Żiyāʾ al-Dīn. *Ladhdhat al-nisāʾ*. MS Ganjbakhsh Library Islamabad (Pakistan) 10958.

Nakhshābī, Żiyāʾ al-Dīn. *Silk al-sulūk*. Delhi: Maṭbaʿ-yi mujtabāʾī, 1895.

Plato. *Gorgias: A Revised Text with Introduction and Commentary*. Edited by E. R. Dodds. Oxford: Oxford University Press, 1959.

Plato. *Philèbe*. Edited and translated by A. Diès. Paris: Belles Lettres, 1941.

Plato. *Philebos*. Translated by Dorothea Frede. Göttingen: Vandenhoeck und Ruprecht, 1997.

Plato. *Philebus*. Translated by Dorothea Frede. Indianapolis: Hackett University Press, 1993.

Plato. *Philebus*. Translated by J. C. B. Gosling. Oxford: Oxford University Press, 1975.

Plato. *Plato: Complete Works*. Edited by John M. Cooper and D. S. Hutchinson. Indianapolis: Hackett, 1997.

Plato. *Platonis Opera*. Edited by J. Burnet. Oxford: Oxford University Press, 1901.

Plotinus. *Theologia Aristoteles* [Uthūlūjiyā]. Edited by ʿAbd al-Raḥman al-Badawī. Cairo: L'Institut français, 1947.

Rāzī, Abū Bakr. *The Spiritual Physick* [al-Ṭibb al-rūḥānī]. Translated by A. J. Arberry. London: John Murray, 1950.

Reid, Thomas. *Essays on the Intellectual Powers of Man*. Ed. Derek Brookes and Knud Haakonssen. State College: Pennsylvania State University Press, 2000.

Ṣādiq, Shākir Khān b. *Hadīqa-yi ḥādiq-i ganjīna-yi Ṣādiq*. MS British Library India Office Islamic 1781, dated 1716.

Sisman, Elaine. *Mozart: Jupiter Symphony*. Cambridge: Cambridge University Press, 1993.

Ṭabrisī, al-Ḥasan b. al-Faḍl. *Makārim al-akhlāq*. Kuwait: Maktabat al-Alfayn, 1987.

Ṭūsī, Naṣīr al-Dīn. *The Nasirean Ethics*. Translated by G. M. Wickens. London: Allen and Unwin, 1964.

Wodeham, Adam. *Lectura secunda in librum primum Sententiarum*. Edited by Rega Wood and Gedeon Gál. 3 vols. St. Bonaventure, NY: Franciscan Institute, 1990.

SECONDARY SOURCES

Adam, J. *The "Republic" of Plato* 2. Cambridge: Cambridge University Press, 1902.

Adamson, Peter. *Al-Kindī*. Oxford: Oxford University Press, 2007.

Adamson, Peter. "Miskawayh on Pleasure." *Arabic Sciences and Philosophy* 25 (2015): 199–223.

Aliquié, Ferdinand. *Le cartésianisme de Malebranche*. Paris: Vrin, 1974.

Allison, H. *Kant's Theory of Taste: a Reading of the Critique of Aesthetic Judgment*. Cambridge: Cambridge University Press, 2001.

Allison, H. "Reply to the Comments of Longuenesse and Ginsborg." *Inquiry* 46 (2003): 182–194.

Alston, W. "Pleasure." In *The Encyclopedia of Philosophy*, edited by P. Edwards, 244–250. New York: Collier-Macmillan, 1968.

Anscombe, G. E. M. *Intention*. Cambridge, MA: Harvard University Press, 1957.

Anscombe, G. E. M. "Modern Moral Philosophy." In *The Collected Philosophical Papers of G. E. M. Anscombe*, vol. 3, *Ethics, Religion, and Politics*, 26–42. Minneapolis: University of Minnesota Press, 1981.

Aquila, R. "A New Look at Kant's Aesthetic Judgment." In *Essays in Kant's Aesthetics*, edited by T. Cohen and P. Guyer, 87–114. Chicago: University of Chicago Press, 1982.

Armstrong, D. M. *Bodily Sensations*. London: Routledge and Kegan Paul, 1962.

Armstrong, J. M. "After the Ascent: Plato on Becoming God." *Oxford Studies in Ancient Philosophy* 26 (2004): 171–183.

Aufderheide, J. "Processes as Pleasures in *EN* vii 11–14: *Ethics* Book VII." *Ancient Philosophy* 33 (2013): 135–157.

Aydede, M. "An Analysis of Pleasure vis-à-vis Pain." *Philosophy and Phenomenological Research* 61 (2000): 537–570.

Aydede, M. "Pain and Pleasure?" In *Routledge Handbook of Emotion Theory*, edited by A. Scarantino. London: Routledge, forthcoming.

Aydede, M. "How to Unify Theories of Sensory Pleasure: An Adverbialist Proposal." *Review of Philosophy and Psychology* 5 (2014): 119–133.

Aydede, M., and M. Fulkerson. "Affect: Representationalists' Headache." *Philosophical Studies* 170 (2014): 175–198.

Aydede, M., and M. Fulkerson. "Affective Qualities." Presentation at the annual meeting of the Pacific Division of the American Philosophical Association, San Francisco, April 2013.

Aydede, M., and M. Fulkerson. "Reasons and Theories of Sensory Affect." In *The Philosophy of Pain: Unpleasantness, Emotion and Deviance*, edited by David Bain, Michael Brady, and Jennifer Corns. Forthcoming.

Bain, D. "What Makes Pains Unpleasant?" *Philosophical Studies* 166 (2013): 60–89.

Barch, Deanna M., Michael T. Treadway, and Nathan Schoen. "Effort, Anhedonia, and Function in Schizophrenia: Reduced Effort Allocation Predicts Amotivation and Functional Impairment." *Journal of Abnormal Psychology* 123.2 (2014): 387–397. https://doi.org/https://doi.org/10.1037/a0036299.

Barrett, Lisa Feldman. *How Emotions Are Made: The Secret Life of the Brain*. New York: Houghton Mifflin Harcourt, 2017.

Barrett, Lisa Feldman, and Ajay Satpute. "Large-Scale Brain Networks in Affective and Social Neuroscience: Toward an Integrative Functional Architecture of the Brain." *Current Opinion in Neurobiology* 23.3 (2013): 361–372. https://doi.org/10.1016/j.conb.2012.12.012.

Bashir, Shahzad. *Sufi Bodies: Religion and Society in Medieval Islam*. New York: Columbia University Press, 2011.

Behl, Aditya. *Love's Subtle Magic: An Indian Islamic Literary Tradition, 1379–1545*. New York: Oxford University Press, 2012.

Berger, Susanna. *The Art of Philosophy: Visual Thinking in Europe from the Late Renaissance to the Early Enlightenment*. Princeton: Princeton University Press, 2017.

Berger, Susanna. "The Invention of Wisdom in Jean Chéron's Illustrated Thesis Print." *Intellectual History Review* 24.3 (2014): 343–366.

Berger, Susanna. "Martin Meurisse's Garden of Logic." *Journal of the Warburg and Courtauld Institutes* 76.2 (2013): 203–249.

Berger, Susanna. "Martin Meurisse's Theater of Natural Philosophy." *Art Bulletin* 95.2 (2013): 269–293.

Berridge, K. "Motivation Concepts in Behavioral Neuroscience." *Physiology & Behavior* 81 (2004): 179–209.

Betegh, G. "Tale, Theology and Teleology in the *Phaedo*." In *Plato's Myths*, edited by C. Partenie, 77–100. Cambridge: Cambridge University Press, 2009.

Blackburn, S. *Ruling Passions: A Theory of Practical Reasoning*. Oxford: Clarendon Press, 1998.

Block, N. "Troubles with Functionalism." In *Readings in Philosophy of Psychology*, vol. 1, edited by Ned Block, 268–305. Cambridge, MA: Harvard University Press, 1980.

Bobonich, C. *Plato's Utopia Recast*. Oxford: Oxford University Press, 2002.

Bostock, David. "Pleasure and Activity in Aristotle's Ethics." *Phronesis* 32 (1988): 251–272.

Bouhdiba, Abdelwahab. *Sexuality in Islam*. London: Routledge, Kegan and Paul, 1985.

Boulnois, Olivier. "Duns Scot: Existe-t-il des passions de la volonté?" In *Les passions antiques et médiévales: Théories et critiques des passions I*, edited by B. Besnier et al., 281–295. Paris: Presses Universitaires de France, 2003.

Boyle, M. "Active Belief." *Canadian Journal of Philosophy,* supp. vol. 35 (2010): 119–147.

Brady, M. "Pain and the Euthyphro Dilemma." Paper presented at the Pain Conference, University of Glasgow, June 18–20, 2013.

Bramble, B. "The Distinctive Feeling Theory of Pleasure." *Philosophical Studies* 162 (2011): 201–217.

Brandt, Richard. *A Theory of the Good and the Right*. Oxford: Clarendon Press, 1979.

Brandwood, L. "Stylometry and Chronology." In *The Cambridge Companion to Plato*, edited by R. Kraut, 90–120. Cambridge: Cambridge University Press, 1992.

Brink, David. "Mill's Moral and Political Philosophy." In *The Stanford Encyclopedia of Philosophy* (Winter 2016 Edition), edited by Edward N. Zalta. http://plato.stanford.edu/archives/fall2008/entries/mill-moral-political/. Accessed June 18, 2015.

Brink, D. *Moral Realism and the Foundations of Ethics*. Cambridge: Cambridge University Press, 1989.

Broad, C. D. *Five Types of Ethical Theory*. London: Routledge and Kegan Paul, 1930.

Busch, Alison. *Poetry of Kings: The Classical Hindi Literature of Mughal India*. Oxford: Oxford University Press, 2011.

Butler, J. "The Arguments for the Most Pleasant Life in *Republic* IX: A Note against the Common Interpretation." *Apeiron* 32 (1999): 37–48.

Butler, J. "On Whether Pleasure's Esse Is Percipi: Rethinking Republic 583b–585a." *Ancient Philosophy* 19 (1999): 285–298.

Byrne, A. "Experience and Content." *Philosophical Quarterly* 59 (2009): 429–451.

Cannon, J. "The Intentionality of Judgments of Taste in Kant's *Critique of Judgment*." *Journal of Aesthetics and Art Criticism* 66 (2008): 53–66.

Carone, G. "Hedonism and the Pleasureless Life." *Phronesis* 45 (2000): 257–283.

Cassam, Quassim. "Contemporary Reactions to Descartes' Philosophy of Mind." In *A Companion to Descartes*, edited by Janet Broughton and John Carriero, 482–495. Malden, MA: Wiley-Blackwell, 2007.

Clark, A. "Painfulness Is Not a Quale." In *Pain: New Essays on Its Nature and the Methodology of Its Study*, edited by M. Aydede, 177–198. Cambridge, MA: MIT Press, 2005.

Clark, A. *Sensory Qualities*. Oxford: Oxford University Press, 1996.

Cohen, Alex S., and Kyle S. Minor. "Emotional Experience in Patients with Schizophrenia Revisited: Meta-analysis of Laboratory Studies." *Schizophrenia Bulletin* 36.1 (January 2008): 143. https://doi.org/10.1093/schbul/sbn061.

Crisp, R. *Reasons and the Good*. Oxford: Oxford University Press, 2006.

Cummins, Phillip D. "Berkeley's Ideas of Sense." *Noûs* 9 (1975): 55–72.

Cummins, Phillip D. "Perceptual Relativity and Ideas in the Mind." *Philosophy and Phenomenological Research* 24 (1963): 202–214.

Cutter, B., and M. Tye. "Tracking Representationalism and the Painfulness of Pain." *Philosophical Issues* 21 (2011): 90–109.

Davis, W. A. "A Causal Theory of Enjoyment." *Mind* 91 (1982): 240–256.

Davis, W. A. "Pleasure and Happiness." *Philosophical Studies* 39 (1981): 305–317.

Delcomminette, S. *Le Philèbe de Platon: Introduction à l'agathologie platonicienne*. Leiden: Brill, 2006.

Delmas, Jean-François. "Estampes et textes imprimés sur tissus de soie. Catalogue raisonné de thèses et d'exercices publics XVIIe–XIXe siècle." *Bulletin du bibliophile* 1 (2005): 85–142.

De Rosa, Raffaella. *Descartes and the Puzzle of Sensory Representation*. Oxford: Oxford University Press, 2010.

Doney, Willis. "Two Questions about Berkeley." *Philosophical Review* 61 (1952): 382–391.

Donner, Wendy, and Richard Fumerton. *Mill*. Oxford: Wiley-Blackwell, 2009.

Drummond, Ian. "John Duns Scotus on the Passions of the Will." In *Emotion and Cognitive Life in Medieval and Early Modern Philosophy*, edited by Martin Pickavé and Lisa Shapiro, 53–74. Oxford: Oxford University Press, 2012.

Duncker, K. "On Pleasure, Emotion, and Striving." *Philosophy and Phenomenological Research* 1 (1941): 391–430.

Ebrey, D. "The Asceticism of the *Phaedo*: Pleasure, Purification and the Soul's Proper Activity." *Archiv für Geschichte der Philosophie* 99.1 (2017): 1–30.

Engstrom, S. *The Form of Practical Knowledge: A Study of the Categorical Imperative*. Cambridge, MA: Harvard University Press, 2009.

Erginel, M. M. "Plato on the Psychology of Pleasure and Pain." *Phoenix* 65 (2011): 288–314.

Erginel, M. M. "Inconsistency and Ambiguity in *Republic* IX." *Classical Quarterly* 61 (2011): 493–520.

Evans, M. "Plato and the Meaning of Pain." *Apeiron* 40 (2007): 71–93.

Evans, M. "Plato's Anti-hedonism." *Proceedings of the Boston Area Colloquium of Ancient Philosophy* 22 (2007): 121–145.

Feldman, Fred. "Hedonism." In *The Encyclopedia of Ethics,* edited by L. C. Becker and C. B. Becker, 662–669. New York: Routledge, 2001.

Feldman, Fred. "On the Intrinsic Value of Pleasures." *Ethics* 107 (1997): 448–466.

Feldman, Fred. *Pleasure and the Good Life.* New York: Oxford University Press, 2004.

Fields, Keota. *Berkeley: Ideas, Immateralism, and Objective Presence.* Lanham, MD: Lexington Books, 2011.

Fletcher, E. "The Divine Method and the Disunity of Pleasure in the *Philebus*." *Journal of the History of Philosophy* 55.2 (2017): 179–208.

Fletcher, E. "Plato on False and Deceptive Pleasures." *Archiv für Geschichte der Philosophie* (forthcoming).

Fletcher, E. "Plato on Pure Pleasure and the Best Life." *Phronesis* 59 (2014): 113–142.

Fletcher, E. "Pleasure, Judgment, and the Function of the Painter-Scribe Analogy."" Unpublished manuscript.

Frankel, Melissa. "Acts, Ideas, and Objects in Berkeley's Metaphysics." *Canadian Journal of Philosophy* 43 (2013): 475–493.

Frede, D. "Disintegration and Restoration: Pleasure and Pain in Plato's *Philebus*." In *The Cambridge Companion to Plato*, edited by R. Kraut, 425–463. Cambridge: Cambridge University Press, 1992.

Frede, D. "Rumpelstiltskin's Pleasures: True and False Pleasures in Plato's *Philebus*." *Phronesis* 30 (1985): 151–180.

Gard, David E., Marja Germans Gard, Ann M. Kring, and O. P. John. "Anticipatory and Consummatory Components of the Experience of Pleasure: A Scale Development Study." *Journal of Research in Personality* 40 (2006): 1086–1102. https://doi.org/10.1016/j.rp.2005.11.001.

Gard, David E., Ann M. Kring, Marja Germans Gard, William P. Horan, and Michael F. Green. "Anhedonia in Schizophrenia: Distinctions between Anticipatory and Consummatory Pleasure." *Schizophrenia Research* 93.1–3 (July 2007): 253–260. https://doi.org/10.1016/j.schres.2007.03.008.

Ginsborg, H. "Aesthetic Judging and the Intentionality of Pleasure." *Inquiry* 46 (2003): 164–181.

Ginsborg, H. "Kant on the Subjectivity of Taste." In *Kants Ästhetik/Kant's Aesthetics/L'esthetique de Kant,* edited by Herman Parret, 448–465. Berlin: de Gruyter, 1995.

Ginsborg, H. "Lawfulness without a Law: Kant on the Free Play of the Imagination and Understanding." *Philosophical Topics* 25 (1997): 37–83.

Ginsborg, H. *The Normativity of Nature*. Oxford: Oxford University Press, 2015.

Gold, James M., Gregory P. Strauss, James A. Waltz, Benjamin M. Robinson, Jamie K. Brown, and Michael J. Frank. "Negative Symptoms of Schizophrenia Are Associated with Abnormal Effort-Cost Computations." *Biological Psychiatry* 74.2 (2013): 130–136. https://doi.org/10.1016/j.biopsych.2012.12.022.

Gold, James M., James A. Waltz, Tatyana M. Matveeva, Zuzana Kasanova, Gregory P. Strauss, Ellen S. Herbener, Anne G. E. Collins, and Michael J. Frank. "Negative Symptoms and the Failure to Represent the Expected Reward Value of Actions: Behavioral and Computational Modeling Evidence." *Archives of General Psychiatry* 69.2 (2012): 129–138. https://doi.org/10.1001/archgenpsychiatry.2011.1269.

Goldie, Peter. *The Emotions: A Philosophical Exploration*. Oxford: Clarendon Press, 2000.

Goldstein, I. "Why People Prefer Pleasure to Pain." *Philosophy* 55 (1980): 349–362.

Gonzalez, Francisco. "Aristotle on Pleasure and Perfection." *Phronesis* 36 (1991): 141–159.

Gorodeisky, Keren. *A Matter of Form: The Significance of Kant's Judgment of Taste*. Unpublished manuscript.

Gorodeisky, Keren. "A Tale of Two Faculties." *British Journal of Aesthetics* 51 (2011): 415–436.

Gorodeisky, Keren, and Eric Marcus. "Aesthetic Rationality." *The Journal of Philosophy*, (forthcoming).

Gosling, J. C. B., and C. C. W. Taylor. *The Greeks on Pleasure*. Oxford: Oxford University Press, 1982.

Guyer, P. *Kant and the Claims of Taste*. Cambridge: Cambridge University Press, 1979.

Hackforth, R. *Plato's Examination of Pleasure*. New York: Liberal Arts Press, 2006.

Hadreas, Peter. "The Functions of Pleasure in NE X 4–5." *Ancient Philosophy* 24 (2004): 155–167.

Hall, R. "Are Pains Necessarily Unpleasant?" *Philosophy and Phenomenological Research* 49 (1989): 643–659.

Hampshire, S. *Freedom of the Individual*. New York: Harper and Row, 1965.

Hardie, W. F. R. *Aristotle's Ethical Theory*. Oxford: Oxford University Press, 1980.

Harte, V. "The *Philebus* on Pleasure: The Good, the Bad and the False." *Proceedings of the Aristotelian Society* 104 (2006): 111–128.

Heathwood, C. "Desire-Based Theories of Reasons, Pleasure, and Welfare." *Oxford Studies in Metaethics* 6 (2011): 79–106.

Heathwood, C. "Desire Satisfactionism and Hedonism." *Philosophical Studies* 128 (2006): 539–563.

Heathwood, C. "The Reduction of Sensory Pleasure to Desire." *Philosophical Studies* 133 (2007): 23–44.

Heerey, E. A., K. R. Bell-Warren, and J. M. Gold. "Decision-Making Impairments in the Context of Intact Reward Sensitivity in Schizophrenia." *Biological Psychiatry* 64.1 (July 2008): 62–69.

Helm, B. "Felt Evaluations: A Theory of Pleasure and Pain." *American Philosophical Quarterly* 39 (2002): 13–30.

Horan, William P., Ann M. Kring, and Jack J. Blanchard. "Anhedonia in Schizophrenia: A Review of Assessment Strategies." *Schizophrenia Bulletin* 32.2 (April 2006): 259–273.

Jesseph, Douglas M. "Berkeley, God, and Explanation." In *Early Modern Philosophy: Mind, Matter, and Metaphysics*, edited by Christia Mercer and Eileen O'Neill, 183–205. Oxford: Oxford University Press, 2005.

Jolley, Nicholas. *The Light of the Soul: Theories of Ideas in Leibniz, Malebranche and Descartes*. Oxford: Oxford Clarendon Press, 1990.

Jolley, Nicholas. "Sensation, Intentionality, and Animal Consciousness: Malebranche's Theory of the Mind." *Ratio* 8 (1995): 129–135.

Juckel, G., F. Schlagenhauf, M. Koslowski, T. Wustenberg, A. Villringer, B. Knutson, J. Wrase, and A. Heinz. "Dysfunction of Ventral Striatal Reward Prediction in Schizophrenia." *Neuroimage* 29.2 (2006): 409–416.

Kagan, S. "The Limits of Well-Being." *Social Philosophy and Policy* 9 (1992): 169–189.

Kahane, G. "Pain, Dislike and Experience." *Utilitas* 21 (2009): 327–336.

Katz, Leonard D. "Hedonism as Metaphysics and Value." Ph.D. diss., Princeton University, 1986.

Katz, Leonard D. "Pleasure." In *The Stanford Encyclopedia of Philosophy* (Spring 2014 edition), edited by Edward N. Zalta. Last modified 2006. http://plato.stanford.edu/archives/spr2014/entries/pleasure/.

Kenny, A. *Action, Emotion and Will*. London: Routledge and Kegan Paul, 1963.

King, Peter. "Aquinas on the Passions." In *Thomas Aquinas: Contemporary Philosophical Perspectives*, edited by Brian Davies, 353–384. New York: Oxford University Press, 2002.

King, Peter. "Dispassionate Passions." In *Emotion and Cognitive Life in Medieval and Early Modern Philosophy*, edited by Martin Pickavé and Lisa Shapiro, 9–31. Oxford: Oxford University Press, 2012.

Kitanov, Severin Valentinov. *Beatific Enjoyment in Medieval Scholastic Debates: The Complex Legacy of Saint Augustine and Peter Lombard*. Lanham, MD: Lexington Books, 2014.

Klein, Colin. "What Pain Asymbolia Really Shows." *Mind* 124 (2015): 493–516.

Korsgaard, Christine M. "From Duty and for the Sake of the Noble." In *Aristotle, Kant and the Stoics*, edited by S. Engstrom and J. Whiting, 203–236. Cambridge: Cambridge University Press, 1996.

Kring, Ann M., and Deanna M. Barch. "The Motivation and Pleasure Dimension of Negative Symptoms: Neural Substrates and Behavioral Outputs." *European Neuropsychopharmacology* 24.5 (2014): 725–736. https://doi.org/10.1016/j.euroneuro.2013.06.007.

Kring, Ann M., Lisa Feldman Barrett, and David E. Gard. "On the Broad Applicability of the Affective Circumplex: Representations of Affective Knowledge among Schizophrenia Patients." *Psychological Science* 14.3 (May 2003): 207–214.

Kring, Ann M., and Janelle M. Caponigro. "Emotion in Schizophrenia: Where Feeling Meets Thinking." *Current Directions in Psychological Science* 19.4 (August 2010): 255–259. https://doi.org/10.1177/0963721410377599.

Kring, Ann M., and Kelly S. Earnst. "Stability of Emotional Responding in Schizophrenia." *Behavior Therapy* 30 (1999): 373–388.

Kring, Ann M., and Ori Elis. "Emotion Deficits in People with Schizophrenia." *Annual Review of Clinical Psychology* 9 (2013): 409–433. https://doi.org/10.1146/annurev-clinpsy-050212-185538.

Kring, Ann M., and Erin K. Moran. "Emotional Response Deficits in Schizophrenia : Insights from Affective Science." *Schizophrenia Bulletin* 34.5 (2008): 819–834. https://doi.org/10.1093/schbul/sbn071.

Kugle, Scott. *Sufis and Saints' Bodies: Mysticism, Corporeality and Sacred Power in Islam*. Chapel Hill: University of North Carolina Press, 2007.

Kurz, Susanne. "Never Just for Fun? Sexual Intercourse in Persophone Medicine, Erotology and Ethics." In *Muslim Bodies: Körper, Sexualität und Medizin in muslimischen Gesellschaften*, edited by Susanne Kurz, Claudia Preckel, and Stefan Reichmuth. Münster: LIT Verlag, 2016.

Labukt, I. "Hedonic Tone and the Heterogeneity of Pleasure." *Utilitas* 24 (2012): 172–199.

Lennon, Thomas. "Malebranche's Argument for Ideas and Its Systematic Importance." In *Minds, Ideas, and Objects: Essays on the Theory of Representation in Modern Philosophy*, edited by Phillip Cummins and Guenter Zoeller, 57–71. Atascadero, CA: Ridgeview, 1992.

Llerena, Katiah, Gregory P. Strauss, and Alex S. Cohen. "Looking at the Other Side of the Coin: A Meta-analysis of Self-Reported Emotional Arousal in People with Schizophrenia." *Schizophrenia Research* 142.1–3 (December 2012): 65–70.

Longuenesse, B. "Kant's Theory of Judgment and Judgments of Taste: On Henry Allison's *Kant's Theory of Taste*." *Inquiry* 46 (2003): 143–163.

Lorenz, H. *The Brute Within: Appetitive Desire in Plato and Aristotle.*
Oxford: Oxford University Press, 2006.

Macleod, Christopher. "John Stuart Mill." In *The Stanford Encyclopedia of Philosophy* (Spring 2018 edition), edited by Edward N. Zalta. http://plato. stanford.edu/archives/spr2018/entries/mill. Accessed March 3, 2018.

Marcus, E. *Rational Causation.* Cambridge, MA: Harvard University Press, 2012.

Martínez, M. "Imperative Content and the Painfulness of Pain." *Phenomenology and the Cognitive Sciences* 10 (2011): 67–90.

McDowell, John. *Mind and World.* Cambridge, MA: Harvard University Press, 1996.

Meyer, Véronique. *L'Illustration des thèses à Paris dans la seconde moitié du XVIIe siècle: Peintres, graveurs, éditeurs.* Paris: Commission des travaux historiques de la ville de Paris, 2002.

Miner, Robert. *Thomas Aquinas on the Passions: A Study of Summa Theologiae 1a2ae 22–48.* Cambridge: Cambridge University Press, 2011.

Moore, George Edward. *Principia Ethica.* Edited by T. Baldwin. Cambridge: Cambridge University Press, [1903] 1993.

Moran, R. "Frankfurt on Identification." In *Contours of Agency*, edited by Sarah Buss and Lee Overton, 189–217. Cambridge, MA: MIT Press, 2002.

Moss, Jessica. "Appearances and Calculations: Plato's Division of the Soul." *Oxford Studies in Ancient Philosophy* 34 (2008): 35–68.

Moss, Jessica. "Pleasure and Illusion." *Philosophy and Phenomenological Research* 72 (2006): 503–535.

Muehlmann, Robert G. *Berkeley's Ontology.* Indianapolis: Hackett, 1992.

Muniz, F. "Propositional Pleasures in Plato's *Philebus.*" *Journal of Ancient Philosophy* 8 (2014): 49–75.

Murata, Sachiko. *The Tao of Islam: A Sourcebook on Gender Relationships in Islamic Thought.* Albany: State University of New York Press, 1992.

Myin-Germeys, Inez, Philippe A. E. G. Delespaul, and Marten W. DeVries. "Schizophrenia Patients Are More Emotionally Active Than Is Assumed Based on Their Behaviour." *Schizophrenia Bulletin* 26.4 (2000): 847–854.

Nadler, Steven. *Malebranche and Ideas.* Oxford: Oxford University Press, 1992.

Nadler, Steven. "Malebranche's Theory of Perception." In *The Great Arnauld and Some of His Philosophical Correspondents*, edited by E. Kremer, 108–128. Toronto: University of Toronto Press, 1994.

Nagel, T. *The Possibility of Altruism.* Princeton: Princeton University Press, 1970.

Nolan, Lawrence. "Malebranche on Sensory Cognition and 'Seeing As.'" *Journal of the History of Philosophy* 50.1 (2012): 21–52.

Obdrzalek, S. "Fleeing the Divine—Plato's Rejection of the Ahedonic Ideal in the *Philebus*." *International Plato Studies* 26 (2007): 209–214.

Olscamp, Paul J. *The Moral Philosophy of George Berkeley*. The Hague: Martinus Nijhoff, 1970.

Olscamp, Paul J. "Some Suggestions about the Moral Philosophy of George Berkeley." *Journal of the History of Philosophy* 6 (1968): 147–156.

Oorschot, Margreet, Thomas Kwapil, Philippe Delespaul, and Inez Myin-Germeys. "Momentary Assessment Research in Psychosis." In "Special Section: Psychopathology in Daily Life: Using Ecological Momentary Assessment Methods." *Psychological Assessment* 21.4 (December 2009): 498–505. https://doi.org/10.1037/a0017077.

Oorschot, Margreet, Tineke Lataster, Viviane Thewissen, Mariëlle Lardinois, Marieke Wichers, Jim van Os, Philippe Delespaul, and Inez Myin-Germeys. "Emotional Experience in Negative Symptoms of Schizophrenia—No Evidence for a Generalized Hedonic Deficit." *Schizophrenia Bulletin* 39.1 (January 2013): 217–225.

Oorschot, Margreet, Tineke Lataster, Viviane Thewissen, Mariëlle Lardinois, Marieke Wichers, Jim van Os, Philippe Delespaul, and Inez Myin-Germeys. "Symptomatic Remission in Psychosis and Real-Life Functioning." *British Journal of Psychiatry* 201.3 (September 2012): 215–220.

O'Sullivan, B., and R. Schroer. "Painful Reasons: Representationalism as a Theory of Pain." *Philosophical Quarterly* 62 (2012): 737–758.

Ott, Walter. "Malebranche and the Riddle of Sensation." *Philosophy and Phenomenological Research* 88 (2014): 689–712.

Panksepp, J., and L. Biven. *The Archeology of Mind*. New York: Norton, 2012.

Parfit, D. *On What Matters*. Vol. 1. Oxford: Oxford University Press, 2011.

Pelosi, Francesco. *Plato on Music, Soul, and Body*. Cambridge: Cambridge University Press, 2010.

Penner, T. "False Anticipatory Pleasures: *Philebus* 36a3–41a6." *Phronesis* 15 (2005): 166–178.

Pickavé, Martin. "Emotion and Cognition in Later Medieval Philosophy: The Case of Adam Wodeham." In *Emotion and Cognitive Life in Medieval and Early Modern Philosophy*, edited by Martin Pickavé and Lisa Shapiro, 94–115. Oxford: Oxford University Press, 2012.

Pickavé, Martin. "On the Intentionality of the Emotions (and of Other Appetitive Acts)." *Quaestio* 10 (2010): 45–63.

Pitcher, G. "Pain Perception." *Philosophical Review* 79 (1970): 368–393.

Pollock, Sheldon. *The Language of Gods in the World of Men: Sanskrit, Culture, and Power in Premodern India*. New York: Columbia University Press, 2006.

Pyle, Andrew. *Malebranche*. New York: Routledge, 2003.

Radner, Daisy. *Malebranche: A Study of the Cartesian System*. Amsterdam: Van Gorcum, 1978.

Raz, J. *From Normativity to Responsibility*. Oxford: Oxford University Press, 2011.

Rickless, Samuel. *Berkeley's Argument for Idealism*. New York: Oxford University Press, 2013.

Riley, J. "Interpreting Mill's Qualitative Hedonism." *Philosophical Quarterly* 53 (2003): 410–418.

Riley, J. "On Quantities and Qualities of Pleasure." *Utilitas* 5 (1993): 291–300.

Rizvi, Sajjad H. "Sayyid Niʿmat Allāh al-Jazāʾirī and His Anthologies: Anti-Sufism, Shiʿism and Jokes in the Safavid World." *Die Welt des Islams* 50 (2010): 224–242.

Robinson, W. S. "What Is It Like to Like?" *Philosophical Psychology* 19 (2006): 743–765.

Rödl, S. "The Form of the Will." In *Desire, Practical Reason and the Good*, edited by S. Tenenbaum, 38–160. Oxford: Oxford University Press, 2010.

Rödl, S. *Self Consciousness*. Cambridge, MA: Harvard University Press, 2007.

Rolls, E. T. *Emotion and Decision Making Explained*. Oxford: Oxford University Press, 2014.

Roskill, Mark W. *Dolce's "Aretino" and Venetian Art Theory of the Cinquecento*. Toronto: University of Toronto Press, 2000.

Russell, D. *Plato on Pleasure and the Good Life*. Oxford: Oxford University Press, 2005.

Ryle, G. "Pleasure." *Proceedings of the Aristotelian Society*, supp., 28 (1954): 135–146.

Sanchez, Amy H., Lindsey M. Lavaysse, Jessica N. Starr, and David E. Gard. "Daily Life Evidence of Environment-Incongruent Emotion in Schizophrenia." *Psychiatry Research* 220.1–2 (July 28, 2014): 89–95. https://doi.org/10.1016/j.psychres.2014.07.041.

Saunders, B. "J. S. Mill's Conception of Utility." *Utilitas* 22 (2010): 52–69.

Scanlon, T. *What We Owe to Each Other*. Cambridge, MA: Harvard University Press, 1978.

Schmaltz, Tad. "Malebranche on Ideas and the Vision in God." In *The Cambridge Companion to Malebranche*, edited by S. Nadler, 59–86. Cambridge: Cambridge University Press, 2000.

Schmaltz, Tad. *Malebranche's Theory of the Soul*. Oxford: Oxford University Press, 1996.

Schroeder, T. "Pleasure, Displeasure, and Representation." *Canadian Journal of Philosophy* 31 (2001): 507–530.

Schroeder, T. *Three Faces of Desire*. Oxford: Oxford University Press, 2004.

Sedley, David. "The Idea of Godlikeness." In *Plato 2: Ethics, Politics, Religion*, edited by Gail Fine, 309–328. Oxford: Oxford University Press, 1999.

Shah, Shalini. *Love, Eroticism and Female Sexuality in Classical Sanskrit Literature: Seventh–Thirteenth Centuries*. New Delhi: Manohar, 2009.

Shaikh, Saʿdiyya. *Sufi Narratives of Intimacy: Ibn ʿArabī, Gender, and Sexuality*. Chapel Hill: University of North Carolina Press, 2012.

Shapiro, Lisa. "How We Experience the World: Passionate Perception in Descartes and Spinoza." In *Emotion and Cognitive Life in Medieval and Early Modern Philosophy*, edited by Martin Pickavé and Lisa Shapiro, 193–216. Oxford: Oxford University Press, 2012.

Shelley, James. "Critical Compatibilism." In *Knowing Art*, edited by Matthew Kieran and Dominic McIver Lopes, 125–136. Dordrecht: Springer, 2007.

Shihadeh, Ayman. *The Teleological Ethics of Fakhr al-Dīn al-Rāzī*. Leiden: Brill, 2006.

Sibley, Frank. *Approach to Aesthetics: Collected Papers on Philosophical Aesthetics*. Oxford: Oxford University Press, 2001.

Sidgwick, H. *The Methods of Ethics*. 7th ed. New York: Macmillan, [1907] 1981.

Simmons, Alison. "Are Cartesian Sensations Representational?" *Noûs* 33.3 (1999): 347–369.

Simmons, Alison. "Guarding the Body: A Cartesian Phenomenology of Perception." In *Contemporary Perspectives on Early Modern Philosophy: Essays in Honor of Vere Chappell*, edited by P. Hoffman, D. Owen, and G. Yaffe, 81–114. Peterborough, Ontario: Broadview Press, 2008.

Simmons, Alison. "Sensation in a Malebranchean Mind." In *Topics in Early Modern Philosophy of Mind*, edited by J. Miller, 105–129. Studies in the History of Philosophy of Mind 9. Dordrecht: Springer, 2009.

Sisman, Elaine. *Mozart: Jupiter Symphony*. Cambridge: Cambridge University Press, 1993.

Skorupski, J. *The Arguments of the Philosophers: John Stuart Mill*. London: Routledge, 1989.

Smuts, A. "The Feels Good Theory of Pleasure." *Philosophical Studies* 155 (2011): 241–265.

Sommerville, B. "The Image of the Jars in Plato's *Gorgias*." *Ancient Philosophy* 34.2 (2014): 235–254.

Sprigge, T. L. S. "Is the Esse of Intrinsic Value Percipi? Pleasure, Pain and Value." *Royal Institute of Philosophy*, supp. vol. 47 (2000): 119–140.

Strohl, Matthew. "Pleasure as Perfection: *Nicomachean Ethics* X.4–5." *Oxford Studies in Ancient Philosophy* 41 (2011): 257–287.

Taylor, C. C. W. "Pleasure: Aristotle's Response to Plato." In *Plato's and Aristotle's Ethics*, edited by R. Heinaman, 1–20. Aldershot, England: Ashgate, 2003.

Tinguely, Joseph. "Kantian Meta-aesthetics and the Neglected Alternative." *British Journal of Aesthetics* 50 (2013): 211–235.

Treadway, Michael T., Joel S. Peterman, David H. Zald, and Sohee Park. "Impaired Effort Allocation in Patients with Schizophrenia." *Schizophrenia Research* 161.2–3 (2015): 382–385. https://doi.org/10.1016/j.schres.2014.11.024.

Trémeau, Fabien, Daniel Antonius, John T. Cacioppo, Rachel Ziwich, Pamela Butler, Dolores Malaspina, and Daniel C. Javitt. "Anticipated, On-line and Remembered Positive Experience in Schizophrenia." *Schizophrenia Research* 122 (2010): 199–205. https://doi.org/10.1016/j.schres.2009.10.019.

Tuozzo, T. "The General Account of Pleasure in the *Philebus*." *Journal of the History of Philosophy* 34 (2014): 495–513.

Tye, M. "Another Look at Representationalism about Pain." In *Pain: New Essays on Its Nature and the Methodology of Its Study*, edited by M. Aydede, 99–120. Cambridge, MA: MIT Press, 2005.

Tye, M. *Ten Problems of Consciousness: A Representational Theory of the Phenomenal Mind*. Cambridge, MA: MIT Press, 1995.

Van Riel, Gerd. *Pleasure and the Good Life*. Leiden: Brill, 2000.

Vogt, K. "What Is Hedonism?" In *Pain and Pleasure in Classical Antiquity*, edited by William Harris. Leiden: Brill, forthcoming.

Warren, J. *The Pleasures of Reason*. Cambridge: Cambridge University Press, 2014.

West, H. R. *An Introduction to Mill's Utilitarian Ethics*. Cambridge: Cambridge University Press, 2004.

White, Kevin. "Pleasure, a Supervenient End." In *Aquinas and the Nicomachean Ethics*, edited by Tobias Hoffmann et al., 220–238. Cambridge: Cambridge University Press, 2013.

Wilson, F. "John Stuart Mill." In *The Stanford Encyclopedia of Philosophy* (Fall 2014 edition), edited by Edward N. Zalta. http://plato.stanford.edu/archives/spr2014/entries/mill/. Accessed June 16, 2015.

Wilson, Margaret Dauler. "Descartes on the Representationality of Sensation." In *Ideas and Mechanism: Essays on Early Modern Philosophy*, 69–83. Princeton: Princeton University Press, 1999.

Wolfsdorf, David. *Pleasure in Ancient Greek Philosophy*. Cambridge: Cambridge University Press, 2013.

Wurth, Kiene Brillenburg. *Musically Sublime: Indeterminacy, Infinity, Irresolvability*. New York: Fordham University Press, 2009.

Wynn, Jonathan K., William P. Horan, Ann M. Kring, Robert F. Simons, and Michael F. Green. "Impaired Anticipatory Event-Related Potentials in Schizophrenia." *International Journal of Psychophysiology,* 77.2 (August 2010): 141–149. https://doi.org/10.1016/j.ijpsycho.2010.05.009.

Zinkin, Melissa. "Kant and the Pleasure of Mere Reflection." *Inquiry* 55.2s (2012): 433–453.

Zuckert, R. *Kant on Beauty and Biology.* Cambridge: Cambridge University Press, 2007.

Index